MB

D0290745

Interpreting Events

Also by Paul Hernadi:

Beyond Genre: New Directions in Literary Classification

INTERPRETING EVENTS

*Tragicomedies of History
on the Modern Stage*

PAUL HERNADI

Cornell University Press

ITHACA AND LONDON

First published 1985 by Cornell University Press

International Standard Book Number 0-8014-1766-X
Library of Congress Catalog Card Number 85-4166
Printed in the United States of America
Librarians: Library of Congress cataloging information appears on the last page of the book.

Permission to quote from the following works is gratefully acknowledged:

Jean Anouilh, *The Lark,* translated by Christopher Fry. Copyright © 1956 by Christopher Fry. Quotations reprinted by permission of Oxford University Press, Inc., and Dr. Jan van Loewen Ltd.

Bertolt Brecht, *Life of Galileo,* translated by Wolfgang Sauerlander and Ralph Manheim. Quotations reprinted by permission of Random House, Inc., and Suhrkamp Verlag.

Albert Camus, *Caligula.* Copyright 1944 by Editions Gallimard. Translated by Stuart Gilbert. Quotations reprinted by permission of Editions Gallimard, Hamish Hamilton Limited, and Alfred A. Knopf, Inc.

Paul Claudel, *Le Livre de Christophe Colomb.* Copyright 1933 by Editions Gallimard. Quotations reprinted by permission of Editions Gallimard and John Calder (Publishers) Ltd.

Friedrich Dürrenmatt, *Romulus der Grosse,* translated by Gerhard Nellhaus as *Romulus the Great.* Copyright © 1957 by Peter Schifferli, Verlag AG Die Arche, Zurich; copyright © 1958 by Verlag AG Die Arche, Zurich. English version copyright © 1964 by Jonathan Cape. Quotations reprinted by permission of Arche Verlag and Tessa Sayle Literary and Dramatic Agency.

T. S. Eliot, *Murder in the Cathedral.* Copyright 1935 by Harcourt Brace Jovanovich, Inc.; renewed 1963 by T. S. Eliot. Quotations reprinted by permission of Harcourt Brace Jovanovich and of Faber and Faber Ltd.

As this page cannot accommodate all copyright notices, the following page constitutes an extension of the copyright page.

Contents

7

Contents

Preface

Ever since 472 B.C., and perhaps even before that approximate date of *The Persians* by Aeschylus, playwrights in the Western tradition have liked to base their plots on memorable events of the past. They have done so for good (if widely differing) reasons. Depending on the way it is handled, historical subject matter will help to elicit admiration, scorn, resignation, nationalistic or revolutionary fervor, and a variety of other emotions that may be in demand at particular times with particular types of audiences. Understandably enough, history has thus served as the apparent source of many twentieth-century plays as well. Yet the period since World War I has witnessed the emergence, not without some earlier instances to be sure, of a new kind of historical drama.

The present book is an attempt to explore that relatively recent development in the European and American theater. Fine observations about some of the pertinent issues can be found in many specialized articles and in such more general studies as Peter Szondi's *Theorie des modernen Dramas* (1956), Eric Bentley's *Life of the Drama* (1967), Herbert Lindenberger's *Historical Drama* (1975), and Bruce Wilshire's *Role Playing and Identity* (1982). It seems to me, however, that the importance of shared characteristics in outstanding dramatizations of history since the 1920s has not received sufficient notice. This is quite surprising because the detached, ironic, often paradoxical, and almost always tragicomic spirit in which some of the most influential mid-twentieth-century

9

plays treat historical events and figures is fundamentally different from the typical attitudes of earlier playwrights toward history. In part no doubt as a backlash against nineteenth- and twentieth-century efforts to turn historiography into an objective and predictive or even quantifiable science, some of the best historical plays of the last decades *conspicuously fictionalize history*. Rather than attempt and fail to conceal, they flaunt the parallels between storytelling and historytelling, stress the role of the ''teller'' and ''listener'' in the ''tale,'' and generally imply that re-presentations of the past show us far less How It Really Was than How It Shall Be Remembered.

In keeping with the title of the book, I hope to have addressed each one of the twelve discussed plays in its own terms both as an interpretation of events and as an event of interpretation. But I mainly wished to explore the remarkable similarity of approach that characterizes the work of most major historical playwrights of our century despite the no less remarkable diversity to be found in their ideological commitment, favored dramatic structure, and verbal style. To demonstrate likeness amid apparent disparity, I have chosen to consider one work each by twelve very different but, by and large, equally successful and respected authors. They are, to name them in the rough chronological order of the works under study, Bernard Shaw, Paul Claudel, T. S. Eliot, Bertolt Brecht, Thornton Wilder, Albert Camus, Max Frisch, Friedrich Dürrenmatt, Jean-Paul Sartre, Jean Anouilh, Peter Weiss, and Peter Shaffer. Partly because several of these authors kept revising their plays significantly, I have decided against discussing them in what would have been a somewhat fictive historical sequence. Without ignoring the question of possible influence or adverse reaction altogether, I have yoked the plays into contrastive pairs with a view to highlighting what all of them, more or less explicitly, suggest concerning the re-presentation of past events (Chapter 1), tragicomic mood (Chapter 2), the relationship between myth and history (Chapter 3), dramatic and theatrical enactment (Chapters 4 and 5), and the constant making of history by interactive perceivers (Chapter 6).

It is, of course, far from easy to genre-alize about the diverse plays to be discussed in the following pages. Almost any general (or generic) statement that can be made about them and about the dozens of similar contemporary plays will appear paradoxical: their alleged historicity is conspicuously spurious; their dramatic structure tends to oscillate between what is known as "epic breadth" and "lyric depth"; their comic delights give most of us the aftertaste of tragedy while their at least partially tragic view of history tends to evoke—within or below or above the sequence of the represented events—insight into nontragic aspects of human existence. It is as if the authors of what may be called, without pejorative connotations, pseudohistorical drama had tried to follow the paradoxical hint young Friedrich Schlegel gave his generation almost two hundred years ago: "It is equally lethal for the mind to have a system and to have none. It may very well have to decide to combine the two" (*Athenaeum Fragments*, no. 53).

The first theoretician of romantic irony would have been pleased, I think, with the manner in which modern historical playwrights combine, or rather contrast, various systems of philosophy and taste within the dynamic framework of a tragicomedy. After all, every conceptual or aesthetic frame of reference suggested by their constant juxtaposition of different sets of views and values seems to be claiming relative significance only. Thus, to use Schlegel's term, each such system includes (and is in turn included by) other systems. As a result, recourse to the author's stated interpretation or programmatic pronouncements is likely to blur rather than sharpen our focus on a particular play. Such statements do, of course, belong to each text's context, and I have cited and interpreted them on several occasions. Yet some prefaces, postscripts, and other types of authorial commentary to the contrary notwithstanding, the intellectual and moral pattern of the most representative modern tragicomedies of history is merely sketched; its completion requires the eye of the beholder. In this respect, too, the plays under study reveal their affinity with Friedrich Schlegel, who said of the historian— but would probably have been prepared to say about the interpreter of certain kinds of texts as well—that he is *ein rückwärts gekehrter Prophet:* "a prophet turned backward" (*Athenaeum Fragments,* no. 80).

Some of my own acts of hermeneutic beholding, verbalized in the interpretations to follow, date back to the early 1960s, when two of the discussed plays (and some of the most valuable critical studies about all of them) had not yet been written. As a student of the history of the theater, I was then preparing my first doctoral dissertation, "Pseudohistorische Gestalten in der Nachkriegsdramatik" (University of Vienna, 1963). My subsequent exposure to advanced literary theory and the history of criticism in the Department of Comparative Literature at Yale University resulted in a second dissertation on which my book *Beyond Genre: New Directions in Literary Classification* (Cornell University Press, 1972) is based. That book has some less obvious but no less pertinent intellectual ties to the present study, in which the close reading of individual passages is coordinated with general observations about what the interpreted plays imply when they are perceived from the vantage point of current theorizing in some of the human sciences. Needless to say, it is for the reader to decide whether I have stirred up too much interpretive dust of practical criticism, got lost in the clouds of cross-disciplinary speculation, or managed to make those two types of intellectual endeavor supplement and illuminate each other.

When dealing with foreign plays and some other non-English texts relevant to my topic, I found it useful in most cases to offer my own renderings of the quoted lines and to refer the reader to those pages in readily available books where the original wording, as well as a slightly or not so slightly different English translation, can be consulted. Whenever two sources of this kind needed to be indicated, the first parenthetical reference identifies the original and the second the published translation; the bibliographical information about both texts appears at the end of the book. The English versions of the quotes from Peter Weiss's *Marat/Sade,* however, are taken verbatim from the cited verse translation. In order to avoid burdening my arguments with the citation of alternative explorations of the twelve much-considered plays, I have largely refrained from discussing the critical literature about them. My debt is great, however, to several translators and hundreds of reviewers and scholars who have tilled some of the same soil from which, it is to be hoped, a better understanding of the texts and contexts of modern historical tragicomedy will continue to grow.

In the intermittent process of working on the present book I have incurred a large number of more tangible debts too. Leaves and grants from the University of Rochester and the University of Iowa, as well as fellowships from the Wesleyan Center for the Humanities and the National Endowment for the Humanities, have enabled me to concentrate on reading and writing (rather than teaching and administration) at crucial phases of the necessary research. But the solitary hours spent at a desk have been usefully supplemented by many more that were spent in the stimulating company of students and colleagues in classrooms, coffee lounges, lecture halls, professional meetings, and the lively sessions of my two NEH Summer Seminars for College Teachers on modern historical tragicomedy.

Since a fifth or so of this book represents the condensation of articles and elaboration of brief remarks that I have published elsewhere, I must also thank several editors and readers who, either before or after initial publication, cared to comment on the ideas now appearing in modified form. Each source of such borrowings, whose respective length ranges from a couple of phrases to a few recast paragraphs, is identified in the appended bibliography by means of the references, under my name, to the journals *Critical Inquiry, History and Theory, New Literary History,* and *Poetics,* and to five multi-authored books published by Indiana University Press, the Modern Language Association of America, the Pennsylvania State University Press, and the University of Toronto Press. Earlier versions of the entire manuscript were expertly read and (more or less gently) criticized by Bert O. States, Philip R. Berk, Herbert Lindenberger, and Scott McMillin. Their comments have been very helpful, and it is not their fault if I have not managed to make greater improvements between the "dress rehearsals" they

13

have reviewed and the "opening night" of publication. My debt to Lorna Olson and David Lasocki in Iowa City and to Kristina Nash, Linda Sanchez, Michael Weber, and Kymberly Williams at the Santa Barbara campus of the University of California is in turn comparable to the playwright's debt to an expert stage crew: without their care and skill in word processing and proofreading, this show would not have gotten on the road.

PAUL HERNADI

Santa Barbara, California

Interpreting Events

Re-presenting the Past:

Saint Joan and *L'Alouette*

"Well, if you will burn the Protestant, I will burn the Nationalist." So says the Earl of Warwick to Bishop Cauchon about the title
character in the fourth scene of George Bernard Shaw's *Saint Joan*
(1923). During the entire conversation, Joan's principal opponents
express their misgivings in clearly anachronistic terms. In the summer of 1429, just before the coronation of Charles VII by The Maid,
no language had words for "protestant" and "nationalist." Nor is
it likely that any of Joan's contemporaries perceived her as representing what Warwick describes as "the protest of the individual
soul against the interference of priest or peer" with the private
person's relationship to God and the state (1971:107). But Shaw's
preface to the play defends the conceptual anachronism of his dialogue with a remarkable argument: "It is the business of the stage
to make its figures more intelligible to themselves than they would
be in real life; for by no other means can they be made intelligible to
the audience." In order to secure "sufficient veracity," the playwright must incur a "sacrifice of verisimilitude" and portray his
characters as saying "the things they actually would have said if they
had known what they were really doing" (52–53).

This line of thought has far-reaching implications not only for
historical drama or the craft of playwriting at large. It points to the
inevitable hindsight involved in any re-presentation of past events.
The skillful historian will convey a sense of how certain men and

women of a past period understood themselves and their relationships to each other. Yet he or she will also suggest certain patterns of cause and purpose of which the participants in the narrated events could not have been fully aware. In short, the historian will try to make us see the past both from within and from without—as evolving drama and as the fixed target of distanced retrospection. Such a dual mode of vision is, of course, sustained by the historian's favored verbal medium: narrative discourse. Historiography typically turns the untold *dramas* of history, in which many a disconcerted player "struts and frets his hour upon the stage," into intelligible *tales*. These tales may well be "full of sound and fury" but escape Macbeth's charge of "signifying nothing" (V.v. 24–28) by being channeled through a narrator's unifying consciousness. Indeed, most readers are inclined to doubt the reliability of historians providing verbatim reports of what was said or thought on a given occasion—a practice for which even Thucydides (1928:1, 39) felt called upon to offer a somewhat apologetic justification:

> As to the speeches that were made by different men . . . it has been difficult to record with strict accuracy the words actually spoken, both for me as regards that which I myself heard, and for those who from various other sources have brought me reports. Therefore the speeches are given in the language in which, as it seemed to me, the several speakers would express, on the subjects under consideration, the sentiments most befitting the occasion. [l.xii.i]

By using a narrative rather than dramatic mode of communication, modern historians conspicuously refrain from pretending to mirror what they in fact mediate. When they indulge in the mimetic luxury of direct quotation, they usually quote written documents postdating the events under consideration, and such documents themselves are verbal mediations of largely nonverbal events. In pronounced contrast to the narrative historian's predilection for *indirectly presenting envisioned action,* the author of dramatic work is engaged in *directly representing action.* Except for the "side text" of stage directions, the playwright is typically absent from the lin guistic surface of his play. In the colorful words of young Stephen Dedalus, he remains, "like the God of the creation, within or behind or beyond or above his handiwork, invisible, refined out of existence, paring his finger-nails" (Joyce 1916:252). In performance, even the stage directions (as well as such clearly authorial utterances as prefaces and postscripts) become submerged. From staged historical drama, therefore, an obviously imaginative version of what happened in the past can emerge without any overt intervention by a present consciousness. The result is a paradoxical relationship between historiographical narrative and historical drama. While the dialogue form of history plays and the documentable content of history books claim to offer unmediated insight into what really happened, the imaginative content of drama and the narrative form of historiography typically acknowledge that the re-presented events have been produced, or at least reproduced, in a human mind.

Beyond Verisimilitude

Shaw's concern for "veracity" as opposed to "verisimilitude" highlights the generic tension between the dialogue form and the imaginative content of earlier dramatizations of history. Generally speaking, serious historical drama before the late nineteenth century attempted to conceal rather than betray, let alone flaunt, the playwright's imaginative role in re-presenting the past. Shakespeare's debased and Schiller's romanticized Joan of Arc, for example, presumably reflected their authors' view of the character. But the iambic pentameters of neither Joan—one speaking in English, the other in German to boot—strike us as pointing to an authorial stance outside the imaginative worlds evoked in *Henry VI* or *Die Jungfrau von Orleans*. By contrast, Warwick and Cauchon in *Saint Joan* discuss the Maid in frankly anachronistic language, and Shaw's dreamlike Epilogue—of which more will be said later—relies completely on authorial hindsight.

In *The Lark* (1953), Jean Anouilh made an even bolder attempt to combine retrospective vision with the prospective orientation of the represented characters. As his Cauchon orders Joan's coronation of King Charles to be performed *after* the scene at the flaming stake, the King (rather than, as in Christopher Fry's English version, Cauchon himself) has the dubious privilege of explaining why:

> The real end of Joan's story . . . the end which they will always tell, long after they have forgotten our names and confused them all together: it isn't the painful and miserable end of the cornered animal caught at Rouen: but the lark singing in the open sky, Joan at Rheims in all her glory . . . . Joan of Arc: A story which ends happily. [227/103]

Remarkably enough, the modern playwright's overt departure from historical verisimilitude does not interfere with our willing suspension of disbelief as regards his representation of past events. Quite to the contrary: when Schiller's Joan dies on the battlefield, *history* is felt to be violated; but when Anouilh explicitly disrespects the only possible chronology (coronation before death) of two very historical occurrences, most readers and spectators are pleased to contemplate his *story* of Joan, with its happy "real end," from the bird's-eye view of a retrospective authorial perspective.

The same applies to Shaw's Epilogue, in which Joan, twenty-five years after her death, discusses her recent rehabilitation with half a dozen characters from the play and with a "clerical-looking gentleman in black frock-coat and trousers, and tall hat, in the fashion of the year 1920" (159). Much to Joan's surprise, this Gentleman announces her canonization by the Catholic church. Much to Joan's grief, however, her offer to "rise from the dead and come back . . . a living woman" provokes general rejection or evasion for a number of all too human reasons. Bishop Cauchon's plea must exasperate her the most: "Mortal eyes cannot distinguish the saint from the heretic. Spare them" (162). In 1456 as in 1920, the world can live with Joan's statues—the one in Winchester Cathedral and the one in front of Rheims Cathedral even become visible through the window of Charles's bedchamber. But as a "living woman," who might once more act as an early (and thus too early) proponent of the future, she would have to be burned, crucified, or otherwise disposed of all over again. Since the burning of Joan we have seen many a victory of Protestantism and nationalism, but as a renewed incarnation of whatever at a given time struggles to become the order of the day, she must forever forgive or despair. This is why Shaw makes her speak some of the last words of Jesus ("Father, forgive them; for they know not what they do" and "My God, my God, why hast thou forsaken me?") in characteristically revised version: "They were as honest a lot of poor fools as ever burned their betters" (153) and, at the very end of the Epilogue, "O God that madest this beautiful earth, when will it be ready to receive Thy saints? How long, O Lord, how long?" (164).

Such an epilogue fully defies the principle of verisimilitude. Upon her astonishing entrance Joan tells King Charles that she is but a dream of his; yet this "psychological" explanation for Shaw's complete departure from the quasi-realistic tradition of historical drama is no doubt offered tongue in cheek. Joan significantly remains on stage after Charles and the other characters have disappeared. Her presence in the final "white radiance" and her concluding appeal to God (just quoted) clearly indicate that she is not Charles's dream but Shaw's. Only as a figment of the playwright's historical imagination, which he endeavors to share with us, can the Maid emerge from the Epilogue as the unwanted harbinger of the time to come, another genius cast by the less gifted bulk of humanity in the gloriously thankless role of the crucified Messiah.

Anouilh's Joan, too, is a harbinger of daybreak: she is *l'alouette,* the lark. But Anouilh refuses to see her as championing any particular cause (such as Shaw's "Protestantism" and "Nationalism," for example). In a note for the program of the first French production, quoted here from the unnumbered pages preceding the play in Christopher Fry's translation, he declared:

The play that follows makes no attempt to explain the mystery of Joan. The persistent effort of so-called modern minds to explain

21

mysteries is, in any case, one of the most naive and foolish activities indulged in by the puny human brain since it became overstocked with shallow political and scientific notions, and can yield nothing, in the long run, but the nostalgic satisfaction of the small boy who discovers at last that his mechanical duck was made up of two wheels, three springs, and a screw. The little boy holds in his hands three springs, two wheels, and a screw, objects which are doubtless reassuring, but he has lost his mechanical duck, and he has usually not found an explanation.

Privileging the historical imagination of collective memory over the latest findings of scholarly research, Anouilh holds fast to the popular image of Joan as "haggard and thin (yes, I know she was a big healthy girl, but I couldn't care less)." At the same time, his own imagination attempts to penetrate deeper layers of the past than his (or anybody else's) notion of what actually happened. For example, King Charles, his mistress Agnes Sorel, and Queen Yolande, the delightfully unconventional mother of his lawful wife, visit Joan in her prison. As with Shaw's Epilogue, it *could* be argued that their obviously pseudohistorical conversation takes place in the mind of one of the characters. Once again, however, a much more natural location suggests itself: the playwright's and the reader's or spectator's minds contemplating subliminal aspects of historical causation and motivation.

JOAN: Take care of Charles. Let him keep his courage.
AGNES: Of course he will, silly girl. I am working at it the same as you. Do you think that I want to be the mistress of a poor little king who is always being beaten? You shall see, I will make our little Charles a great King yet, and without getting myself burnt for him. [206/92]

What most pre-twentieth-century historical plays occult and what even Shaw's *Saint Joan* merely suggests becomes explicit in *L'Alouette:* the present mode of existence of men and women of the past belies our ordinary frameworks of space, time, and personal identi-

22

ty; it is a complex mode of becoming by dint of being imaginatively re-called in a retrospecting consciousness. The very structure of Anouilh's play is designed to evoke not an actual sequence of past events but their imagined presence in *memory*—be it the playwright's memory and the spectator's or the memory of each and every stage figure. To Warwick's urging, "The sooner she is found guilty and burned the better for all concerned," Anouilh's Cauchon replies: "But, my lord, before we do that we have the whole story to play: Domrémy, the Voices, Vaucouleurs, Chinon, the Coronation" (9–10/1). So the play of Joan's life, as recalled in the course of a playfully staged trial, is ready to commence:

JOAN: May I begin wherever I like?
CAUCHON: Yes.
JOAN: Then I'll begin at the beginning. The beginnings are always the best. At my father's house, when I am still a little girl. In the field where I am looking after the sheep and hear the Voices for the first time. [12/2]

From this early point on, the almost bare stage will serve to represent many places, and the spacial simultaneity of different locations is paralleled by Anouilh's stress on the synchrony of all remembered time. In a play like *L'Alouette*, therefore, anachronism—whether intended or unintended—cannot be an issue. Shaw's Joan nonpluses the medieval Captain Baudricourt, who has dismissed her voices as merely coming from her imagination, with this postromantic answer: "Of course. That is how the messages of God come to us" (69). By contrast, Anouilh's Joan replies to "Who is going to play the Voices?"—a question shouted at her from the crowd of as yet unidentified actors—"I am, of course" (13/2), and proceeds to speak "in the deep voice of the Archangel [Michael]" (15/3) whenever the occasion arises. The difference between the two playwrights' respective approaches to Joan's calling could hardly be more pronounced. To be sure, Shaw's principle of veracity makes him represent his characters as saying "the things

23

they actually would have said'' had they known what, in the play-wright's restrospective estimation, they were really doing. Yet Anouilh's memory play expressly fuses the multiple perspectives of the little girl in the field and the young woman on trial with those of Joan's judges, chroniclers, and her more or less skeptical present and even future admirers into a single acoustic phenomenon within the massive here and now of every performance: Joan's voice and Joan's Voices are emphatically identified as the voice of the actress playing the part.

The counterpoint of voices within a remembered event is particu-larly suggestive when it allows Joan to interiorize the future opinion of others. As the following "exchange" implies, genuinely interior dialogue and the assessment of the self by fellow human beings can converge in a single stream of consciousness:

> JOAN: You see, holy St. Michael, it isn't possible; they won't ever understand. No one will. It would be better if I gave up at once. Our Lord has said that we have to obey our father and mother. (*She replies in the voice of the Archangel.*)
> —But first you have to obey God.
> —But if God commands the impossible?
> —Then you have to attempt the impossible, calmly and quietly. . . .He doesn't ask the impossible of everybody, but He does ask it of you. He thinks that nothing is too difficult for you. That's all. (*Joan rises and says simply.*)
> —Well, I will go.
> A VOICE (*from somewhere out of the dark background*): Arrogant girl!
> JOAN (*disturbed*): Who is calling me arrogant? (*After a pause, in the voice of the Archangel.*)—It was you, Joan. And when you have begun to do what God is asking, it will be what the world calls you. [48–51/18–19]

It should be sufficiently clear by now that Shaw and Anouilh deviate from the standard of verisimilitude in two essentially differ-ent directions. The main thrust of Shaw's deviation is sociological. To quote once again from his Preface, *Saint Joan* is intended to make us see "not only the visible and human puppets, but the Church, the Inquisition, the Feudal System." Pulling the strings behind the stage of the puppet show, those institutions seem to Shaw "more terrible in their dramatic force than any of the little mortal figures clanking about in plate armor or moving silently in the frocks and hoods of the order of St. Dominic" (51). Anouilh's characters, too, have certain strings attached to their visible limbs. But they are manipulated, so to speak, from within their psyches.

When, for instance, Cauchon's indulgent treatment of Joan promises to result in her compromising willingness to recant, the Inquisitor falls to his knees, oblivious of all around him, and expresses what is best understood as an unconscious psychological motivation for his institutional orthodoxy:

> O Lord! It has pleased You to grant that Man should humble himself at the eleventh hour in the person of this young girl. . . . But why has it also pleased You to let a shameful tenderness be born in the heart of this hardened old man who was supposed to judge her? Will you never grant, O Lord, that this world should be relieved of every trace of humanity, so that at last we may in peace consecrate it to Thy glory alone? [200/89]

Anouilh thus attributes the Inquisition as an aggressive social institution to a self-consuming urge, reminiscent of Freud's "death drive" (*Todestrieb*), in its human representatives. By contrast, his Joan's psyche appears to propel her toward death by an existential impulse to be what she is: Anouilh's Joan steers away from public repentance and proceeds to the flames because of her strong sense of personal identity and the concomitant fear of entering what, for her, would be an inauthentic mode of existence. In talking to Warwick she verbalizes that fear, as far as the style of the speech is concerned, very much in character; yet her words express what is, strictly speaking, the playwright's rather than Joan's own psychological insight into why she is about to revoke her previous recantation:

25

My life isn't lavish like yours, my lord, running orderly and smoothly between war, hunting, divers pleasures, and your beautiful fiancée. . . . What will be left for me when I am not Joan any longer? . . . Can you see Joan . . . set free, perhaps, vegetating at the French Court on her small pension? (*Almost laughing, yet sadly.*) Joan accepting everything, Joan with a big belly, a glutton. . . . Can you see Joan all made up, entangled in her gowns, busying herself with her little dog or with a man courting her, or who knows, Joan getting married? [214–15/96–97]

Veracity as Composite Vision

Just as it is the case with Shaw's institutional puppeteers ("The Church, the Inquisition, the Feudal System"), the existential-psychological motives stirring Anouilh's "visible and human puppets" are, of course, ultimately mobilized by a master puppeteer—the playwright. T. S. Eliot once remarked that we discern such manifestly poetic lines of drama as Macbeth's speech beginning "To-morrow and to-morrow and to-morrow" as if they were spoken by the character and the playwright "in unison" (1954:34–35). The last sentences just quoted from *The Lark* seem to call for an analogous observation except that the authorial voice heard in them becomes audible in a quasi-narrative rather than Shakespeare's quasi-lyrical register. "Can you see Joan. . . ?": Joan is being heard here as referring to her imagined, inauthentic future self in the third grammatical person characteristic of storytelling. And she addresses her interpretation of her historical prototype's unconscious motivation to Warwick, if not indeed to each member of the audience, as a narrator would appeal to the "dear reader"—in the second person. Along with the deliberately conspicuous use of anachronisms, which Anouilh shares with all the playwrights under present study, such quasi-narrative rhetoric makes us perceive clairvoyant *figures of drama* as capable of intellectually penetrating (rather than simply

26

embodying) the *historical characters* whose lives are being supposedly re-presented on the stage.

Instead of saying what the "real" Joan, Warwick, and Cauchon could have said, heard, or at least thought in their actual historical situation, the dramatic figures in both *Saint Joan* and *The Lark* give verbal expression to the playwright's vision of the action of the persons they are invoked to represent. As Shaw explains in the Preface, his characters should make intelligible not only "themselves"—that is to say, their historical prototypes—but also the institutional imperatives of history governing their way of thinking and their manifest behavior. "Obviously," he adds, "the real Cauchon, Lemaître, and Warwick could not have done this: they were part of the Middle Ages themselves, and therefore as unconscious of its peculiarities as of the atomic formula of the air they breathed" (53). Much of what his characters are made to *say* is really *meant* by the playwright, whose vantage point is that of a different and presumably better-informed era. For the most part, however, Shaw appears to abide by the verisimilar convention of historical drama. Despite what may be called a newly added sound track, what Shaw's characters do up to the Epilogue remains, roughly speaking, in the realm of that which could have been filmed by a candid camera *avant la lettre*. By contrast, Anouilh's entire play evolves along lines similar to Shaw's Epilogue, in which all pretense of historical "verisimilitude" is sacrificed in the author's search for historical "veracity."

Consider the two playwrights' respective dramatizations of a well-known sequence of supposedly miraculous events. Having recognized the Dauphin among his much more lavishly dressed courtiers, Joan succeeds in persuading the insecure young man to allow her to lead the army, against the will of his overbearing councilors, to beleaguered Orléans. This theatrically effective scene, transmitted in Joan's legendary history, is dramatized by Shaw and Anouilh in rather similar fashion. But Shaw forestalls the supernatural interpretation of Joan's prodigious success merely through an anachronistically enlightened exchange about the nature and function of miracles (79–80) between the Archbishop ("nourish their faith by poetry") and La Trémouille, commander of the army ("Poetry! I should call it humbug"). By contrast, Anouilh makes a laughing Warwick comment on and thus defuse the impressively represented events (I quote Christopher Fry's delightful, though far from literal, English version):

> In point of fact, that wasn't exactly how it happened. They called a meeting of the Council, and discussed the matter for hours. In the end they agreed to use Joan as a sort of color-bearer at popular demand. An attractive little mascot, well qualified to charm the general public into letting themseves be killed. [131/56]

Their different treatment of Ladvenu, the Dominican friar who appears to have shown sympathy for Joan during the 1431 procedures, also manifests the same contrast between the approaches taken by the two playwrights: while Shaw introduces his "veracious" hindsight mainly in the realm of diction, Ahouilh permits the composite vision required for any re-presentation of the past to permeate all dramatic action. In response to Warwick's remark about Joan's execution, "I am informed that it is all over," Shaw's Ladvenu "enigmatically" declares: "We do not know, my lord. It may have just begun." Even when Warwick asks him to elaborate, Ladvenu continues to anchor the playwright's retrospective "prediction" of the future in a reasonably verisimilar account of what has just happened:

> When the fire crept round us, and she saw that if I held the cross before her I should be burnt myself, she warned me to get down and save myself. My lord: a girl who could think of another's danger in such a moment was not inspired by the devil. When I had to snatch the cross from her sight, she looked up to heaven. And I do not believe that the heavens were empty. I firmly believe that her Savior appeared to her then in His tenderest glory. She called to Him and died. This is not the end for her, but the beginning. [147–48]

Anouilh's Ladvenu in turns interrupts the reenactment of an early scene from Joan's life, the savage disciplining of the young girl by her father, who is enraged because she wants to join the army to save France. Joan's defender at the court proceedings sets out to defend her, prematurely, in her home town against her father: "Stop him right away! He is hurting her!" Cauchon, likewise disrespecting chronology, puts the preposterous intruder in his—Ladvenu's—chronological "place": "We can do nothing, Brother Ladvenu. We don't get to know Joan until the trial. We can only act our parts, each his own, good or bad, as it is written, and each in his turn. And soon, you know, we shall do worse things than this to her" (41/15).

Such passages, informed by the interplay between the personal core and figural circumference of Anouilh's major characters, highlight the dialectic between history's past "text" and any subsequent "reading" of it. The quotation marks around the key words of the last sentence are, of course, required by the circumstance that history (the "text") is always fleeting and largely nonverbal while its imaginative reconstruction (the "reading") is made permanent by being verbalized: historians, historical playwrights, and dramatic figures expressing the unspoken attitudes of their historical prototypes all translate, so to speak, from a shadowy "original version"—the world of events forever past—into the idiom of a continually present discourse. Thus it may seem surprising that neither Shaw nor Anouilh attempted to stay very close to the language of the extant documents concerning Joan's trial. After all, the re-presentation of the past would have required relatively little "translation" from the medium of occurrences into the medium of words in the case of such a "dramatic" and predominantly verbal event. The "natural affinity between drama and trials" (Lindenberger 1975:21) has indeed appealed to many modern playwrights with documentary or otherwise realistic ambitions. Even Peter Weiss, whose *Marat/Sade* (1964) is far from being a docudrama in any sense of the word, based his next play, *Die Ermittlung* (1965; *The*

Investigation, 1966), almost verbatim on selected excerpts from the 1963–65 Frankfort trial of eighteen former staff members of the Auschwitz concentration camp. By contrast, Shaw and Anouilh are allied with the Weiss of *Marat/Sade* (to be considered in chapter 5), of *Trotzki im Exil* (1970), and of *Hölderlin* (1971) in refusing to conceal the editorial, retrospective aspect of the production, transmission, and any later use of such historiographical materials as trial transcripts and archival records. As a result, their plays unmistakably dramatize history by turning private acts of *envisioning action* into public events of *enacting vision.*

Let me clarify the italicized terms by elaborating on some implications of my earlier study, *Beyond Genre: New Directions in Literary Classification* (1972), where I contrasted Action and Vision as two poles between which the sparks of imaginative literature are generated. I used proverbs and realistic conversational dialogue as my respective literary examples for the thematic presentation of vision and the dramatic representation of action. I have also noted, however, that vision and action interconnect even in those relatively "pure" thematic and dramatic modes of discourse, and that predominantly narrative and lyric texts or passages integrate vision and action—those organizing principles of predominantly thematic and dramatic texts or passages—into the presentation of envisioned action and the representation of enacted vision, respectively (cf. esp. pp. 156–70).

I wish to stress now what I merely implied a dozen years ago: only methodological considerations warrant the privileging as "basic" of any one (or two or three) among *four* constitutive dimensions of human life and consciousness out of which, in addition to much else, four distinct yet combinable modes of discourse have evolved. These dimensions are the (protodramatic) continual interaction between self and other, the (protolyric) instantaneous awareness of what is happening both within and outside the evolving self, the (protonarrative) molding of all experience including imaginative experience into sequential patterns, and the (protothematic) systematizing of all experience including imaginative experience into more or less explicitly articulated world views. The four dimensions intersect in all human activity, but their respective prevalence can be seen, to use a homely set of illustrations, in each player's interaction with other players during a ball game, the radio announcer's "blow-by-blow coverage" of the game and of his emotional response to it, the Monday-morning quarterback's sequential account of what was going wrong and what ought to have been happening on the field, and the bookmaker's (or some other well-informed gambler's) systematic overview of recent game scores and of additional factors affecting the odds in a proposed wager.

It is clear that historical chronicles re-present past events primarily from the Monday-morning quarterback's vantage point of envisioned action and that a great deal of historical drama is aligned with documentary plays in appearing to represent action as if directly from the unmediated points of view of the interacting "players." To continue with the same analogy, annals offering a year-by-year account of frequently unrelated occurrences (for example, "720. Charles fought against the Saxons. 721. Theudo drove the Saracens out of Aquitaine. 722. Great crops") approximate within their larger chronological framework the structure of the sportscaster's highly selective running commentary; and philosophers of history as well as those historians who attempt to explain or even quantify events by subsuming them under general laws aspire to the systematic coherence underlying the predictive operations associated with bookmaking. It should also be clear, however, that each of those approaches to history can and usually does include in its favored structure of re-presentation features favored by the others. How else, indeed, could its practitioners hope to avoid impoverishing their understanding of human life and consciousness, which, as I have suggested, always involve continual interaction, instantaneous awareness, sequential orientation, and systematic overview? It is by adding lyric, narrative, and/or thematic components to their primarily dramatic orientation that playwrights moderate the demand of "strict" drama for unmediated interaction among the characters with the respective compensatory demands of "subjective" experience, "objective" historiography, and "pure" philosophy for intense awareness, structured progression, and systematic theorizing. It takes a different set of verbal strategies for most historians to temper their predilection for presenting envisioned action in the objectifying narrative pattern of unilinear time. But historical playwrights and narrative historians alike enact their present, future-bound vision of the past by always placing received history in a new context of authorial hindsight concerning the present and future significance, as they see it, of past words and deeds. As Goethe's Faust points out to his literal-minded assistant Wagner:

> Mein Freund, die Zeiten der Vergangenheit
> Sind uns ein Buch mit sieben Siegeln.
> Was ihr den Geist der Zeiten heisst,
> Das ist im Grund der Herren eigner Geist,
> In dem die Zeiten sich bespiegeln.

> To us, my friend, the ages of the past
> Are like a book with seven seals protected.
> What you the spirit of the ages call
> Is but the scholars' spirit, after all,
> In which the ages are reflected.

> [575–79]

Must we share Wagner's presumably great discomfort with this state of historical affairs? I think not. Precisely because history as we can ever hope to know it is "reflected" in human minds, it can teach us important lessons about the mind's method of critically translating the sealed book of How It Really Was into the anthology—still incomplete, always to be revised—of How It Shall Be Remembered.

The Erotics of Retrospection

The most pervasive shared trait of such "translations" is, perhaps, that they are mostly stories that, in terms of plot structure, character delineation, and audience response, invite the kind of analysis that is applied by literary critics to works of both drama and narrative fiction. It is worth remembering that Shaw himself rejected some historical accounts of Joan that were casting her in the role of "melodramatic heroine" while making her antagonists look like "villains of melodrama" (7); his own play had been intended, rather, to combine "the romance of her rise, the tragedy of her execution, and the comedy of the attempts of posterity to make amends for that execution" (46). In another set of comments on aspects of genre within his play, Shaw claims that, since Joan was burned "by normally innocent people in the energy of their right-eousness," her death resulted from one of those "pious murders" whose inherent contradiction "brings an element of comedy into the tragedy: the angels may weep at the murder, but the gods laugh at the murderers" (52). Of course, Shaw's risible divinities can amuse themselves not only at the expense of Joan's antagonists, whose attempt to stay the progress of history was doomed to eventual failure. The "law of God," which Shaw's Preface defines as "a law of change" (39), prompts its apostles always to engage in uphill battles against the social establishment of their day. Many such battles will be lost because, as a friend points out to Joan, "God is no man's daily drudge and no maid's either. . . . For he has to be fair to your enemy too—don't forget that" (114–15). In this most tragicomic of his tragicomedies, Shaw seems to be implying that the frequent frustration of "progressive" saints entails, as a corollary, the temporary fulfilment of some of humankind's more conser-vative, less inspiring, but by no means less human aspirations.

Shaw was, of course, neither the first nor the last person to genre-alize about historytelling in this fashion. Ancient rhetoricians, as well as modern philosophers of history, have often been characteriz-ing remembered or recorded historical occurrences as "tragic," "farcical," and the like. In the next two chapters I shall have more to say about a large variety of generic moods that plays, as well as other representations of human events including historiographical narratives, convey to their responsive readers. At this point I merely wish to suggest that the often-noted resemblance between stories

33

and histories invites contrary interpretations. We may assume that life itself has such qualities as epic breadth and tragic depth, and that therefore the structure of history has given rise to literary genres. Or else we may assume that all narratives follow the generic patterns of myth and literature, and that therefore the structures of historiography ultimately stem from the human imagination. Let me sidestep the question of temporal priority between stories and histories. Why argue which came first and smash both the chicken and the egg under the spinning wheels of just another history that may turn out to be fiction? It should be more rewarding to consider whether storytellers and historytellers are not closely allied agents of what might be called the erotics of retrospection; in other words, whether our reactions to events evoked by historiographical narratives and to events evoked by imaginative literature are not in fact determined by similar strategies of desire.

In recent decades there has been much discussion of the marked contrast between historiography as an essentially *narrative* endeavor and the more readily *quantifiable* findings of natural or even social science. At the same time, historical research has usually been assimilated to scientific inquiry on the basis of their presumably shared capacity to yield knowledge. It is true, of course, that all knowledge is being generated for some purpose, and Jürgen Habermas (1971) has plausibly distinguished three kinds of motivation for knowledge as the "human interest" in, respectively, our (technological) domination over nature, our (hermeneutic) participation in culture, and our (self-consciously critical) alteration of the very framework of human nature and culture (cf. esp. 301–17). It seems to me, however, that the connection between human interest or desire and historical knowledge is far more intimate than Habermas and most other writers on the subject appear to assume. Indeed, to the extent that historiographical narratives share with overtly imaginative works of literature their quasi-mythic narrative focus on the fulfillment and/or frustration of human projects, they are primarily answerable to the principle of desire rather than the principle of knowledge. Sure enough, different stories will be found in greater or lesser agreement with "historical evidence" as the latter is extracted from other, perhaps earlier and more rudimentary stories about the past. But the primary reason why we tell and listen to such stories does not lie in their presumed truth value.

Why, indeed, should we want to know the kinds of things histories are about? The slim chances of using—and thus plausibly validating—such knowledge hardly warrant the vast effort required to reach what is a tentative, and probably rather distant, approximation of it. To be sure, the most inclusive scientific theory is only hypothesis awaiting additional corroboration, and even the most profound insight into an intimately known mind or object leaves further depths unplumbed. Yet the application of a basically appropriate theory or of a roughly adequate insight tends to follow more or less generalizable methods of technological or sociopsychological "engineering." In contrast, the historian never knows just how far he is from a comprehensive understanding of all pertinent occurrences or the ultimate understanding of a single life or event. His only advantage over theoretical scientists and over such interpreters of individual people as practicing psychoanalysts and practiced poker players is that he need not even strive for complete coverage and complete penetration. Precisely because total knowledge of the Every and total knowledge of the Each conspicuously elude the historian, his stories may claim assent on the basis of reasonable probability about the Many and persuasive plausibility about the Some. In other words, the historian can, and his readers will, be satisfied if he shows, for instance, that *many* successful revolutions were started by active minorities or that *some* people would have thought and acted the way he suggests (but cannot prove) Luther or Napoleon thought and acted in particular moments of their lives. Even under the best of circumstances, however, the historian's appeal to the Many (rather than the Every or the All) can promise only very imperfect knowledge of a statistical kind, and his appeal to the Some (rather than the Each or the One) should make us expect of him such very partial verdicts as juries or judges render in response to courtroom rhetoric.

35

The persistent concern of historiographers and their readers with the past can thus be explained much more plausibly in terms of another question, namely, *Why is it that we enjoy telling and hearing or reading histories?* One answer to this question is suggested by the recognition that storytellers and historytellers avail themselves of comparably structured narrative forms and that (to anticipate an argument that will wind its way through the next two chapters) the correspondence between the moods conveyed by such forms and the desire for self-asserting entertainment and self-transcending commitment can help us to understand why we "like" both literature and historiography. But even a secondary reason for the popularity of historytelling has more to do with the conative motives of cognition than is generally supposed. The very notion that the human agents of a story I am contemplating actually existed allows me to react to the already determined fate of other people with the survivor's sense of superior vitality and increased hindsight. Even when I follow fictive representations of actions, my attitude is not unlike that of the unobserved observer standing behind a one-way mirror. But such privileged status over people actually believed to have existed will enhance my self-esteem even if— or rather, especially if—I am made to admire them. To the extent that a historian *persuades* me that he has understood the life and times of Luther or Napoleon, he offers to share with me both his (presumed) intuition of what it felt like to be Luther or Napoleon and his (presumed) hindsight into more than what Luther or Napoleon could fully grasp about his own situation. The ego trip involved hardly requires commentary. But it testifies to the reality of pleasure rather than to the pleasure of reality because, clearly, the rhetorical effectiveness of a historiographical work is hardly evidence for its mimetic accuracy.

Many people will, of course, object to a view of historical knowledge as tentative supplement—now you believe it, now you don't— of hard and fast literary pleasure. One powerful objection runs as follows: even the pleasures of great fiction are ultimately pleasures of a deeper insight into the same reality whose surface is traced by historiographers. Arguments based on that objection tend to invoke Aristotle's remarks about the pleasure we derive from any truthful representation and his favorable view of the poet's mimesis of actions as "more philosophical" than the historian's (cf. *Poetics*, chaps. 4 and 9). But can we really claim that the acquisition of nonpractical knowledge—a "knowing that" without bearing on some "knowing how to"—is in fact pleasurable? Learning a new skill—learning to ride a bicycle, for instance, or to play a difficult piece on the piano—may indeed give me a great deal of pleasure. Yet I rather suspect that whenever a piece of new but, in practical terms, inapplicable information fills me with unadulterated pleasure (rather than with the agony accompanying the process of any conversion against the grain of one's mental fabric) I have either acquired additional confirmation for a preconceived conclusion—new ammunition for shooting at an old target—or only abandoned tenets that, subconsciously at least, I had wished to abandon in the first place. Thus the satisfaction derived from an actual or imagined increase of knowledge by means of both literature and historiography requires a more plausible explanation than the alleged pleasure of coming face to face with reality, and I will graft such an explanation on my ensuing consideration of audience response to dramatic works, only some of which claim to offer insight into history.

Tragicomic Mood: *Murder in the Cathedral* and *Romulus der Grosse*

The primary purpose of this chapter is to explore the sense in which a great deal of modern historical drama can be called tragicomic. As far as possible, I will couch my remarks in the current vocabulary of drama critics interested, as we all should be, in elucidating (1) significant similarities between individual plays and (2) significant differences between different kinds of plays. I am also convinced, however, that the genre critic's main task is continually to sharpen, alter, or even replace our conceptual tools and thus to contribute to the ongoing endeavor better to understand individual texts and productions as well as the basic principles of textual and theatrical communication and representation. Furthermore, the present book's concern with historical drama as just one of several vehicles of historytelling makes it especially desirable to place the tragicomic qualities of the discussed plays in close relation to what are, or can be perceived as, the tragicomic qualities of historical events. In the next section, therefore, I will offer an abbreviated and refocused version of my earlier proposal of a reception theory of literary genres (1981a) so as to prepare the reader for the ensuing juxtaposition of T. S. Eliot's *Murder in the Cathedral* and Friedrich Dürrenmatt's *Romulus the Great*—two plays that are quite dissimilar in many respects—as exemplary tragicomedies of history.

Complex Mood through Composite Vision

Any attempt to come to terms with tragicomedy implies that we know or almost know what tragedy and comedy are. Let me therefore begin by rejecting a few and endorsing some other concepts of those supposedly unmixed, simple genres. I will do so by relating tragedy and comedy to each other and to romance and satire not as fixed entities but as major directional signals within the conceptual space surveyed by drama criticism. The first recorded occurrence of the word "tragicomedy" may well serve as my point of departure. In the Prologue of Plautus' *Amphitryon,* Mercury announces that the play to follow should be considered a tragicomedy since such traditionally tragic characters as gods and kings and such comic figures as slaves will appear in it side by side. As a matter of fact, Mercury himself, a god, will be ordered by Jupiter to take on the outward appearance of a slave for much of the play's action. Yet the reason why later adaptations of the Amphitryon story by Molière, Heinrich von Kleist, and Jean Giraudoux have increasingly assumed tragicomic overtones has nothing to do with the mixed social status of the dramatic characters. Indeed, few modern critics would assert that a distinction between tragedy and comedy on the basis of the social standing of the main characters is useful. Developments in the drama of the last two hundred years or so likewise preclude a definition of tragedy or comedy in terms of the time-honored distinction between stylized diction and everyday language. Another familiar touchstone, subject matter, seems to me hardly more reliable. Who is to tell in the abstract how a play involving jealousy or ambition, for example, ought to be classified from such a thematic point of view?

Of all traditional criteria, the effect of a work on its reader or spectator strikes me as the least objectionable. For the most part, tragedy and comedy will dispose us, respectively, to weep and laugh, whether or not our aesthetic experience actually results in one or the other kind of audible and visible behavior. The intriguing question is, of course, *just what* is likely to elicit an incipient or full-fledged version of either response from the congenial reader or spectator of a play. Before considering three pertinent aspects of plot structure, I wish to suggest that our perception of a literary work as primarily tragic or comic is largely due to our perception of its implied author's predominantly "pathetic" or "humorous" attitude toward the represented world.

Pathos in tragedy tends to result from measuring the infinite with a finite gauge—the kind of procedure for which Job is repudiated by his Creator and latter-day promoters of a "tragic philosophy" are repudiated by Karl Jaspers. Jaspers concedes that tragedy is a valid mode of responding to the world as long as our response remains in the realms of myth and art; he rejects only speculative attempts at "systematizing tragic knowledge" and "turning it into a philosophic absolute" (1952:102). The implication seems to be this: the human need to measure the universe with a finite gauge is very real even though such a gauge is not an adequate instrument for the purpose. A fully developed sense of humor is, then, the very opposite of the pathetic (and ostensibly tragic) world view. It makes us measure everything finite by standards of the infinite. As Jean Paul Richter put it in the first decade of the nineteenth century: "Humor, as the sublime in the reverse, annihilates not the individual but the finite by contrasting it to the Idea. There is no individual foolishness, there are no individual fools for Humor, only foolishness at large and a crazy world" (125). In the light of this statement it becomes clear why most comedy (as opposed to almost all tragedy) does not lead to the death of individuals: from its humorous vantage point in the infinite, they do not really exist to begin with.

Now, the humorist's ostensibly detached attitude makes us look at things and people from the outside, while pathos leads through empathy to sympathy by the adoption of a fictive or real person's finite perspective—the way he sees himself and his world from within. To be sure, some of us lean toward humor and others toward pathos because, as Horace Walpole repeatedly paraphrased a French

40

proverb—*Qui sent, pleure; qui pense, rit*—"This world is a comedy to those that think, a tragedy to those that feel!" (1:315, 344;
2:444). Yet most people simultaneously engage in at least some
"thinking" and some "feeling" most of the time. As Blaise Pascal
noted in his *Pensées*, B. 112: "Things have divers qualities and the
soul has divers inclinations, for nothing that offers itself to the soul
is simple, and the soul never offers itself to anything simply. Hence
people will weep and laugh about the same thing" (13:39). Such
insights into the complementary nature of weeping and laughing
may well make us expect to find incipient forms of tragicomedy
even in the greatest examples of tragedy and comedy or, perhaps,
especially in those greatest—the most penetrating and most circumspect—manifestations of pathos and humor.

The dichotomies weeping / laughing and pathos / humor correlate
the responsive reader's or spectator's mood and the implied author's
attitude. (I prefer not to speculate about what went on in the actual
author's mind.) Just as the author implied by the tragicomic aspects
of a play integrates the basic orientation of pathos with that of
humor, the congenial reader or spectator implied by them has a
likewise flexible attitude enabling him or her to view individual
characters, as well as the natural and cultural force field of their
interaction, both from within and from without. Three further pairs
of useful critical concepts focus on plot structure—the chief dramatic vehicle of turning authorial challenge into audience response.
They contrast frustration to fulfillment, self-consummation to self-
preservation, and the linear flux of time to cyclical temporality
within the worlds evoked by literary works.

Frustration and fulfillment are particularly useful concepts for both
distinguishing and interrelating tragedy and comedy. Tragedy highlights the frustration of great and unique individuals who cannot
avoid running up against their restrictive natural or social confines.
By contrast, comedy tends to show ways and means whereby relatively "little" people adjust to the circumstances imposed upon them
by nature and culture. This is why the tragic hero tends to assert his
will but seldom stays alive while the often pale comic hero prevails

over his usually more memorable chief opponent, who serves as an impressively colorful target for our ridicule. But the contraposition of frustration and fulfillment also suggests why tragedy and comedy so easily mix or fade into one another. The widespread dualistic view of the human being as soul and body (or "angel" and "beast") naturally provides for the simultaneous frustration and fulfillment of different motives within the same person. Indeed, Victor Hugo based the concept of tragicomedy implicit in the celebrated preface to his play *Cromwell* (1827) on just that dualism (1:416). A more subtle theory of tragicomedy might rely on such tripartite concepts of the soul as Plato's charioteer with the two horses (*Phaedrus,* 246a and b) or Freud's stratification of the psyche into id, ego, and superego (1967:76–86/1965:69–80). But even if we consider every character as a solid and ultimate unit, it is clear that one person's fulfillment is (or can be) another's frustration. Unless our sympathies and aversions are unequivocally (and somewhat childishly) divided between the two sides of every serious conflict, our respective sense of potential tragedy and comedy will enter various combinations in our response to life and literature alike.

At least two modern philosophers have explicitly connected tragic frustration with self-consummation as it manifests itself in the deathward progress of living organisms (Langer 1953:351) or in the destruction of social structures through the very forces to which they owe their existence (Simmel 1968:43). This dialectic process of self-annihilation through the actualizing of one's own potential (cf. Szondi 1961:50–52, 60–61) involves linear temporality—the irreversible movement from a unique past through a unique present toward a unique future. Comic fulfillment, by contrast, can be seen as the preservation of a self: the recycling, so to speak, of deconstructed texture within a larger structure of cyclical time (cf. Watts 1955:154–70). What we look forward to in those long North American winters is, of course, the self-preservation of trees, not of leaves. Closer to everybody's home, it is the growing fingernail that "survives," not the clipping. Likewise, the human species is perpetuated, not the individual organism—except in the rudimentary form in which nature recycles cells and molecules and culture recycles some of our attitudes and institutions. In each instance, a "tragic" view from within the recycled can be combined with the recycler's "comic" view from without, and the resulting tragicomic perspective of empathetic distance will integrate the extreme responses elicited by single-minded tragedy and comedy.

Now, human beings, including characters in literary works, can be adjusted to or crushed by either nature or culture. By *nature* I mean all nonhuman forces operating in the universe rather than anything strictly and specifically physical, chemical, or biological. *Culture* may then be taken to refer to the order (or disorder) of human societies. To put it simply, nature is what has made us; culture, what we have made. But this dichotomy is far from clearcut. Our sense of what is natural is a product of our culture, and it seems to lie in the nature of human beings as symbol-using animals to develop certain forms (and not others) of culture. Thus nature and culture are to some degree in the eye of the beholder. What matters is how individuals, groups, or entire societies look upon a certain force or institution, whether they see it as humanity-making or human-made, as constitutive of their world or merely regulative in it. In this qualified sense of the two concepts, nature and culture suggest two principal directions in which tragedy and comedy can approach each other. On the one hand, frustration and self-consummation, as well as fulfillment and self-preservation, can be treated as natural phenomena—things that must and in a sense should be. On the other hand, they can be treated as cultural phenomena— things that tend to but need not and often should not be. To the extent that a play stresses either nature or culture as the general framework of all human fulfillment or frustration, either the acquiescent marvel of romance or the indignant analysis of satire will eclipse comic humor or tragic pathos in it.

Admiration for nature, indignation over culture: I may appear to have endorsed a pair of unqualified proto-Romantic attitudes of the kind that make us describe the granting of citizenship to foreign-born persons as "naturalization." Yet I am just as sympathetic toward a contrary, proto-Classicist argument whose gist is contained in the following three assertions: culture, in the best sense of the word, is a constructive elaboration of "raw" nature; almost any mask is preferable to the apelike grin of the uncultivated, demasked human face; the cure for cultural evils is more, not less, culture. On balance, I find myself sharing the hope of Friedrich Schiller and other "romantic classics" that it is possible to mediate between the two extreme positions. In his profound essays *On the Aesthetic Education of Man* (1793) and *On Naive and Sentimental Poetry* (1797), Schiller seems to have assumed that culture ideally is and should actually become our second nature. At a hypothesized future stage of social and literary history, Schiller's satire and elegy— those "sentimental," self-conscious responses to the perceived contradiction between the Real and the Ideal—may well be superseded by a form of romance: the newly attained idyl of the Realized Ideal. Until then, however, satire—which in Schiller's scheme is closely related to tragedy and comedy (1962:444–46/1966:120–22)—will do better justice than idyllic romance to our everyday experience; hence our uneasiness about the mandatory happy endings that rewards virtue both in eighteenth-century bourgeois comedy and in its allegedly proletarian second cousin with the fancy stage name "Socialist Realism." Eventual happiness in a green Shakespearean forest or in the evergreen world of the City of God proves more acceptable, since it overtly transcends, rather than claims to mirror, ordinary social reality. But in its most profound literary manifestations, even romance will retain both aspects of the sublime expressed in the twofold meaning of the Greek word *deinos:* wonderful and terrible.

I hardly need to point out that my use of the terms *comedy, satire, tragedy,* and *romance* has much in common with Northrop Frye's use of them in his *Anatomy of Criticism* (1957:158–293) and other writings. I, too, see tragedy and comedy on the one hand and romance and satire on the other as "opposed pairs" (162): much like North and South against West and East at the bridge table, the two concepts belonging to each pair face one another as limiting values of two perpendicular coordinates. But there are at least three fundamental differences between Frye's scheme (from which I have learned a great deal) and mine.

First of all, I do not think that it is helpful to contrast romance and satire as genres of innocence and experience and to say that tragedy moves from innocence to experience and comedy from experience to innocence. Rather than follow Frye in adopting that Blakean juxtaposition to the study of literature at large, I think of romance as principally informed by marvel at whatever appears natural or supernatural in the world and see satire as informed by an obverse critical and analytical attitude toward presumably human-made culture. On such a view, tragic frustration and comic fulfillment within the represented world emerge as the chief mimetic vehicles of combining the romancer's admiration with the satirist's indignation—considered as attitudes ascribable to the authors implied by certain texts— into diverse forms of thrilling or gratifying entertainment offered to responsive spectators and readers.

Second, I doubt whether a useful purpose is served by associating each of the four genres or, as Frye calls them, ''narrative pregeneric elements of literature'' (1957:162), with one of the four seasons. In *Anatomy of Criticism* we read about comedy as the mythos of spring, romance as the mythos of summer, tragedy as the mythos of autumn, and irony or satire as the mythos of winter. This is, however, a rather northern—or shall we say Canadian?—way of looking at things. There are periodic agricultural chores and delights under every climate but nature is not ''dead'' during winter (for which season some languages do not have a special word) in the southern Mediterranean or several of the United States. Rather than derive literary genres from four seasonal segments of a natural cycle, I prefer to think of the typical plot structures of comedy, romance, tragedy, and satire as functioning within a twofold cultural framework of entertainment and commitment. In a sense that is to be refined in the first section of the next chapter, a particular play or performance should be seen as ''tragic'' or ''comic'' to the extent that it affords us entertainment through thrill or gratification, and it

45

should be seen as "satirical" or "romantic" to the extent that it fills us with indignation or admiration, thereby committing us to attempt to change either the world or ourselves. On such a view, the audience may watch one or more than one character's self being "tragically" hardened and consummated or "comically" softened and preserved, but it may also contemplate selfhood as being transcended through the implied author's "satirical" or "romantic" commitment, potentially shared by readers and spectators, to certain social or cosmic values.

Finally, I relate tragicomedy to four additional categories occupying intermediate conceptual space between adjacent pairs of Frye's four *mythoi:* melodrama between tragedy and satire, farce between comedy and satire, festivity between comedy and romance, and mystery (in a sufficiently capacious sense to include non-Christian mysteries and not only of the Sherlock Holmes type) between tragedy and romance. Within this framework, tragedy emerges as integrating the effect of melodrama with that of the mystery play into the Aristotelian combination of pity and fear or—if one prefers Wolfgang Schadewaldt's rendition (1955) of *eleos* and *phobos* as *Jammer* and *Schauder*—woe and awe or even distress and shudder. Correspondingly, comedy elicits the integrated response of punitive derision and celebratory joy characteristic, in separation, of farce and festivity. Romance in turn evokes a response in which the moods of joy and awe are combined, while our reaction to satire tends to be a mixture of scornful derision (directed at the satirist's potentially dangerous targets) and woeful pity or distressed self-pity (for the potential victims of the derided actual or would-be victimizers). My approach to the various moods evoked by tragicomic drama presupposes, therefore, four rather than just two "opposed pairs." Besides laughing (comedy) and weeping (tragedy) and besides gaze (romance) and frown (satire), I see tragicomedy as capable of also integrating various combinations and degrees of cheer (festivity), sob (melodrama), jeer (farce), and throb (mystery) in the highly complex mood it conveys to a responsive audience.

As the reader cannot fail to have noticed, I propose to replace

Frye's "anatomy" of plot structure by a "physiology" of audience response. To be sure, responsible critics will always try to justify the generic categories that emerge from their reading experience as relying on a legitimate response to a given sequence of words. Yet I feel warranted in stressing the importance of reception because, clearly, we must notice how a work works before we can tell in what way its form or subject matters. How, indeed, can I tell whether Molière's *Miser,* for example, portrays the "tragic" downfall of Harpagon or the "comic" rise to pleasure and power of his children's generation? Only by examining the play's impact on responsive readers or spectators—at first and particularly on myself. In the last analysis, I will have to explore whether the text or a given production of the play strikes me as portraying the frustration or the fulfillment of aspirations with which it makes me identify. Thus no anatomy of plot structure can avoid being based on the physiology of a response to the work in question.

Does this state of affairs make the impact of drama subject to the personal whim of individual readers and to the idiosyncrasy of particular performers and audiences? No one familiar with the history of taste (or lack thereof) is likely to deny that, to a certain extent, it does. Yet it is well to remember that the history of the literary and theatrical reception of drama is no more whimsical or idiosyncratic than most other strains in the motley fabric of human history. Indeed, mindful of the relatively recent work of Wolfgang Iser, Hans Robert Jauss, and other scholars reinvigorating the study of audience response with a hermeneutic concern for the interaction between texts and readers, I feel justified in making the following assumption: the response that my present place in the literary, theatrical, and critical tradition predisposes me to evolve to a particular text or performance may fairly count for me and for those who are predisposed or can be persuaded to share it as the kind of response that, owing to historically changing horizons of expectation, the play demands of its historically changing implied audience.

There are good reasons why, long before the current reawakening of general interest in literary reception, drama was providing the most fertile ground for affective criticism. Since most plays focus on a "change . . . of fortune" (Aristotle 1968:15) and contrast a happy or unhappy end to an initially very different situation, the final moods conveyed even by their unperformed texts tend to be particularly pervasive. Moreover, a congenial performance can impose additional "unity" on the represented action, and live audiences further homogenize the response of individual spectators: who would not be somewhat embarrassed to laugh when most others are on the verge of weeping and vice versa? But poems, novels, or even proverbs and works of expository writing including historiography may well elicit some of the same basic moods. To be sure, worthwhile works—whether dramatic or nondramatic—will not convey exactly the same mood to us from their beginning to their end. In most instances, however, one mood can serve as our point of critical orientation throughout a diversified text or performance just as one key characterizes a tonal piece of music as being, for example, in G major despite possibly frequent harmonic alterations and modulations. Much as in music, the final key or mood of a play or nondramatic work is likely to be the one to which previous keys—as, for instance, the "subdominant" or "parallel minor"—can be most meaningfully related.

The musical analogy should also help to restrain the drama critic's urge to pigeonhole entire works as belonging to a given genre. It can serve to remind us that the initial assignment to plays of a generic "key" such as tragedy or comedy is not more important than the subsequent effort to establish whether the congenial reception of a particular work "modulates" within adjacent categories (pity and fear, for example) or jumps back and forth among rather divergent moods and thus demands discussion in terms of tragicomedy. To facilitate communication, I myself have been using such reifying nouns as "tragedy" and "romance" as if individual plays might actually "belong" to a given generic category rather than "participate" in any number of them (cf. Staiger 1963:241 and Derrida 1981:61). It should be clear, however, that I have been interested chiefly in various types of receptive experience, which are best designated in adjectival terms (say "tragic" or "romantic") as a set of moods whose total expanse, like the musical octave or the color spectrum, could of course be sliced differently. I have sliced it the way I have in keeping with my own, I trust, widely sharable perspective on European and American drama.

Once we realize that even the supposedly "simple" genres tragedy, comedy, satire, and romance are interrelated and composite categories, the "mixed" status of tragicomedy (cf. Guthke 1966:40–42) need not strike us as a particularly difficult problem. Recalling Plato's insight into the "mixed feeling of pleasure and pain" elicited by both tragedy and comedy (*Philebus,* 48–50), we may even say that the tragicomic mood is a complex *Urphänomen* from which simpler responses to life or drama must be distilled, so to speak, by philosophical abstraction or artistic stylization. This could well be why tragicomedy is such a protean, hard-to-define phenomenon: the spirit of a particular tragicomedy may be "closer" to farce, for example, than to another tragicomedy that approximates a mystery play. Furthermore, most tragicomedies defy attempts to approximate their mood by just one of such neatly opposed terms as *admiration* and *indignation* or *fulfillment* and *frustration.* Almost always, one reader will find that the main thrust of a particular tragicomedy goes in one direction, while another reader will find that it goes in another. There is considerable disagreement among critics, for example, as to how thoroughly the festive finale of *Measure for Measure* manages to qualify Shakespeare's melodramatic satire against Angelo and other pseudo-angelic manifestations of human nature and culture. In the case of *Romulus the Great* (as well as in Eugène Ionesco's *Rhinoceros* and some other plays discussed by Martin Esslin in *The Theatre of the Absurd*), it is easier to miss the tragic than the farcical aspects. Conversely, the somber tones of *Murder in the Cathedral* may make some readers overlook how the "mystery" of Thomas Becket merges into a tragicomic backgound whose elaborate pattern is estabished by the melodrama of the Chorus ("living and partly living" [Eliot 1963:19]), the indecorous farce of the shortsighted Priests "dragging off" Becket into presumed safety

(70–71), the ironic satire of the self-vindication of the Four Knights (78–84), and the festive celebration following the Martyr's *imitatio Christi* (86–88).

While the contemporaries of Shakespeare and those of Molière probably approached *Timon of Athens* as a tragedy and *The Misanthrope* as a comedy, many modern readers appreciate the tragicomic implications of what the two plays have in common: the representation of a more or less justified yet grotesquely exaggerated hatred of humankind advocated by (and dehumanizing) a human being. Of course, the shared characteristics of Shakespeare's Timon and Molière's Alceste ought not to blur our view of significant differences between them—differences that in fact highlight an intriguing problem of drama criticism and invite being addressed in the present context. Why does the single-minded rigidity of one character strike us as a predominantly tragic trait and that of another as a predominantly comic one? According to the traditional distinction that can be found already in John Dryden's *Essay of Dramatic Poesie* (1668), the tragic hero gradually succumbs to an overwhelming *pathos* while the comic character is under the irresistible influence of a preponderant "humour" (1971:57–60; the British spelling is retained here in order to differentiate the Ben Jonsonian theory and practice of the "comedy of humours" from Jean Paul Richter's general concept of humor adopted earlier in my characterization of the implied author's attitude toward the world seen and represented as comic). To be sure, the postulated links between tragedy and moral struggle and between comedy and quasi-medical affliction raise as many questions as they propose to answer, the most troubling of which concerns our presumed propensity to laugh at a hopelessly afflicted fellow human being; after all, no one laughs at terminal cancer patients as such. But if we integrate two additional observations, one by Aristotle and one by Henri Bergson, to the "humour" theory of comedy, we may be able to understand and justify our different responses to tragedy's "passionate" monomaniac and to his comic, "humourous" counterpart. According to Chapter 5 of the *Poetics* (1968:9), the character's rigidity ought not to be harmful to himself or to others and, according to Bergson (1956:150–59), his intransigence ought not to spread across an entire, fully delineated personality if he is to become the object of our ridicule. If either of those "oughts" is violated, fear and pity (rather than derision) are likely to be aroused, and we approach the realm of tragedy rather than comedy. Clearly, Shakespeare's misanthrope is more harmful to himself and to others than Molière's; and since we are shown why and how Timon has assumed his intransigent hatred of humanity, his rigidity does not strike us as a foreign body in a "round" character or as the single determinant of a "flat" one. To stay within the medical analogy, Alceste's misanthropy is more amusing and less pitiable and fearful than Timon's insofar as it seems less like a malignant tumor spreading to the afflicted man's vital organs than like bad breath or some other odor expected to be suppressed in polite society.

Needless to say, a high degree of generic purity is quite uncharacteristic of the most mature representatives of any of our briefly discussed genres. "Unadulterated" tragedy and comedy would especially tempt us not to exert the effort required for composite vision but to look at dramatic characters—and, through identification with them, at ourselves—either from within or from the outside only. In contrast, our human (and humane) gift of "seeing it both ways" is especially exercised by plays whose tragicomic import reminds us that human beings trying to be all they can be and more are equally fulfilled and frustrated by complete alienation from their world and by the illusion of total integration with it. When perceived through the bifocal lens of tragicomic vision, both the dogged manifestation and the unconditional surrender of selfhood highlight the predicament of a finite being who is a particular human being and yet also part of several larger, natural as well as cultural contexts. It seems to me that playwrights can proceed in two directions as they combine the characteristic visions of the potentially tragic isolation of the self and its potentially comic insufficiency. They can make us frown upon the ways in which frustration and fulfillment as well as nature and culture appear *grotesquely inter-*

twined; or else they can elicit our astonished gaze into a universe where frustration and fulfillment as well as nature and culture seem *paradoxically identical.* The first method relates tragicomedy to the world as we feel it should not be; it stresses strife and incongruity; it tends toward satire. The second method relates tragicomedy to the world as we feel it should be; it stresses pattern and reconciliation; it tends toward romance. Of the two plays to be discussed in the next section of this chapter, T. S. Eliot's exemplifies the latter alternative, Friedrich Dürrenmatt's the former.

Before turning to those two plays, however, I wish to conclude my somewhat abstract typology of generic moods with an invitation to the persevering reader to embark with me on a brief imaginary cruise in time and space to the Primal Scene of Western drama theory, described at the end of Plato's *Symposium* (223c and d). As we arrive, most guests lie about sound asleep while Socrates is forcing two drowsy fellow revelers, the playwrights Aristophanes and Agathon, to admit "that the same man ought to understand how to compose both comedy and tragedy, and that he who has skill as a tragic poet has skill for a comic poet." Remarkably enough, not even Aristophanes and Agathon, a comic and a tragic poet, are kept awake for long by the philosopher's discourse concerning the identical essence of their art. Fortunately for both, however, kindly Socrates does not go off to the Lyceum to have a wash without first "making them comfortable." Consider for a moment: the alert critic finds a cozy nook for the authors representing comic and tragic drama as their creative slumber continues to turn shared private drives and shared public experience into separate dreams. Plato's attention to such a curious and seemingly insignificant detail may not directly corroborate my own attempt to place that odd couple, tragedy and comedy, at close quarters within a comfortable conceptual design. But the events reported at the end of Plato's *Symposium* greatly extenuate my guilt feelings for having possibly done to some of my readers what even Socrates could not avoid doing when his discourse on the same topic—the relationship between tragedy and comedy—put his listeners to sleep.

History and Self-Sacrifice

Shared subject matter justified comparative discussion of *Saint Joan* and *The Lark* even at first glance. A second, deeper look at *Murder in the Cathedral* (1935; 4th rev. ed. 1938) and *Romulus the Great* (1949; 3d version 1964) is required to discern what Eliot's revival of serious liturgical drama and Dürrenmatt's "unhistorical historical comedy," pioneering the theater of the absurd in its very subtitle, have in common. After all, Eliot's Thomas Becket dies convinced that he has escaped the temptation of self-imposed martyrdom while Dürrenmatt's Romulus survives with the realization that he has succumbed to it. Yet both plays make us aware of the same unsettling paradox: transcending the self through acts affirmed by the self may not mean genuine self-transcendence. And both plays deal with the tragicomedy of self-sacrifice against the background of history, which, according to their mutually corroborative testimony, is far too serious a concern to be taken, as if it did not point beyond itself, with utmost seriousness.

To be sure, the murder of Eliot's Becket by four agents of King Henry II could not take place outside of history. Yet it is not within secular history that the blood of the martyrs can, at the same time, "enrich the earth" (1963:87) and be "upon our heads" (88). In view of that transhistorical paradox, the historical causes and effects of Becket's death emerge as incidental adjuncts of spiritual decisions that occur in individual souls and/or rest with God. Thus the course of history appears to run between private pathos and cosmic humor: historical events constitute a series of contact points between potential tragedy and potential comedy, correlating the fate of each part with the destiny of the whole. Even the passive Chorus ("We do not wish anything to happen" [19]) is painfully entangled in the approaching murder. The Women of Canterbury agonize before the event: "Have I not known, not known, / What was coming to be?" And the self-accusation continues:

> What is woven on the loom of fate
> What is woven in the councils of princes

Is woven also in our veins, our brains,
Is woven like a pattern of living worms
In the guts of the women of Canterbury.

[68]

In Eliot's framework, then, whatever is recorded as having happened requires interpretation below, at, and above the level of history. The easy life whose divers pleasures the First Tempter offers to Becket so unsuccessfully (23–26) is surely below the plane of noteworthy historical events. But the former chancellor and present archbishop of Canterbury is not spared history's typical temptations of established and revolutionary power either. First we witness his refusal to make up with the King and, in the Second Tempter's words, to "Disarm the ruffian, strengthen the laws, / Rule for the good of the better cause" (28). Becket then refuses to ally himself and the church with the insurgent barons who claim to represent the people. He tells the Third Tempter, that "rough straightforward Englishman" (31) and early spokesman of "a happy coalition of intelligent interests" (33):

If the Archbishop cannot trust the Throne,
He has good cause to trust none but God alone.
It is not better to be thrown
To a thousand hungry appetites than to one.
At a future time this may be shown.

[34]

The last three lines just quoted are among those that Eliot has been persuaded—"by experiment in the course of production" (7)—to delete from the text of the fourth edition. Even without them, however, Becket's response to the Third Tempter, who insists that "Church and people have good cause against the throne" (34), echoes the Third Priest's previously expressed depreciation of what counts as history:

I see nothing quite conclusive in the art of temporal government,
But violence, duplicity and frequent malversation.
King rules or barons rule:
The strong man strongly and the weak man by caprice.
They have but one law, to seize the power and keep it,
And the steadfast can manipulate the greed and lust of others,
The feeble is devoured by his own.

[14]

Yet Becket has strained his eyes to penetrate the meaningless surface of events. He realizes what the Women of Canterbury, who serve as the choral background for *Murder,* "know and do not know," namely, "that action is suffering / and suffering is action." On such a view, of course, "neither does the agent suffer / Nor the patient act." From this carefully worded negative symmetry a double implication of identity in difference emerges: he who acts is merely an "agent" or, in the earlier versions of the play, an "actor" (presumably playing an assigned *part* on the stage of world history); yet he who patiently refrains from making history is also a disabled "patient" (deprived of the haleness or *wholeness* of health). Furthermore, the ensuing lines presently reveal that the neither/nor disjunction results from a temporary fragmentation of eternal action and eternal patience into temporal agent and patient and that the unity of the broken "both" is ultimately "fixed" in the repeated equation of *must* and *may,* destiny and freedom:

But both are fixed
In an eternal action, an eternal patience
To which all must consent that it may be willed
And which all must suffer that they may will it,
That the pattern may subsist, for the pattern is the action
And the suffering, that the wheel may turn and still
Be forever still.

[21–22]

55

Becket thus seems to have discerned the divine pattern behind human history. But has he really? His only formidable adversary in the quartet of Tempters, the Fourth, will soon apply the Archbishop's words about the Chorus to Becket himself:

> You know and do not know, what it is to act or suffer.
> You know and do not know, that acting is suffering,
> And suffering action.
>
> [40–41]

And so forth, repeating the Archbishop's previously quoted lines almost literally, until the wheel once again "may turn and still / Be forever still." The well-nigh identity of their language corroborates the Fourth Tempter's claim, "I offer what you desire" (40). In other words, while the first three temptations are feeble memories from Becket's past, the fourth represents an aspect of his present personality. Even before the Fourth Tempter assumed independent stage existence as a projection of the Archbishop's egotistical desire for "eternal grandeur" (40), the celebrated lines about the pattern and the wheel, about willed submission and self-fulfilling self-sacrifice, may thus have expressed his own sophisticated rationalization of the temptation to "seek the way of martyrdom" (39) for the sake of "general grasp of spiritual power" (36). But if the Archbishop's death should ultimately result from a misconceived desire for self-fulfillment, he would in fact have jettisoned himself from the divine pattern of history's turning wheel into that "Void" whose prospect is described by the Chorus as "more horrid than active shapes of hell" because, in its total "emptiness, absence, separation from God," there is nothing "to divert the soul / From seeing itself, foully united forever, nothing with nothing" (71–72).

Such diabolic fornication with his own beloved self reduced to nothingness would be the truly Dantesque eternal punishment of the willful (rather than willing) renouncer of temporal human existence. Does Becket's transcending of the wheel of history expose him to such punishment or has he, rather, escaped from committing "the greatest treason: / To do the right deed for the wrong reason" (44)? Consulting only the conceptual patterns of the dialogue, we would have to conclude: "we know and do not know." Eliot's elaboration on traditional Christian paradoxes (freedom in submission, elevation through self-humiliation) and especially his powerful battery of oxymora shortly before the murder ("spiritual flesh of nature," "animal powers of spirit," "lust of self-demolition," "ecstasy of waste and shame" [68]) sustain the ambiguity by contributing to a bold association of the martyr's death with the imagery of rape as fructifying the victim and, as it is often alleged, even enjoyed by her. Becket experiences "a tremour of bliss" before "all things / Proceed to a joyful consummation" (70), which can come about only after he has repeatedly commanded the Priests first to unbar and then to open the door of the cathedral; and while the church "lies bereft, alone, desecrated, desolated" by the intruding murderers, it is also left "triumphant in adversity" (84), since the blood of the martyrs and saints "shall enrich the earth, shall create the holy places" (87).

Perhaps subliminally affected by such ambivalent sexual implications, some critics have argued that the more strongly Becket feels that he has overcome the temptation of self-willed martyrdom, the more profoundly he succumbs to it in wishful blindness. But this argument ignores the dramatic logic of the play. Having been resisted by the hero, the Four Tempters—modernized allegorical figures of medieval morality plays—do not so much disappear as transmogrify into the melodramatic foursome of "slightly tipsy" knights, whose parts are usually played, "as was originally intended" (7), by the same four actors. Having slain Becket, the Four Knights revert to being tempters again: now tempters of each member of the audience and the reading public. As a result, the sob of melodrama gives way to the frown of bitter satire against the self-righteous murderers addressing the audience in apologetic speeches that ironically reveal the subtle yet shallow vileness of their character.

This holds especially for the Fourth Knight's insinuations, reminiscent once again of a rape trial: Becket is supposed to have "used every means of provocation'' and thus to have ''deliberately exasperated us beyond human endurance'' (83). Shifting the burden of guilt from the transgressors to the victim, the Fourth Knight asks the audience to ''render a verdict of Suicide while of Unsound Mind'' (84). The dramatic implication is clear: we would be siding with murderers if we were to endorse the Fourth Knight's claim that Becket, having pathologically ''determined upon a death by martyrdom,'' succumbed to the Fourth Tempter. The more appropriate interpretation of the play as resolving tragicomic tensions on a note of festivity is, aided by the musical accompaniment of the action. Before the murder, an awesome Dies Irae was ''sung in Latin by a choir in the distance'' (71). At the end, a celebratory Te Deum reinforces the English words of the Chorus on stage: ''We praise Thee, O God. . . . Thy glory is declared even in that which denies Thee; the darkness declares the glory of light'' (86).

Beyond doubt, Eliot has not spelled out in detail how Becket overcomes the temptation of transcending history by the dubious means of throwing away his life. But the play contains at least one clear hint, once again in terms of the carefully ordered sequence of speeches as dramatic events rather than in terms of purely textual meaning. After his harrowing encounter with the Fourth Tempter, Becket falls silent. There follows a whirlwind of alternatingly chanting Women, Tempters, and Priests. Finally Becket's silence is broken in response to the Chorus of women, representing the passively suffering bulk of humankind:

> CHORUS . . . : O Thomas, Archbishop, save us, save us, save your-
> self that we may be saved;
> Destroy yourself and we are destroyed.
> THOMAS: Now is my way clear, now is the meaning plain:
> Temptation shall not come in this kind again.   [44]

The emphatically repeated ''Now is . . . now is . . . '' indirectly answers the twice expressed appeal ''Save us, save us.'' Presumably recognizing once again that ''they speak better than they know'' (21), Becket resolves to comply with the spirit rather than the letter of the women's supplication. Far from deciding to save his earthly life in order to save theirs, he now realizes how profoundly the Low and the High depend on each other and embarks on a course of simultaneously saving his soul and the spiritual health of his flock by dying as Jesus died: neither selfishly for his own sake nor first and foremost, vaingloriously, for His, but humbly for theirs. A true martyr, Becket dies for the sake of ''subdued, violated'' (68) humanity, which, ''living and partly living'' (19) below the level of recorded history, looks for peace and justice beyond it.

In Dürrenmatt's view, at least according to the testimony of *Romulus the Great,* peace and justice ought to be sought *under* the historical level of momentous events. This realization comes too late to the title character. As the last emperor of Rome, Dürrenmatt's Romulus has spent the twenty years of his reign in a secret but ''historically'' successful effort to undermine the Roman resistance against the approaching Teutons because he has decided that his empire is too guilty of bloody oppression to deserve survival. When the enemy forces arrive, Romulus must discover that their humane leader, Odoaker, in turn wants to submit to Roman rule lest the idol of the troops, his warlike nephew Theodoric, erect ''a Teutonic empire, just as transitory as Rome and just as bloody.'' Romulus despairs:

> I took it upon myself to be Rome's judge, because I was ready to die.
> I asked of my country an enormous sacrifice because I, myself, was
> willing to be sacrificed. By rendering my country defenseless, I have
> made it bleed because I was ready to spill my own blood. And now I
> am to live. And now my sacrifice is not being accepted. . . . All I
> have done has become absurd. Kill me, Odoaker.

That mercy is denied by the sensible Teuton: ''Your death would be senseless. It would only make sense if the world were as you imagined it to be. But it isn't. Your enemy, too, is a human being who would do what is right, just as you do'' (1965b:72–73/1965a:112–14).

59

Since Romulus refuses to relieve Odoaker of the burden of world power, the Teutonic leader decides to send the Roman emperor into retirement and to begin his own reign as king of Italy with the murder of his still obedient yet ominous nephew. At this point it is Romulus' turn to speak a word of resigned wisdom: "If you kill your nephew, a thousand Theodorics will rise. Your people's views are different from yours. They desire heroism. You cannot change that." Romulus then ascribes the blame for the shared predicament of the two enlightened rulers to their having taken history too seriously, each in his own way:

> I have destroyed Rome because I feared its past; you [have wanted to destroy] Germania because you shuddered at its future. Two specters ruled us, for we have power neither over what was nor over what will be. We have power only over the present. Yet we did not think of the present, and now we founder on it.

Finally he suggests to Odoaker: "Try to give sense to nonsense in the few years that will still be yours. . . . Provide peace for the Teutons as well as the Romans. . . . World history will forget these years because they will be unheroic years. But they will be among the happiest this confused world has ever seen." A mellowed Romulus even accepts his bitterly ironic "happy end" as he resigns himself to the embarrassing retirement ceremony: "Let us do it quickly. Once more and for the last time, let us play comedy. Let us act *as if* final accounts were settled here on earth, as if the spirit won over the material called man" (74–75/114–15). As the two "as if" clauses indicate, Romulus no longer thinks that there is more to historical events than meets the eye. Indeed, the human task emerges from the play as the effort to withdraw from the visible surface of history in the downward direction of that kind of apparently trite but potentially meaningful day-to-day existence which is symbolized by the Emperor's preoccupation with the breeding of prize chickens.

Romulus' plea for this earthly kind of transcendence is in obvious contrast not only to Becket's Christmas sermon delivered to his community—embodied by the spectators—during the Interlude (1963:47–50). It also deviates from the religious spirit of Dürrenmatt's own first two historical plays, *Es steht geschrieben* (*It Is Written*, 1947) and *Der Blinde* (*The Blind Man*, 1948)—unorthodox Protestant equivalents of Eliot's Anglo-Catholic verse drama. Those two plays further resemble *Murder* in that they convey the modern playwright's world view without too frequently introducing conspicuous anachronisms into their ostensibly historical dialogue and action. *Romulus* in turn explodes the historical illusion of his Roman setting completely. The little we know about the last emperor of Rome, for example, includes the fact that he was dubbed Augustulus—the Little Emperor—and that he ruled for about eleven months as an adolescent figurehead. On the Teutonic side, Theodoric the Great was in fact Odoaker's eventual killer and successor but, far from being Odoaker's nephew, belonged to a different tribe and was not even in Italy at the presumed time of the action. Dürrenmatt's total disregard for the archives even permits him to introduce such fully anachronistic secondary characters as Caesar Rupf, head of an international corporation manufacturing trousers, who offers to buy off the Teutonic invaders in exchange for the hand of Romulus' daughter and a mandatory shift from the toga to his firm's products in Roman legwear fashion.

Just as Anouilh's *Lark* can be seen as applying the spirit of Shaw's Epilogue as a central structural and stylistic principle, Dürrenmatt's entire play is built on that deliberately anachronistic approach to the past which Eliot now and then employs to demonstrate the shared essence of different periods. Such pseudohistorical phrases as "the prize awarded for the English Essay" (1963:41) are relatively rare in *Murder*. They are the unruly rule rather than the occasional exception in *Romulus*. In the first act, for example, Rupf proposes to save the otherwise hopeless Roman Empire through "solid affiliation with an experienced business firm" (30/65); in the third, the Emperor describes the alternatives presented by that offer as the choice "between a catastrophic capitalism and a capital catastrophe" (53/92). Neither formulation represents a foreign ver-

61

bal body in the satirical mainstream of Dürrenmatt's dialogue, whose anachronistic diction articulates the playwright's awareness of the current alternative threats to human dignity by Big Business and Big Brother—the unscrupulous pursuit of the objectives either of economic profiteering or of oppressive government.

The latter threat is perceived by the Romulus of the first three acts as tied only to the power structure of his own political system. He remains blind to the fact that his lifelong deliberate inaction has helped Rome's world-historical rival to assume imperialistic ambitions of its own. That is why he can proudly reveal to his indignant wife that he married her merely to become emperor and to destroy the empire from above: "This was the only way in which my doing nothing could make sense. To be idle as a private citizen is completely ineffectual" (51/89). That is also why he can demand that his daughter remain loyal to her fiancé, who has just returned from Teutonic captivity with a mutilated body, even though patriotic Emilian himself insists that Rea leave him and save the Fatherland by marrying Rupf. And that is, finally, why he feels he can stand up to Emilian, in whom he sees "the great ultimate argument against the man who, like myself, refuses to defend himself" (60/99). The Emperor hurls the following rejoinder at the tortured patriot when Emilian appears with a dozen conspirators in the imperial bedchamber to kill Romulus, the traitor:

> I didn't betray my empire; Rome betrayed herself. Rome knew the truth but chose violence. Rome knew humaneness but chose tyranny. Rome doubly demeaned herself: before her own people and before the other nations in her power. You are standing before an invisible throne, Emilian; before the throne of all the Roman Emperors, of whom I am the last. Shall I touch your eyes that you may see this throne, this mountain of piled-up skulls, these rivers of blood streaming on its steps, the eternal cataracts of Roman power? . . . We have shed the blood of others; now we must pay back with our own. . . . Answer my question: Do we still have the right to defend ourselves? Do we still have the right to be anything but a victim? [60–61/100–101]

The German word for victim, *Opfer,* also means sacrifice, and Dürrenmatt is skillful in exploiting the implications of that homonymy. His Romulus victimizes the Roman Empire as a sacrificial act of atonement since he has determined that it is time for "the curses of Rome's victims" (61/100) to be fulfilled. But, as Dürrenmatt shrewdly noted in a postscript to the play, "if Romulus sits in judgment over the world in Act Three, the world sits in judgment over Romulus in Act Four" (79/119). Even his daughter and Emilian, two people he dearly loved, lose their lives while attempting to escape from the approaching Teutons; thus Romulus ultimately confronts the ironic consequences of his refusal to be cast in the melodramatic role of "those heroic fathers who say 'good appetite' to the state when it wants to devour their children" (54/93). Hiding his own tragic project from both his court and the audience, the Romulus of Act One might disingenuously declare: "People at their last gasp like us can only understand comedy" (19/106). Yet the osten tatiously farcical Emperor is being prepared by the humorous indifference of history to what he has considered fair play and poetic justice for the tragicomic role of "Rome's judge" (72/112) whose self-imposed death sentence is commuted contrary to his faith in the appropriateness of the verdict. Hence the disillusioned bitterness of his complaint, already quoted, about his sacrifice "not being accepted."

We must imagine Eliot's Becket in Romulus' situation to comprehend fully what Dürrenmatt called the tragic quality in the comedy of the Emperor's retirement (79/119). With the Chorus and the Priests rather than Becket himself killed by the King's men, how would the retired Archbishop feel about a small pension granted to him by the King in appreciation of his past political accomplishments? Furthermore, the slaying of Becket could only result in genuine martyrdom if it had not been willed as such by Becket but had been so willed by God. What, then, can be said of the fate of Romulus, whose self-willed sacrificial death the god of his frustrated project—world history—refuses to accept?

Toward the end of Act I Romulus concludes his leisurely breakfast with the declaration "I do not wish to disturb the course of world history" (31/67) and proceeds ceremoniously to demand a finger bowl and to wash his hands, presumably almost until the curtain falls, with fastidious cleanliness. The scenic allusion to Pontius Pilate is hardly accidental. It allies Romulus, who fancied himself as the servant of the divine justice manifested in history, with a highly objectionable prototype of the policy of shaping the world's fate by means of consequential noninterference. In deliberate mockery of what his bustling compatriots regard as the tragic downfall of the empire, Romulus has spent the comic phase of his life raising and consuming prize chickens and retailing or otherwise distributing such last relics of Rome's greatness as the sculpted busts of his predecessors on the throne and the golden leaves of the imperial wreath. Yet in the final scene of the play, the tragic shadow of Eliot's Fourth Tempter hovers triumphantly over Romulus' bitterly farcical exit. Having announced to the assembled and respectfully amazed Teutons, "Gentlemen, the Roman Empire has ceased to exist" (77/117), this martyr *manqué* walks away slowly, with bent head, carrying the unmarketable bust of his namesake, the founder of Rome, under his arm. His self-sacrifice having been rejected, Romulus must realize that no human design justifies the willful sacrifice of a self. The contrast between Eliot's "romantic" and Dürrenmatt's "satirical" yoking of pathos and humor could hardly be more pronounced. While Becket, after his potentially tragic inner struggle with the Tempters, is permitted to merge into the transhistorical pattern of cosmic romance, *Romulus the Great* leads us from delightful amusement at a clownish emperor through derisive scorn toward his selfish subjects to bemused pity for Romulus the Little, who has even failed in his melodramatic aspiration to die the sacrificial death of a tragic hero.

3

Myths of Progress and Recurrence:

Le Diable et le bon dieu and

Die chinesische Mauer

"The play begins! Place of the action: this stage. Or one might also say: our consciousness" (1967:12/1969:7). At the end of the Prelude to Max Frisch's tragicomic "farce" *The Great Wall of China,* which is quoted here from the 1967 reprint of the fullest second version (1955) rather than the first (1947) or the third (1972), the Man of Today thus identifies the two ideal loci of all historical drama: "this stage" (or page) and "our consciousness" are the poles between which the sparks of the make-believe world of any re-presented past must now be generated. Throughout the play Frisch stresses the present ("this stage") but imaginary ("our consciousness") existence of his characters. This is hardly surprising since he has culled them from the history and literature of various periods. We see Columbus, Pontius Pilate, Don Juan, Brutus, Cleopatra, Romeo and Juliet, Napoleon Bonaparte, and others as guests of Hwang Ti, emperor of China in the third century B.C., at a fancy-dress ball celebrating the start of construction work on the Great Wall.

Such dreamlike simultaneity of all ages naturally originates in the playwright's consciousness. But the dream is an *Angsttraum* rather than a *Wunschtraum* because the playwright's mouthpiece, the Man of Today (*Der Heutige*), is at the mercy first of the despotic emperor and later of the prince Wu Tsiang, the no less dictatorial leader of a victorious uprising. Indeed, those two characters created by the playwright with precious little help from historians represent fearfully real powers over him and his audiences. As Hwang Ti tells the spectators:

> I know precisely what you are thinking, you out there. But your hope makes me smile. You're thinking, this very evening I will be hurled from this throne, for the play must have an end and a meaning, and when I have been dethroned you can go home reassured and have a beer and pretzels. That would suit you just fine. You with your dramaturgy! I must smile. Go out and buy your newspaper, you down there, and on the front page you will see my name. For I won't let them dethrone me. I don't observe the rules of dramaturgy. [51/40–41]

In a literal sense, of course, Hwang Ti is dethroned shortly after this speech by the forces of Prince Wu Tsiang. But in the fancy-dress ball of world history he will, or so he predicts, remain in power simply because he *is* power—the dramatic incarnation of the fact that the decisions and actions of some people largely determine the fate and consciousness of others.

Historytelling and the Strategies of Desire

The "making" of all human history by just some human beings is a central concern of both Max Frisch and Jean-Paul Sartre in *The Great Wall of China* and *The Devil and the Good Lord*. But it is also subtly hinted at in Faust's lines quoted earlier:

> Mein Freund, die Zeiten der Vergangenheit
> Sind uns ein Buch mit sieben Siegeln.
> Was ihr den Geist der Zeiten heisst,
> Das ist im Grund der Herren eigner Geist,
> In dem die Zeiten sich bespiegeln.

In the context of Chapter 1 I found it meaningful to use Walter Kaufmann's translation of the key phrase, *der Herren eigner Geist,* as "the scholar's spirit." That rendering is justified on the basis of the dramatic situation at hand: Faust is challenging his assistant's blind faith in the academic discipline of history. But Walter Arndt's more literal translation, "the gentlemen's own mind," highlights the connection that Goethe's carefully chosen words also suggest between history and power. Before the apocalyptic removal of its *sieben Siegel,* the seven seals mentioned in Revelation (5:1), the book of the past cannot be opened. What we now think of as its contents are highly ambiguous mirror images of *die Zeiten*—"the ages" but also "the [current] times"—in *der Herren eigner Geist:* the masters' "own" (but also "peculiar") mind. Goethe seems to be reminding us that all history is written and rewritten by and for the victors: if not those who have already won, then those who have at least survived in the struggle for political and intellectual domination. This association of historiography with willful mastery suggests at least two considerations relevant to the present study of modern historical drama. As vocal survivor, the playwright, like any other history-teller, prevails over the past; as influential myth-maker, he helps to shape the present and even the future. When Frisch's Man of Today announces, "Time of the action: this evening" (12/7), he is also telling us that the most significant action of any performed historical play is the positive or negative effect of its proposed mythmaking on the spectators.

In the broadest and recently current sense of the word, a myth is a firmly held conviction that claims and often gains credence without being demonstrably true. In this solid form—a set of unquestioned assumptions that feed on private or collective desires—"myths" provide both the best targets and, I hasten to add, the best guns for the intellectual shooting matches known as critiques of ideology (cf. Barthes 1957/1972). More typically, however, we encounter myths in the fluid state of narrated or enacted stories that are hardly, if at all, distinguishable from certain works of narrative or dramatic fiction. It is in this narrower sense of the word that myth and history have been interrelated by contemporary students of religion and anthropology. Mircea Eliade, for example, called attention to the analogy between the recollection of prehistoric, mythical events in traditional societies and the "recollection of *all that took place in historical Time*," the ultimate aim of historiography in the modern West: "Both types of *anamnesis* project man out of his 'historical moment'" and thus open "on a primordial Time, the Time in which men established their behavior patterns" (1963:138). Claude Lévi-Strauss has likewise argued that the self-styled "historical consciousness" of members of a modern class or state is comparable to mythic explanatory constructs of the "savage mind"; like all ideological superstructure, it is built out of "*faulty acts* which have 'made it' socially" (1966:253–54). According to Lévi-Strauss, wisdom consists in living one's present life in the "spurious intelligibility" derived from one's internalized interpretations of the relatively recent past "while at the same time knowing (but in a different register) that what one lives so completely and intensely is a myth—which will appear as such to men of a future century, and perhaps to oneself a few years hence, and will no longer appear at all to men of a future millenium" (255).

It is easy to see why the less wise among us tend to "rationalize" our favorite versions of what has happened into rationally unassailable bastions of aggressive or even self-destructive inclinations: those myths of history help organize our experience, which without them would be either too chaotic or too closely bound to instinctual automatisms to remain human. The frequent appearance in older histories of such stereotypes as the just ruler or the bloodthirsty tyrant unmistakably points to the confluence of mythic archetypes and ideological oversimplifications. While modern historians prefer a less fairy-tale-like vocabulary, their collective agents (such as the exploited peasantry or the victorious bourgeoisie) and explanatory constructs (such as the will to power or the class struggle) still emerge from the collective consciousness of a given historian's society and serve quasi-mythic needs of self-orientation within that society. In other words, present hopes and fears are reflected in the

68

narrative structure, if not in much of the very content, of the chronicled fulfillments and frustrations of the past.

This holds, I believe, both for those historians who attempt to *explain* events in the scientific terms of generally applicable laws of historical causation and for those who attempt to make us *understand* events in the mythic terms of purposive human action. As Arthur C. Danto pointed out in his *Analytical Philosophy of History,* "phenomena *as such* are not explained, it is only phenomena *as covered by a description* which are capable of explanation" (1968: 218). Danto further notes that "we can cover an event with a general law only once we have covered it with a general *description*" (220), and it seems clear that historians have considerable freedom—if, indeed, they are not causally determined—to cover the same phenomena with descriptions of quite different kinds. Some historians favor a scientific approach, which is most fruitful when applied to objects lacking intentions of their own, others approximate the mythic principle, best suited to stories about supernatural beings who are not subject to causal determination. But even if one historian should see men and women as involved in completely determined processes and another should see them as exercising complete freedom in essentially open situations, each would have to describe past events as he or she sees them—that is to say, as past events envisioned by a present consciousness. In so doing, both will correlate a retrospective point of view from which the narrated events can be seen as irretrievably determined (what has *occurred, has* occurred) with a present-oriented, future-bound perspective (analogous to the prospective point of view animating the intentions and expectations of the historical agents themselves who consciously participate in *occurring* events) from which historiography turns "what really happened" (cf. Ranke 1973:137) into "how it shall be remembered."

The historian thus appears to labor under two sometimes conflicting jurisdictions: whereas science evolves through the competition of more or less demonstrable explanations, myth develops through the competition of more or less preferable objectives. Since changing conditions codetermine what is demonstrable and what is preferable in a given instance, both science and myth have histories of their own from which their respective and apparently opposed principles emerge as interrelated in the realm of historiography. While science claims, "All things are determined," and myth insists, "All things are purposeful," the historian's scientific mythmaking suggests that causality and teleology are complementary idioms in which the question "Why?"—the question each of us has so frequently asked ever since, in early childhood, we learned to gripe and to wonder—can be answered.

In the last section of Chapter I I suggested that "to the extent that historiographical narratives share with overtly imaginative works of literature their quasi-mythic narrative focus on the fulfillment and/or frustration of human projects, they are primarily answerable to the principle of desire rather than the principle of knowledge." Ordinarily, of course, we think of knowledge as keeping desire in its place, and of the reality principle as setting viable limits to the pleasure principle. But in an important sense the very opposite is true. From a human point of view, the most universal principle of reality is that there is too much of it for wholesome consumption. This holds for both the body and the mind: our well-nigh insatiable appetite for both food and information would destroy us if our modes of metabolism, sensory perception, emotive response, and conceptual understanding were not restricted to a relatively limited number. Beyond doubt, selectivity is particularly important in matters pertaining to what is assumed to have happened. Through archives, oral traditions, memories, and even dreams, an ever bulkier past keeps crowding in on our fragile present. Only by relentlessly reducing what happened to what shall be remembered can we escape unbearable emotive and conceptual chaos.

In his monumental *Metahistory: The Historical Imagination in Nineteenth-Century Europe* (1973), Hayden White adopted Northrop Frye's classification of four fundamental mythic and literary story patterns—the *mythoi* or "pregeneric" plot structures of tragedy, comedy, romance, and satire (1957:158–239)—as the blueprint according to which historians erect the explanatory edifices of followable narratives on the neutral ground of the "unprocessed historical record" (1973:5, 7–11). In keeping with my amplification, in Chapter 2, of Frye's theory of *mythoi* from the vantage point of audience response, I wish to suggest that some recurrent patterns of historytelling prevail over the life-sustaining blockade against stimuli of all kinds because they fit in especially well with our desire for the kinds of thrill, gratification, indignation, and admiration that partly or predominantly tragic, comic, satirical, and romantic works of literature afford to their responsive audiences. We like plays and stories, *as well as* histories, because they help us to replace boredom and indifference—those nearly vacant states of mind that bring us frighteningly close to Eliot's Void, the infernal experience of nonexistence—with the thrill or gratification of self-assertive entertainment and with the social or cosmic commitment to bypass or surpass selfhood. Ultimately, therefore, two kinds of desire—the desire for self-assertion and the desire for self-transcendence—impose narrative order on the "historical field," which by dint of this imposition becomes pleasurably knowable. In other words, our getting to know the past entails either the desirable assertion or the equally desirable transcendence of selfhood or else, to conclude with the most desirable alternative, some combination of the two.

By conveying one or more than one of the moods distinguished in Chapter 2, dramatic texts and performances thus appeal to our desires for self-assertive entertainment and/or self-transcending commitment. But they do so with different degrees of single-minded intensity. Works characterized by just one mood (festive joy, farcical derision, melodramatic pity, or fear-ful mystery, for example) represent coarser varieties of entertainment and commitment than the more complex works conveying comedy's cheer *and* jeer, tragedy's sob *and* throb, satire's jeer *and* sob, or the throb *and* cheer of romance. But even the more complex and more dignified genres—Northrop Frye's foursome of *mythoi*—display a good deal of family resemblance to such embarrassing second cousins of civilized drama as glamorous burlesque, violent slapstick, blood-curdling whodunit, and tear-jerking soap opera. Each of the last-mentioned offsprings of today's entertainment industry, as well as the corresponding instruments of easy gratification and cheap thrill employed in other cultures, titillates one of four impulses whose thrust comedy and tragedy attempt to domesticate. In their different ways, however, the more and the less dignified genres attest to the power of the same set of ultimately dehumanizing tendencies in the human psyche. To give relatively recent names to those gray eminences of show business, both ancient and modern, we may call them voyeurism, sadism, masochism, and *Schadenfreude*—one person's gloating over another's misfortune.

It is clear that the same four tendencies may reach psychotic and antisocial extremes when they operate outside the culturally sanctioned realms of thrilling or gratifying entertainment. They can also provide forceful motivation for pursuing a cosmic or social commitment to its extreme of radical disrespect for the value of individual human life. Indeed, a careful analysis of just why certain kinds of plays (as well as comparable myths, stories, and histories) are so successful in entertaining or committing their congenial audiences could call needed attention to the voyeuristic and masochistic aspects of certain forms of religious adoration and mortification, as well as to the element of sadism or self-congratulatory condescension in some of our violent or charitable dealings with the evils of society. For our present purpose it will suffice to insist that the various areas and formations of human culture are by no means discontinuous; for example, while the quasi-romantic genres of the medieval miracle play and morality play hark back to drama's religious origin, the quasi-satirical genres of the ubiquitous lampoon and the modern docudrama signal drama's political potential.

Willing self-exposure to large doses of unalloyed endurance, indulgence, indignation, or admiration characterizes the respective devotees of melodramatic soap operas, glamour pageants, incriminating videotapes, and the faith healer's miraculous mysteries (to stay within the familiar realm of what, thanks to the Nielsen ratings, gets so frequently televised). Tragedy and comedy, in con-

trast, offer more complex versions of thrilling or gratifying entertainment as they affect us in the respective ways contraposed by
Edmund Burke in 1757 as the sublime and the beautiful; and neither
romance nor satire needs to lure its creators and audiences to the
"ultraviolet" or "infrared" extremes of the spectrum of commitment allegorized by Arthur Koestler as the yogi and the commissar
(1945:3–14). Yet only tragicomic (or "satiromantic") works are
likely to lead to a dynamic equilibrium of two or more of the
following attitudes in their reader's or spectator's psyche: the tragic
endurance of the frightfully limiting, the comic indulgence in the
amusingly pleasurable, the satirical indignation over the revoltingly
incongruous, and the romantic admiration for the inexhaustibly
splendid aspects of the human condition.

My obvious preference for complex over simplistic ways of entertaining and committing an audience is in line with Horace's advice to the poet who aspires to please both the younger and older
members of his potential audience: try to combine the sweet (*dulce*)
and the useful (*utile*), try to delight (*delectare*) as well as benefit
(*prodesse*) your readers ("Ars Poetica," ll. 333–44). Properly understood, such advice suggests that simultaneous rather than selective appeal can also be made to the agelessly young and old—the
more vigorous and the more mature capacity—in each of us. Since
the "young" wants to be entertained through thrill or gratification
while the "old" wants to be committed within social or cosmic
contexts, fictive as well as historical representations of events may
well attempt to promote in their audience a delicate balance between
the self-assertive desire for "sweet" or at least suspenseful entertainment and the self-transcending desire for "useful" or otherwise
beneficial commitment. In associating entertainment with self-assertive and commitment with self-transcending impulses, I have
followed hints from Arthur Koestler, who in *The Act of Creation*
(1964) contrasted self-assertion and self-transcendence as "opposite tendencies" manifesting "part-behavior" and "whole-be-
havior" in the human psyche. Koestler's impressively far-reaching
extrapolation of the "dynamic equilibrium" of those tendencies

from the level of a living organism "both upward into the hier-
archies of the body social and downward into stable inorganic systems" (1976:290) may well have overshot the mark. My own much
more limited objective here is to suggest that a general theory of
human moods could be based on some typical responses of twentieth-century occidental readers and spectators to drama—and to
life as drama—in the library, at the theater, and beyond the confines
of art.

When such "moods" as pity, fear, and the others I named in
Chapter 2 function in a more active than contemplative fashion,
they tend to be referred to as emotions or even passions. As such,
they motivate behavior as well as purposive action and can be
studied from a biological perspective on human existence as well as
from an existential perspective on human biology. Not long ago,
Robert Plutchik (1962) indeed classified the emotions according to
eight "dimensions" of animal behavior: destruction, reproduction,
incorporation, orientation, protection, deprivation, rejection, and
exploration. More recently still, Robert Solomon (1976) discussed
the passions from an existentialist point of view as "constitutive
judgments according to which our reality is given shape and structure." In partial agreement with Plutchik and Solomon, I would say
that my "moods" and their "emotions" or "passions" manifest,
respectively, responses to the recent past and motives for the immediate future. But I wish to add that each mood as well as each
emotion or passion typically aims at some form of self-assertion
through thrill or gratification or else at some form of self-transcendence toward social or cosmic horizons. Just like our actions, our
moods, emotions, and passions are thus various "ways of worldmaking," as the title of Nelson Goodman's thought-provoking book
(1978) calls our creations and supposed representations of reality.
As mental acts of self-assertion and self-transcendence, they converge with other events within the worlds that our moody minds
tentatively make and our active bodies terminally inhabit.

It follows from the preceding remarks that the principle of self-assertive and self-transcending desire bears on both the methods and the subject matter of historiography. As regards historical knowledge that twofold principle underlies the differences between two kinds of cognition: the objectifying and the hermeneutic. Desire for self-assertion motivates historiography as an objectifying science that aims at the knower's mastery over the known by keeping the two as separate as the cognitive interaction between subject and object will allow. Desire for self-transcendence motivates historiography as a hermeneutic discipline that entangles—if not, indeed, constitutes—the knower and the known in a ceaseless dialectic of interrelated questions and answers. The two kinds of desire and the two kinds of cognition motivated by them may well be humanized manifestations of two animal instincts of survival: the self-assertive drive for the preservation of the existing organism and the self-transcending drive for the perpetuation of the developing species and perhaps even of its life sustaining environment. More over, the same two drives seem to provide biological energy not only for self-assertive and self-transcending cognition but also for self-assertive and self-transcending action. From the stories historians tell, the human past emerges as constant competition and cooperation between efforts to maintain and to enhance individual identity. Most of the time our selfish instinct for individual survival and the entertaining pleasures of self-assertion win the upper hand. Yet the power of Desire's second, selfless impulse is palpably demonstrated whenever people subordinate physical or economic well-being to their—occasionally misguided—social or cosmic commitments.

This state of affairs invests the analogous genres of storytelling and historytelling with human significance whose esthetic and epistemological aspects cannot be analyzed apart. After all, certain kinds of plays and narratives may well have won their struggle for literary survival in the generic jungle because they have proven to be the fittest containers of the kinds of knowledge that Desire makes or allows us to generate about the kinds of action through which human beings carry Desire's flag into the previously uncharted temporal wasteland of the Not-Yet-Desirable. Since every desire can be partially or completely fulfilled or frustrated, it is hardly surprising that rise, fall, and the cyclical seesaw of rise and fall should be the basic patterns underlying most historiographical narratives. The rising or falling hero of a particular historical narrative may be a person, a class, a state, or some such entity as literary censorship or the gross national product. But either significant change or cyclical recurrence will provide the universal standard against which the reader is expected to measure or even evaluate the particular vicissitudes of the "hero."

Of these two master myths of history, irreversible progress or regress is often felt to be fraught with potential tragedy whereas periodic recurrence is usually seen as potentially comic. It is even tempting to carry these genre-alizations beyond human history into the sphere of thermodynamics and speak with William Holtz (1971) of a "tragic" development toward entropy or the perpetual "comic" rejuvenation of energy and matter through dynamic equilibrium. In any event, the myths of radical change and eternal return merely delineate the backdrop against which dramatic actions of various kinds may take place. Theoretically speaking, linear tragedy is linked to the loss of freedom adumbrated in our foreknowledge of death and in our realization that every human choice entails committing innumerable alternatives to a state of nonbeing; the comic cycle of eternal return can in exchange be affirmed (if not, indeed, activated) through self-transcending acts of love—be it intellectual or spiritual agape, be it psychological or biological eros. But in the concrete, contrapuntally tragicomic instances of *The Devil and the Good Lord* and *The Great Wall of China* both Sartre and Frisch seem to be working against the grain of any such simplifying theory. To invoke the more precise generic terms suggested in Chapter 2, Sartre's melodramatic celebration of existential freedom shows Goetz fulfilled by rejecting just what the frustrated Man of Today achieves in Frisch's awe-inspiring farce of human impotence: self-transcendence through love.

Situated Freedom

The Devil and the Good Lord (1951) offers clear evidence for the gradual reorientation of Sartre's existentialism from the post-Husserlian phenomenology of *Being and Nothingness* (1943) to a largely Marxist *Critique of Dialectical Reason* (1960). Yet no study of Sartre's intellectual biography can be attempted here. As I shall focus on the play's complex world of interacting images and characters, my awareness of parallels or contrasts with Sartre's philosophy and politics will be kept in the relatively unlit background. Such a perspective on the play is in line with Sartre's express demand for a theatrical approach to it. Soon after the first performance of *The Devil and the Good Lord,* he protested against interpretations of the play as a mere variation on some philosophical theme (for example, *"nietzschéisme hégélienisant"*). Sartre's argument is persuasive: if he had wished to "prove" the nonexistence of God or some other philosophical tenet, he would have used the essay as the appropriate medium for such a message; once he has chosen to write in dramatic form, the primary question to be asked by readers and spectators is not "What does this play amount to?" (*Que vaut cette pièce?*) but rather "What's going to happen?" (1973:276).

Drama, of course, can take many different shapes and forms, and one critic has perceptively described the play as an "atheist allegory" in which the hero, "tempted by God or Being, lives in 'sin' until he sees the truth, rejects all absolutes, and is saved" (McCall 1969:38). Undoubtedly, *The Devil and the Good Lord* allegorizes the logic of Sartre's own existentialist rebellion against externally imposed standards for human conduct. At the same time, however, the largely fictive history of his Goetz—a sixteenth-century German warrior first trying to be evil, next trying to be good, and then trying to pass beyond the moral and religious dichotomy of good and evil—is presented to us as a psychologically and sociologically interpretable sequence of events.

Unlike his historical prototype, whose autobiography inspired Goethe's play *Götz von Berlichingen* (1773), Sartre's Goetz is a bastard who can describe himself as follows: "I have been a double agent from birth; my mother gave herself to a no-account, and I am composed of two halves that do not fit together; each one is repulsive to the other" (1951:57/1960:33). As the most ambitious dramatic expression of its author's world view, *The Devil and the Good Lord* has been called Sartre's *Faust,* and the second half of the sentence just quoted even echoes the famous lines in which Goethe's Faust laments his predicament:

> Zwei Seelen wohnen, ach, in meiner Brust,
> Die eine will sich von der andern trennen.

> Alas! two souls within my breast abide,
> And each from the other tries to separate.
>
> [1112–13]

But much more than Goethe does in either of his plays set within the same historical period, Sartre stresses the connection between the public realm and the private—the extensive social upheavals and the intensive religious agonizing prevalent in the early years of Luther's Reformation. This is particularly obvious in the plight of Heinrich, whose private inability to enter meaningful commitments is projected as stemming from the discrepancy between two public roles. Heinrich is a member, however subordinate, of the priestly hierarchy but also of the unprivileged class of peasants and impoverished townspeople, whose life he has shared ever since his childhood. This is why, during their first encounter, Goetz can treat him as a fellow bastard: "You, too, are a bastard. To engender you, the clergy coupled with misery; what joyless fornication." And Goetz also insists that, by the very logic of their ambivalent situation, "bastards betray, what else do you want them to do?" (57/33).

Heinrich is, indeed, faced with a choice between two kinds of betrayal. The Bishop of Worms, fatally wounded by the rebellious crowd, has entrusted to him the key to a secret underground passage through which Goetz's soldiers may enter the fortified city. If they do, they are likely to "massacre the poor"; but if they do not, "the poor will massacre the priests." Heinrich's dilemma has readily quantifiable social implications: "Two hundred priests or twenty thousand men. . . . The question is how many men equal a priest" (40/23). Given the conflicting allegiances of his bastardly existence, Heinrich cannot choose well but choose he must. Once he has delivered the key to Goetz, who in turn decides not to make use of it, despair drives him further and further into isolation from the human world around him; he believes himself to be constantly accompanied by the devil and, at the end, his sole remaining hope is that an "infinite being" rather than his equals will judge him (239/142).

Being the embodiment of such "bad faith," Heinrich serves throughout the play as a foil to Goetz, as the latter's alter ego. Early on, he is responsible for the first sea change in Goetz's attitude toward good and evil. When Goetz prepares to burn down the city of Worms and kill its inhabitants, his claim to uniqueness ("Sometimes I imagine Hell as an empty desert waiting for me alone") in thwarting God's supposedly benign master plan is mocked by Heinrich:

But Hell is overflowing, you fool! . . . Every night the soil of Germany is illuminated by living torches; tonight, as on every night, cities are going up in flames by dozens, and the captains who pillage them don't make nearly so much fuss about it. . . . The world itself is iniquity; if you accept the world, you are an accomplice, if you change it, you are a hangman. . . . We are equally guilty, bastard, we are all equally deserving of Hellfire, but the Lord forgives when it pleases Him to forgive. [105–8/61–63]

At the end of Act I, this argument provokes Goetz to wager that, against all odds, he will be able to embark on a course of good deeds. Yet, in deciding to submit henceforth "to the will of God" (111/65), Goetz leaves nothing to blind chance. He manipulates the dice when the wager is initiated and must thus feel responsible for

79

the dire consequences of his subsequent actions. The play makes it very clear that the "good deeds" of Goetz—the giving away of his lands to his serfs and the establishing of a pacifistic community of brotherly love in "one corner" of war-torn Germany—lead to more and more destruction, suffering, and death not because, as Heinrich insists, "God has willed that the Good be impossible on this earth" (107/62). Rather, Act II and much of Act III prove Goetz's project to be unsuccessful because it is a misconceived project, based on the reified phantoms of good and evil that haunt Heinrich and, through him, can also haunt Goetz as long as the wager's outcome is to be judged by Heinrich and, through him, by God. "For lack of a judge" (239/142), however, the supposed trial turns into a final battle that Heinrich and Goetz fight first with verbal, then with physical force.

From their shared failure to elicit any response from God to their human plight, Heinrich concludes that man doesn't matter; Goetz, that God doesn't exist. As if to highlight the irreconcilable opposition between their respective views of who is ultimately responsible for human decisions (Goetz has come to exclaim: "If God exists, man is nothing; if man exists . . . " [238/141]), one of the two "bastards" must die in one of two suggestively symbolic ways: first Heinrich attempts to kill Goetz by *choking* him, but Goetz liberates himself from the deadly embrace by *stabbing* Heinrich to death. With Heinrich and his constant stifling talk of heaven and hell gone, Goetz's words over the dead body of his impaled alter ego are meant to apply to the devil and the good Lord as well: "You are dead, and the world is as full as ever; you won't be missed by anyone" (240/143). His newly invigorated sense of existence needs corroboration only through commerce with other human beings. Giving up his inauthentic attempt at celibacy, Goetz now pleads with his consort, Hilda: "Look at me, don't stop looking at me for a moment. . . . If you turned away your head, I should be afraid of annihilation." In his present frame of mind, even the approach of his enemies is something to look forward to: "Let us stay: I need the sight of men" (241/143).

Goetz's conclusion that man's existence as a free agent entails the nonexistence of God does seem to resolve, if not indeed dissolve, the play's first dispute about freedom and determination. In an attempt to console a woman whose child starved to death in the beleaguered city of Worms, Heinrich has said: "Nothing happens without God's permission" (21/10). "Nothing except evil, which is born out of the wickedness of man," retorts the baker Nasty, who emerges as the leader of the incipient rebellion (24/12). If Heinrich is right, man could be considered what Goetz later calls a mere "optical illusion" (223/132). But even Nasty's less omnipotent God would have to be thought of as deciding what man ought to do and leaving man the far lesser choice between acting and not acting as he should—doing what is good or else causing evil to be "born out of the wickedness of man." As a champion of presumably total human freedom, Goetz progresses from defying external oughts (Act I) through trying, against what he believes are overwhelming odds, to conform to them (Act II and much of Act III) to abandoning the very notion of their existence. The scene next to the last yields this penultimate insight: "Silence is God. Absence is God. God is the loneliness of man. There was no one but myself; I alone decided on Evil, I alone invented Good" (238/141). Yet this individualistic concept of freedom, propounded by Goetz in the penultimate scene of the play, is eventually qualified. The last scene makes abundantly clear that we are free in predetermined situations and that every human decision is potentially a decision for other human beings whose freedom is diminished by it.

Goetz wants to join the rank and file of rebellious peasants but is told by Nasty that he is welcome only as their general in the ever more desperate war against the barons: "For a year and a day, your place has been waiting for you. Take it!" (246/146). Much against his expressed desire to be an ordinary "man among men" (245/145), Goetz eventually realizes that he is meant to be their lonely and bloody leader; he takes command of Nasty's demoralized army, stabs a recalcitrant captain, and proclaims that deserters will be hanged: "We shall be sure of victory when your men are more afraid of me than of the enemy'' (251/149). In what sense, to what extent, can Goetz then be considered free? Of course, he could have allowed the peasant army to disintegrate without at least attempting, regardless of the chances of success, to stem the course of events. Yet the play leaves no doubt that Goetz would thereby have acted in a wrong way. The fact that his ''place'' had been unoccupied for a mythical ''year and a day'' points to an external Ought: Goetz might have decided to go on defying his existential obligation to realize his full historical potential as a leader, but he could not have ignored that obligation out of existence. Whether or not he will play his proper part in the drama of his historical situation, whether or not he will play it to the best of his ability, the part has been irrevocably assigned to him by his private and public circumstances.

The parts in Sartre's secularized world theater are, of course, not distributed by a supernatural being as they are in Calderón's *Gran teatro del mundo* (1645). Yet the men and women in Sartre's theatrical world, too, are performers who deviate from the ''script'' of their full human potential at their own peril—the peril of failing to really, authentically, exist. In terms of the imagery of Act I, Goetz has access to certain keys and no access to others. Moreover, just as the dying Bishop was staring at mortified Heinrich, the watchful gaze of all people whose self-fulfillment through their own situated freedom depends on what Goetz locks or unlocks imposes on his freedom a set of externally defined and sometimes conflicting Oughts. And unlike nonhuman entities with which Fortuna plays dice, he must always cast the dice himself and decide whether or not, and if so how, to ''cheat.'' To invoke three crucial concepts from Sartre's *Being and Nothingness,* the decision not to cheat, to let the dice roll as they may, would still be a decision—one made in the ''bad faith'' of assuming that the freedom of man's conscious ''being-for-itself'' can be reduced to the determined state of an unconscious ''being-in-itself'' (1949:85–127/1956:47–84).

Goetz's development has thus not come, as it may appear to have come, full circle. The nonviolent partisan of the Good has not simply turned, once again, into an obdurate ''butcher'' or habitual "hangman." No longer does he blindly defy what he assumes God wants him to do. He now wishes to live by self-made principles. Rather than accepting or rejecting standards of conduct imposed on him, he proposes to set his own standards for how the world shall become. Having come to the conclusion that "on this earth at present good and evil are inseparable," Goetz accepts "being bad in order to become good." Giving up the desire for "pure love" as "ridiculous nonsense," he declares: "To love anyone is to hate the same enemy; therefore I will espouse your hates" (245/145). Before the final fall of the curtain, he expressly reassures Nasty: "Never fear, I shall not flinch. . . . There is this war to fight, and I will fight it" (251–52/149).

The question remains, of course, what it is in Nasty's cause that commands Goetz's newly acquired allegiance just as the French resistance against the Nazis could command Sartre's a few years before writing the play. Surely not the *conviction* that the side chosen *will* prevail but rather the *desire* to *make* it prevail; otherwise, the existentialist choice would amount to no more than jumping on history's bandwagon. But if the choosing up of sides involves ethical commitment rather than historical divination coupled with self-serving realpolitik, looking to future historical developments for justifying one's decisions is highly problematical even if, for the sake of argument, it were granted that Goetz or anyone else could in fact predict the future in whose light an individual's past and present actions will fall into a definitive pattern of significance. In an illuminating discussion of the function of history in Sartre's *Critique of Dialectical Reason,* Claude Lévi-Strauss has challenged the "abstract schema of men making history of such a kind that it can manifest itself in the trend of their lives as a synchronic totality." Such reification of manifold temporal processes into a single object of "historical consciousness" will not serve, Lévi-Strauss has argued, as a criterion to distinguish the "primitive" from the "civilized"; on the contrary, "in Sartre's system, history plays exactly the part of a myth" (1966:254).

It seems to me that the same charge cannot be leveled against the concept of history emerging from *The Devil and the Good Lord.* Here the revolutionary's familiar claim that history is on his side is subtly repudiated as just another attempt to evade one's full responsibility for one's decisions and actions. In the course of Act I Nasty repeatedly invokes his revolutionary myth of history in terms appropriate to a prophet of the sixteenth century: "For God's chosen the news is never bad" (12/5). "For seven more years, the Evil One will reign on earth; but if each one of us fights valiantly we shall redeem ourselves and God with us" (25/12–13); "God *cannot* command anyone to betray the poor—he is with them" (102/58). In Act II, Nasty's complete faith in the happy end of history even restrains him from condemning the conduct of his enemies on ethical grounds: since exploitation will eventually lead to revolution, "there aren't any wicked rich men; there are rich men, that's all" (121/72). By the end of the play, however, local uprisings instigated by Karl have forced Nasty prematurely to engage the superior force of the barons in decisive combat, and Nasty's myth of universal revolution leading to divinely ordained victory in seven years can no longer keep the intimidated peasants from deserting their decimated army. Karl thus proposes to make the peasants feel invulnerable here and now by having a witch rub their bodies with a wooden hand. In a climactic dispute, down-to-earth Karl acknowledges being a "false prophet" while the frustrated idealist Nasty insists: "I am not a false prophet but a man the Lord has deceived" (244/145). On the evidence of the play, of course, those who reify, or rather deify, History by prophesying in Its name are not deceived by their Lord; they are simply deceiving themselves as well as others. Having been rubbed by the witch on Karl's insistence, the prophet of revolution stands reduced to facing a paradoxical predicament: "I who hate lies, lie to my brothers to give them the courage to be killed in a war I detest" (249/148).

It is at this point that Goetz decides to take on the desperate task of reinvigorating the spirit of the peasant army—not because he presages victory but because he cannot bear the sight of the human agony involved with history's apparent betrayal of its prophet. He tells

Nasty: "Suffering, anguish, remorse, are all very well for me. But if you suffer, the last candle goes out: darkness will fall. I take command of the army" (250/148). I read Goetz's decision as motivated by a refusal to acknowledge the meaninglessness of history. At one level, this refusal simply means the internalizing by Goetz of an alien Ought, namely, the standards of conduct predicated upon Nasty's vision of worldwide revolution. At a deeper level, the same refusal is an existentialist counterpart to Pascal's celebrated "wager" (*Pensées*, B. 233; 1904:141–55) affirming the existence of God: Goetz now hazards his freedom in sharing Nasty's effort—the effort of making history meaningful as a process of humankind's increasingly large-scale self-liberation—without any assurance as to whether his line of action will be retroactively justified by history.

Freedom and Love Today

Even at this deeper, existential level, human freedom remains situated as the specific freedom available, here and now, to a "man of today"—the name given by Max Frisch to his central character. This Man of Today, who "plays the role of an intellectual" (12/7), perceives history as being made in the shadow of anticipated mushroom clouds. After an initial compromising period of cowardice, he speaks up against Hwang Ti's attempt to impose his totalitarian imperialism upon the world as "the Great Order, which we call the True Order and the Happy Order and the Final Order" (44/34):

For the first time in human history . . . we are faced with the choice whether or not there should be mankind. The Flood can be manufactured. . . . The more, thanks to technology, we are able to do what we want to do, the more nakedly we stand where Adam and Eve stood: before the question "What do we want?"—before the moral decision. And if we decide, "Mankind should exist," that means that your way of making history is no longer feasible. We can, it is clear, no longer afford a society that considers war unavoidable. [90/73]

85

The same point needs to be made vis-à-vis another historical figure haunting the "place of the action . . . , this stage . . . , our consciousness." The Man of Today confronts King Philip of Spain just as the enlightened Marquis Posa did in Friedrich Schiller's *Don Carlos* (1787): "not prepared to clothe the thoughts of a citizen of the world into the words of a subject" (25/19). In moving lines well known to German-speaking audiences, Posa had been demanding freedom of thought. Yet the monarch remained unmoved and, as a black-clad symbol of the Inquisition, carries his intransigence from the sixteenth century through Schiller's eighteenth into Fisch's contemporary world:

PHILIP: I know the heretics. I burned them, thousands and tens of thousands of them. There is no other way.

MAN OF TODAY: You are wrong, Sire. There is another way. Of late, we have the hydrogen bomb.

PHILIP: What does that mean?

MAN OF TODAY: That means that the others have it also. . . . Anyone who wants to burn others because they hold different beliefs burns himself. It is no longer so simple, Sire, not so simple to save Christendom. There only remains to us, in fact, the Christian procedure. [26/19]

The last words allude, of course, to the injunction to love or, at any rate, not to take the lives of one's neighbors, on whichever side of the Great Wall they may reside. What used to be perceived as divine dispensation now appears, however, as a pragmatic rule of conduct for an endangered species. Rather than conclude with Goetz, "There is this war to fight, and I will fight it," the Man of Today would have to plead with him, too, not to return from the past because today's Nasty and Karl may soon find themselves in possession of technological products designed to shorten the seven-year period between what they see as today's reign of evil and tomorrow's apocalypse.

To be sure, the Man of Today despises tyrants who claim to represent the will of the "real people" and label their opponents mere "agitators, spies, terrorists, [subversive] elements" (59/47). Yet he is also forced to witness how the revolution against Hwang Ti is being abused. From one scene to the next, the ancient Chinese prince Wu Tsiang turns into the modern leader of "men with armbands and submachine guns" (93/76) who liberate Wang, the mute lad falsely accused by the ancien régime of being Min Ko, the Voice of the People, the author of widespread revolutionary rhymes against the emperor. The experienced Man of Today sees through the scheme: it would, of course, suit the new rulers if the "voice of the people" were henceforth reduced to a tortured mute with a burned-out tongue. But he cannot even bring Wang's simple-minded mother to acknowledging the truth. The old peasant woman believes what, after a whole life spent in the economic and intellectual misery of deprivation, she wants to believe: "Oh Wang, my sweet Wang, my unhappy Wang, why have you never told your mother, my proud Wang, that it was you? . . . Why shouldn't my son be an important man? Yes—it's him. Yes! Yes!" [95–96/78]

The next scene suggests even more forcefully that the dialectic of injustice might forever prevent those sinned against by their oppressors from becoming as truthful and just as Brutus, Frisch's Shakespearean archetype of the uncorruptable yet forever frustrated revolutionary. The Brutus of today confronts, instead of a single tragic Caesar, a farcical couple, dressed in tailcoat and cutaway, representing among Hwang Ti's masked guests the "leaders of the economy" (*Wirtschaftsführer*)—history's latest candidates for top position in society. Just before he stabs the unprincipled upstarts with the bitterly reassuring words "Fear not—your sort will always stay in power" (99/80), he also tells them in updated Shakespearean diction why they have nothing to fear from the oppressed:

> Wie täglich Brot, glaub ich, so unerlässlich
> Sind ihnen Willkür, Hochmut, Fehl und Unrecht
> Der andern nämlich, die man Grosse nennt.
> Wer Unrecht leidet (fragt die eigne Brust),
> Dünkt selber sich, bloss weil er leidet, schon
> Gerecht, kann fordern, was er selbst nicht leistet.
>
> [98]

> As much as daily bread, methinks, they need
> The arrogance, injustice, and oppression
> Inflicted by the ones they call the great.
> For he who suffers injustice can regard
> Himself as just—without having to be so.
>
> [80]

On such a view, the interchangeable "great" of the past—Alexander the Great has been replaced, for the sake of wardrobe economy, by Napoleon Bonaparte (8/3)—can indeed claim that the people themselves want them to return. "I hear their call, day after day" (18/13), says temporarily exiled Napoleon, and the Man of Today appears to have been correct in predicting that his own anti-tyrannical efforts on behalf of the tortured mute (and of human survival in general) would remain ineffective: "Has any intellectual ever been able to forestall destiny by foreseeing it? We can write books and make speeches, even courageous speeches about why things must not go on like that any longer. And yet they go on. Precisely that way" (80/65). Why, then, does he intervene during Wang's show trial, risking torture and death at the hands of Hwang Ti's henchmen?

The play suggests both a social and a psychological answer to that troublesome question. In the first place, the temporal cycles of (more or less subtle) oppression and (more or less abused) revolution recycle sufficient human substance to warrant even utterly desperate efforts for averting our suicide as a species—the foreseeable result of the spiraling of history's pattern of senseless recurrence into a still deathlier pattern of nuclear absurdity. For this point to be made, Hwang Ti's guest list includes some historical and literary figures who represent human attitudes eminently worth preserving. Columbus and Don Juan, for example, appear as legendary manifestations not of greed and debauchery but of a noble desire to discover new truths, to acquire new experience. Frisch's Columbus "didn't voyage in the name of the Spanish crown to discover a piece of land which they nowadays call (I don't see why) America";

for him, "it was not a question of India, the treasures of India—it was a question of truth" (23/17). And Frisch's Don Juan, in keeping with his role in another play by Frisch, *Don Juan or the Love of Geometry* (1962), shows no excessive interest in the pleasures of the flesh. Rather, he deplores that the earth itself is no longer a mysterious bride but a handy globe on everybody's desk. He pleads with Columbus to open up new spheres of the unknown, but Columbus replies that the India he wanted to reach is not yet discovered: "There still remain for you, young man, the continents of your own soul, the adventure of truthfulness. I never saw any other spaces of hope" (62–63/50).

The human substance worth preserving from a nonfuture in which "the rest is silence—radioactive silence" (18/12) can never outrun, of course, its insubstantial, all-too-human shadow. We are reminded of this both by Pontius Pilate, condemned to repeat the self-condemning question ("What is truth?") with which he once tried to evade responsibility and by the equally disturbing, if nameless, archetype of L'Inconnue de la Seine—the unfortunate girl who once threw her tubercular, pregnant body into the river but is now eager not to miss out on the next polonaise: "I love exciting parties . . . , I love the pleasure gardens that I have never entered; I love the silk, the music that makes all things possible. I love the life lived by fine people. I know all this, you see, from reading the magazines" (19/13). The high Passion of His story and the lowlier passion of hers thus emerge as complementary episodes—one told in the gospels, the other in countless popular romances and soap operas— from the history of suffering love. The best-known literary embodiments of such love are also among the "guests" or, rather, hostages of Hwang Ti, because

> whoever sits on a throne these days holds the human race in his hand, its whole history, beginning with Moses or Buddha, including the Acropolis, the temples of the Mayas, Gothic cathedrals, including all of Western philosophy, Spanish and French painting, German music, Shakespeare and this young couple: Romeo and Juliet. [17/12]

The quasi-Shakespearean language of these "children of love from a divided world" allows them to enter the paradoxically compelling plea of two suicides for human survival: "Oh blessed world! O bitter world! Oh world! / We love you so; you must not cease to be" (110–11/81–82).

But the oxymoric claim of suffering love that this bitter world is, after all, blessed impels the Man of Today to take his stand not only as a highly educated defender of human culture including "the classic pair" (15/14), Romeo and Juliet. He gets entangled in a romance of his own with Mee Lan, the play's most original variation on one of its many archetypal themes. Mee Lan first appears on stage as Hwang Ti's pampered daughter who refuses to marry one prince after another despite their warlike exploits on Papa's behalf. Soon enough, however, she falls out of her initial role—the role of the "princess as reward" familiar to us from countless fairy tales— and addresses the spectators as a disillusioned teenager of today:

> You look at me and are silent. The eighth prince! I don't deny it: I hope he never returns. . . . Do you think you can fool me? Do you think I haven't noticed that I'm in disguise? And you, who are grown up and know everything, do you really believe, for example, that Papa is always in the right? I am not stupid. Do you think I haven't noticed that everything here (for example, this throne—every school-girl can see that) that everything here is just theatre? But you sit there and watch, you who are grown up and know everything, you sit with your arms crossed and keep silent—and no one comes forward and says how things really are, no one dares and is a man? [32/24–25]

Upon this cue, Mee Lan's long aside is interrupted by the Man of Today, who steps forward from his hiding place. Half frightened, half fascinated, the princess first believes that he may be the mysterious Min Ko, the Emperor's archenemy, who calls himself the Voice of the People. But the prospect of talking with a man who comes from another time and, knowing the future, might tell her whom she is going to marry seems equally intriguing. Their subsequent (rather lopsided) conversation touches on such subjects as the speed of light, the strange behavior of electrons, and God—how he could not be found in the microscope but may still have to be taken into account since matter turns out to be a "dance of numbers, a figure of the mind" (37/28). So much physics—or is it metaphysics?—sweeps Mee Lan off her feet. She vows to come into his marvelous time, and her next costume, ten scenes later, is indeed a contemporary evening dress. It is fitting that she be dressed as a woman of today in the scene in which she rejects her eighth princely suitor, Wu Tsiang: "I did fall in love with your new helmet like girls nowadays fall in love with a Porsche or Mercedes, [but] one wakes up one morning and doesn't believe in princes any more" (64/52). And the modern clothes particularly suit her lines when she begins to fear that the Man of Today may not be the man of her waking dreams either, for he has registered his protest far too mildly to bring the show trial of Wang to an end.

MEE LAN: You know that he is mute.

MAN OF TODAY: Yes.

MEE LAN: And you have permitted a mute lad to be tortured—you, who know everything?

MAN OF TODAY: Permitted?

MEE LAN: You shrug your shoulders. And that's all! Shrug your shoulders, light another cigarette, while they torture a mute and make him scream because you, who can speak, stand by and keep silent—and that's all!

MAN OF TODAY: What could I do?

MEE LAN: You people with your knowledge! Time and space are one; how comforting! Thermal death of the world; how exciting! And the speed of light cannot be exceeded; how interesting! Energy equals mass times the speed of light!

MAN OF TODAY: (Squared.)

MEE LAN: And what's the outcome of all this: You with your great formulas! You shrug your shoulders while a man is being tortured and light another cigarette! [79/64]

The Man of Today can, of course, return the charge: "And you— what did you do? I see you have changed clothes. You want to be a woman of today, I see, and yet you expect the miracle to come from a man?'' (81/65). Ultimately, however, it is Mee Lan's lucid disapproval of the discrepancy between his advanced physics and underdeveloped ethics, as well as her dancing away from him with Don Juan, that prompts the Man of Today to speak up against Hwang Ti and his entourage in no uncertain terms: ''Stop torturing a mute just to find out what people think. I will tell you. Listen to me'' (80/72). As he delivers his spirited speech, quoted earlier in part, about the need to abolish tyranny and to renounce warlike attitudes in the nuclear age, the Man of Today no doubt expects to be tortured and killed in Wang's place as the ''real'' Min Ko, the voice of the people. Instead, the incipient martyr play turns into tragic farce as events take an astonishing (although apparently not unprecedented) turn. The Emperor has the Man of Today decorated with a golden chain representing ''the Great Kung Fu Tse Award . . . , annually bestowed upon the powerful mind capable of portraying to the world what awaits this world, should it dare to be our enemy'' (92/75).

Hwang Ti has thus managed to co-opt the Man of Today's ''powerful mind'' for his own cause against ''the tyrants beyond the Great Wall of China'' (93/75). In the very next scene, Prince Wu Tsiang likewise succeeds in co-opting the popular uprising for his self-serving liquidation of a status quo that has denied him supreme power as well as the promise of such power through marriage with the Emperor's daughter. Not even the sight of raped Mee Lan moves the spiteful prince-turned-revolutionary: ''Forward! A savior of the world cannot worry about individuals! Forward!'' (96/78). In contrast, the play as a whole is very concerned about individuals who in turn must transcend selfish, ''individual'' purposes if they are to respect and love each other. At the end, after the historical and literary maskers have circled about on the stage—''our consciousness''—once more ''like figures on a musical clock'' (101/83), the man and woman of today find themselves alone in the foreground: he (the contemporary intellectual) with Hwang Ti's ''golden chain around his neck,'' she (Mee Lan) ''with disordered hair and torn clothing.'' Even though he feels and says that he has "achieved nothing," she now knows and says that she loves him. As the curtain falls or the stage lights go out, the once "arrogant" woman kneels before the once loquacious man who, hiding his face, has become speechless; having been the playwright's spokesman from the outset, he is now, as the play is over, "the mute" (103/84). In a world where only individual fulfillment seems to reward frustrated social action, the rest may have to be silence, even radioactive silence. Yet the Man of Today, first prompted and then rewarded by the love of suffering Mee Lan—a more profound manifestation of the Eternal Feminine than Hwang Ti's mistress, flighty Cleopatra, who "loves men who make history" (52/41)—has done more than passively suffer history "to pass over us." As Mee Lan tells him: "You have said what you have had to say" (103/83); he has exercised his situated freedom in showing himself ready to give it up for the sake of securing Mee Lan's love by attempting to enhance the situated freedom of others.

From *The Great Wall of China* both freedom and love thus emerge as rooted in but transcending the absurdity of historical events. *The Devil and the Good Lord,* by contrast, treats freedom or taking as the motor and love or giving as the brakes in the progress of history toward human-made meaning. The "evil" Goetz's principle, "Nothing belongs to me except what I take" (66/38), comes back to haunt the "good" Goetz in the form of Nasty's rejection of his plan to give away his lands; property will "belong" only to those who can "take" it:

NASTY: You—save the poor? You can only corrupt them.
GOETZ: Then who will save them?
NASTY: Don't concern yourself with the poor; they will save themselves. [121/71]

While Goetz now claims to love the poor and wants to make them "big and fat" so that they will have no excuse for not loving their neighbors (131/77–78), Nasty hangs on to his initial belief that "it is too early to love; we shall buy the right to do so by shedding blood'' (36/20), and Karl even warns the peasants: ''You were beasts, and hate has changed you into men. If they take hate away from you, you will again fall down on all fours and rediscover the mute misery of beasts'' (207/122). As if to endorse Sartre's English punning with German names in a French play—the leader of Worms must be Nasty—Goetz ends up with this paradoxical position toward the oppressed: ''I shall make them hate me because I have no other way of loving them'' (252/129).

Only the two major female characters of the play adopt positive attitudes toward love, seen here as one person's either completely belonging to or totally sharing with another. It is clear that Catherine fails to command the playwright's admiration: why should the abused mistress of the ''evil'' Goetz, abandoned by the ''good'' Goetz who does not wish to go on living with a ''whore,'' long for him—belong to him—even on her deathbed? But the case of Hilda is far more complicated. This daughter of a well-to-do miller first renounced relative prosperity to become a nun but, during a famine, gave up her vows in order to live among the starving peasants whom she loves and who idolize her. Her sympathy for suffering mankind turns her against God: ''I have only scorn for Thy elect . . . who have the heart to rejoice while there are damned souls in hell and poor people on earth'' (158/93–94). Since Hilda believes that ''on this earth that bleeds all joy is obscene'' (184/109), love to her simply means sharing burdens and helping those who suffer. This is why her attitude toward Goetz undergoes significant changes. First she loathes him because of the suffering he has caused; next she vies with him in attempting to diminish the suffering of others; finally she tries to soothe his loneliness and suffering by becoming his devoted consort.

Hilda's kind of love, almost identical with pity, is hardly without its problems. In the first place, it waxes and wanes in reciprocal relation to the suffering to which it responds; when Goetz's social experiment appears to succeed and the lot of his liberated serfs improves, she has to confess: ''I have less love for them since they have less suffering.'' More important still, she must admit to "bursting with jealousy" because Goetz, having made the peasants no longer dependent on her love, "has taken away everything" from her (189/111). The implication is clear: since Hilda needs or, in a sense, even uses those who rely on her for love, pity, and help, she is unlikely to become a totally committed fighter for the complete abolition of oppressive class distinctions or any other cause of human suffering. It is thus tempting to interpret Hilda's ardent desire to be needed as a sign that her self-sacrifice is the quasi-masochistic mirror image of an overtly quasi-sadistic attempt to dominate others by depriving them of their self-propelled freedom.

Sartre's philosophical observations about love, desire, masochism, and sadism might even lend support to such an interpretation (1949:428–503/1956:361/430). But the play, once again, seems to point beyond explicit doctrine. Rather than elaborate on the supposedly inevitable reification of every consciousness by every other, it reveals (1) that the best Nasty can do for those who suffer here and now is to offer them easily frustrated hopes of a brighter future after the seven-year reign of Evil; (2) that "a year of patience" is required of Goetz, too, before he can hope to diminish his loneliness by beginning to share his existential humanism, "little by little," with the superstitious, phantom-ridden masses; and (3) that, most significantly, Hilda knows: "in a year we will all be dead" (248/147). In the "year" remaining—that is, in the lifetime of loneliness and suffering—Hilda's love will be sorely needed, just as Hilda's (and Mee Lan's) kind of supportive love continues to be offered and craved by human beings who, whether history rolls over them in a progressive, cyclical, or spiral pattern, continue to suffer.

It is, of course, no accident that both Frisch and Sartre, as well as many other writers, project through female characters the historical futility and human significance of love's power to soothe the pain of deathward temporal existence. Love like Hilda's or Mee Lan's may not "make history" by promoting the formation of large active and effective communities; as selfish Goetz tells selfless Hilda: "You are myself. We shall be alone together" (247/146). But it raises to the level of culture that kind of liberation from the situationally

95

limited freedom of isolated selfhood which, at the level of nature, only a woman can experience when she carries the past into the future—the actual into the potential—by sharing her very body with an incipient human being of the next generation.

To be sure, neither playwright casts his most sharing character in the role of an actual mother. Both seem, rather, to oppose any "myth" that their cultural tradition associates with the biological facts of motherhood. Hilda's love for only those who need her has been portrayed by Sartre as exhibiting some objectionably self-effacing traits of psychological motherhood, and Frisch's satirized Chinese Mother by the name of Olan is a tragicomic parody of her melodramatic namesake, the hard-working and patiently suffering O-lan, who is a central mother figure in Pearl S. Buck's once popular novel *The Good Earth* (1931). Yet neither playwright can escape the "aporia" to which Roland Barthes points when he observes that many targets of his relentless demythologizing (for example, the Tour de France, childhood, and the "good French Wine") are "objectively good" while their "goodness . . . is a myth." Tragicomedies of history, to couple Barthes' terminology with mine, "ideologize" by indignantly satirizing such human-made myths as the myth of motherhood; and they "poetize" by admiringly romanticizing an "*ultimately* impenetrable, irreducible" reality that underlies such myths and resists the mythographer's effort to "demystify." Such plays as *The Great Wall of China* and *The Devil and the Good Lord* could indeed be called satiromances as well as tragicomedies. In contrasting what they (poetizingly) speak about with what they (demystifyingly) say, they suggest what Barthes called the "necessity and limits" of an attempted "reconciliation between reality and men, between description and explanation, between object and knowledge." And in revealing that all human knowledge and explanation fall short of an objective description of reality, they make us share the mythographer's doubt as to whether "tomorrow's truths will be the exact reverse of today's lies" (1957:165–268/1972:156–58).

In fact, such plays can even make us aware of the "myths"

involved in all demythologizing. It is, for example, one of the tragicomic ironies of *The Devil and the Good Lord* that Goetz should need motherly Hilda's negative gospel of love for the overcoming of the infantile, solipsistic phase in the emergence of his existentialist selfhood. Her words "When people love each other, God no longer sees them" (225/133) are merely echoed by Goetz in a different register when he says: "I tell you, God is dead. (*He takes [Hilda] in his arms.*) We no longer have a witness; I alone can see your hair and your brow. How *real* you have become since he no longer exists" (241/143). Indeed, the "reborn" Goetz feels, as we have seen before, that his existence in a godless world depends on Hilda's as a son's depends on his mother's: "Look at me, don't stop looking at me for one moment: the world has become blind; if you turned away your head, I should be scared of annihilation." This plea may not be couched in language that children use in talking to parents. But it is an apt expression of how they feel about those "significant others" who, whether or not they brought them into nature, keep guiding them into (as well as within) the adult life-world of culture.

At the end of the play, Sartre's allusive recourse to a sublimated version of the mother myth is superseded, of course, by what the playwright probably considered a demythologized, materialistic view of history. But when Goetz, on the plane of symbolic action, embraces Nasty and his cause of liberating revolution (rather than Hilda and her cause of supportive love), he only shifts his hope for existential legitimation from a cyclical myth of sustained life through periodic regeneration (the myth of the natural mother) to a linear myth of enhanced life through historical progress (the myth of the spiritual father if not, indeed, the more recent myth of the ideologically infallible leader as Big Brother). And that shift high-lights the tragicomedy of the final stage in the Sartrean hero's intel-lectual and emotive development: whereas the self as "being for itself" lacks direction and legitimacy, the self as directed and legit-imized from the outside is enthralled by myths. It is hardly less instructive to consider why Frisch's eventually muted Man of To-

97

day, while earning Mee Lan's love and respect, ends up having sacrificed what has given rise to the entire play—the contemporary intellectual's recognizably individual and individualistic voice. On the evidence of both plays it would appear that the self (about which more will be said in the final section of Chapter 6) confronts this tragicomic alternative of simultaneous fulfillment and frustration: it may seek to assert its absolute freedom in a transhistorical void where, as in Eliot's hell, it is "foully united forever, nothing with nothing" (1963:72), or else it may situate itself within a mythical pattern of progress or recurrence by embracing some version of a historically conditioned "bad faith"—be it a belief in love, history, revolution, or a likewise self-evasive belief in the devil and the good Lord.

4

Enacting Revisions:

Le Livre de Christophe Colomb and *Leben des Galilei*

More likely than not, the respective authors of *The Book of Christopher Columbus* and *Life of Galileo* would have been quite surprised at the thought that their work might be considered eminently comparable. Yet the total oeuvres of Paul Claudel and Bertolt Brecht, as well as their historical plays considered here, display remarkable similarities. Throughout their entire careers, both men wrote lyric and dramatic works side by side. Both took an active interest in the production of their plays and found important allies against the performance styles prevailing in the commercial theaters of the West in Oriental staging methods and the unpretentious, "anti-Wagnerian" music of their composer friends. To some extent, even their reluctance to institutionalize their respective world views affiliates them: the quintessential Catholic Claudel seriously considered but eventually refrained from entering the priesthood, and the revolutionary Marxist Brecht appears never to have joined a Communist party. Most significantly, their very different ideological allegiances made Claudel and Brecht share a profound doubt as to whether what really happens to human beings happens on the visible surface of their "ever present interpersonal action," to use Peter Szondi's characterization (1956:62) of a great deal of post-Renaissance, pre-Ibsenite drama. Claudel saw God and Brecht saw

History work in ways far less transparent than could be dramatized with unified plots and characters or verbalized by means of some explicit thesis. Hence their shared delight in fragmented story patterns and split or even doubled characters; hence also their provocative treatment of well-known historical figures against the grain, so to speak, of generally accepted opinion. A late-nineteenth-century proposal to beatify Christopher Columbus having been rejected in the course of Vatican proceedings, a rather critical view of him as ambitious adventurer has prevailed in most quarters. Galileo Galilei, whom opponents of the Catholic church have never ceased to regard as an almost martyred hero of free thinking and research, was in turn vindicated by the church itself. Yet Claudel chose to celebrate Columbus as the visionary ''bearer of Christ'' while Brecht chose to repudiate Galileo as a ''social criminal.'' Beyond any doubt, neither playwright considered history as an affair of the past or an affair of past and present historiographers. Rather than what has passed and on what, therefore, definitive judgment can be passed, history (for Claudel as well as for Brecht) is that which remains present in our continued movement toward the future.

The Past Enacts Presence

Claudel's religious concern for the cosmic context of human life and history provided strong personal motivation for him to revive old and to introduce new dramatic means of re-presenting past events in a resolutely nonrealistic, multidimensional framework. As a fervent Catholic, he felt a natural attraction to medieval liturgical drama. But more than twenty years of foreign service in the Far East also familiarized Claudel with the living Chinese and Japanese traditions of likewise symbolic staging, replete with stylized gestures and supported by sparsely orchestrated, dramaturgically significant music. Thus when, in 1927, Claudel's diplomatic career brought him as ambassador to the United States and the project to dramatize the ''discovery'' of the New World must have struck him as particularly appropriate, he responded to Max Reinhardt's invitation to write a "mimic drama with choruses," to be performed in Europe (probably at the Salzburg Festival) as well as in America, by proposing a scenario about Christopher Columbus. The playwright's legendary rather than documentary approach to the subject, stressing the protagonist's early sense of mission and exaggerating his eventual fall into disgrace and poverty, gave no offense. Yet Reinhardt—perhaps because Claudel insisted on asking his congenial friend Darius Milhaud rather than Richard Strauss or Manuel de Falla to compose the music—lost his initial enthusiasm for the project, and Milhaud's operatic version was first produced in 1930 at the Berlin State Opera rather than by one of Reinhardt's companies. To be sure, even this work seems to have fallen short of Claudel's ideal of total theater, for which Oriental staging practices served as an inspiring model (1935:20–27/1972:48–60) and in which none of the contributing arts was to attain supremacy; after all, Milhaud's original score could on some later occasions be performed without stage as an oratorio. Yet the composer agreed to reduce the role of music further for Jean-Louis Barrault's much-admired 1953 production of the play. At the Bordeaux Festival and, for several years thereafter, in Paris and on the world tour of the Compagnie Renaud-Barrault, this production achieved fuller integration of various "sister arts" in yet another important respect. The play's cinematographic component, of which more later, had been screened in Berlin á la Piscator on a neutral backdrop; by Barrault, the filmed symbols and events were more closely tied to the other symbols and events of the play as they were projected, whenever appropriate, to a large sail on the stylized ship of Christopher Columbus (cf. Labriolle 1972).

Claudel, in many ways a great admirer of Richard Wagner, was not alone among twentieth-century playwrights in feeling that Wagner and his followers failed to achieve the equilibrium of performing and other arts because of the dominant role assigned to music in any operatically centered *Gesamtkunstwerk*. A quick glance at the relatively recent history of the Occidental theater may in fact help to explain why such different modern authors as Claudel, Yeats, and Brecht turned to Oriental models of correlating dialogue, music, and stylized decor, props, costumes (including masks), and gestures into a balanced, albeit counterpointed, theatrical performance. Growing out of eighteenth-century enlightened rationalism, the realistic and naturalistic predilections of nineteenth-century Europe were far less conducive than the staging styles prevailing in the Greek, Roman, medieval, Renaissance, or baroque theater to bringing the six aspects of performed drama, distinguished by Aristotle as *mythos, ethos, dianoia, lexis, melos,* and *opsis,* into mutually enhancing interplay. Philosophizing about drama several decades after its Athenean heyday, Aristotle himself privileged the first and slighted the last item on his list (1968:12–14), and excessive preoccupation with just one aspect—whether with plot, character, thought, diction, music, or spectacle—was the rule rather than the exception in theatrical productions typical of the period between, roughly, 1700 and 1900. Under Shakespeare's influence, some European playwrights in the eighteenth and nineteenth centuries (Goethe and Pushkin foremost among them) undoubtedly tapped deeper resources of their integrated dramatic imaginations than those accessible to the majority of their contemporaries. Yet most early performances even of their works would gravitate toward one-dimensional styles more appropriate to a suspenseful well-made play, dramatized psychopathology, highly cerebral drama of ideas, poetic closet drama, opera, or burlesque show as they relied on the respective assumptions that plot, character, thought, diction, music, or spectacle must serve as the chief means of integrating all aspects of a theatrical representation. Recognition of this fact should not entail the denial of, say, the psychological penetration, philosophical insight, or musical genius of many supremely gifted representatives of the period. It is only with respect to the full polyvalent potential of the theater that their work began to be judged unfit for creative emulation by Claudel and some of his contemporaries around and since the turn of our century.

I do not wish to imply, of course, that Claudel was consciously aware of the particular relevance of the six terms, interrelated in the sixth chapter (*et passim*) of Aristotle's *Poetics,* to the endeavor of making various aspects of a dramatic performance more interdependent than they were in the theater of nineteenth-century Europe. In all likelihood, neither he nor most other modern playwrights and directors sharing his theatrical concerns were. Brecht, for instance, did not hesitate to brand the kind of theater he was attacking "Aristotelian" on the sole basis, it appears, of the widespread but possibly erroneous interpretation of Aristotle's concept of catharsis as a highly emotional effect of drama on its audience. He even based much of the theory (although not the practice) of his "non-Aristotelian theater" on the central importance of *die Fabel* or main story line without commenting on the apparent paradox that the same term usually serves in German translations of the *Poetics* to render "plot" (*mythos*)—the most important of the six components of a play according to Aristotle himself. But the lack of direct influence—the circumstance that there seems to have been no need for such influence—only attests to Aristotle's firm general grasp of what goes, beyond peculiarities of Greek tragedy, into the making of any total theatrical representation: the evocation of *mythos, ethos,* and *dianoia* (what is done, by and to whom, and why) through *lexis, melos,* and *opsis* (verbal as well as acoustic or visual but nonverbal means of imaginative worldmaking). It should indeed prove helpful to apply the six Aristotelian categories—plot, character, thought, diction, music, and spectacle—to a pair of plays in which Claudel and Brecht, each in his own way, adapt nonnaturalistic modes of drama and staging to the needs of the modern theater.

It is self-evident that *The Book of Christopher Columbus* is not a plot-centered "well-made play" in the technical sense of the term. It violates every major principle of the *pièce bien faite,* which is expected to guide its audience from an informative exposition of the initial dramatic situation through logically connected and chronologically ordered episodes to an increasingly predictable crisis with a surprising but plausible resolution. By no means do Claudel's first three short scenes serve as an exposition of plot; instead, they inaugurate a masslike ritual of festive celebration. First, a solemn procession carries "the book of the life and voyages of Christopher Columbus" to the stage; next, the Reader (*Explicateur*) prays for "light and competence" to "open and explicate" the book about the man whose name, he tells us, signifies Christ-Bearer and Dove (*la colombe*); and then the Chorus chants the second verse from Genesis, which Claudel's own English version of the play (1930) renders as follows: "And the Earth was void and shapeless, and Darkness covered the face of the Deep, and the Spirit of God hovered over the Waters." Only after one member of the Chorus has added in a shrill voice, "The Spirit of God descended upon the Waters in the shape of a Dove" (44/2) does the plot proper begin, and even now it begins with the *last* episode from the hero's life, at the inn of Valladolid.

Summoned by the Reader, Christopher Columbus enters the stage—old, poor, and sick—but is promptly invited by the Chorus, identifying itself as posterity and the judgment of men, to "leave this sordid place," to "pass the narrow line which is called death" (47/3), and to view his own story from the "throne" set up for him in the proscenium. Since he obliges, another actor will play the part of Christopher Columbus in the subsequent sketchy scenes from his life, which include the calling he receives as a young man to leave Genoa for the Ocean, his later negotiations with creditors, courtiers, and mutinous sailors, and his calming of tempests both at high sea and within his soul. Finally, the Book returns us to the inn, and the two characters designated as Christopher Columbus I and Christopher Columbus II embrace as they utter together words from a letter written by their historical prototype: "May Heaven have pity on me, and may the Earth weep over me" (181/49). The curtain begins to fall, but someone rushes to remind the Reader that the Book is not finished yet. As we saw in Chapter 1, Jean Anouilh was later to employ a similar coup in order to conclude *The Lark* not at the burning stake but with the coronation scene as a more appropriate happy ending of *his* story of Jeanne d'Arc. Such simple rearrangement of a historical sequence could not suffice for Claudel, whose *Book of Christopher Columbus* is not about one man attempting to "place the Globe under the Cross" and unwittingly discovering a "new" world but about "all people who have the calling of the Other World and that farther shore" (43/2). His play must end on a note of radical break with everything temporal. This is why, in the final scene, the reckless voyager's only true supporter on earth, a now transfigured Queen Isabella the Catholic, proceeds from the Paradise of the Idea to the Paradise of Love, pleading (as Beatrice for Dante or Mary for all humankind) for the salvation of her "brother Christopher" (197/56) until the Chorus intones a triumphant "Alleluia!" and the screen shows a dove flying away from the revolving globe.

Claudel's story of Christopher Columbus—a *mythos* in the pre- and post-Aristotelian sense rather than a conventional "plot"— thus starts with a dove identified as the Spirit of God descending upon the newly created waters and ends with a dove interpretable as the divine spirit in the hero's saved soul ascending from the earth, whose "perfect" spherical shape his quest was designed to demonstrate. A plot of this kind hardly allows for characters in the realistic sense of unique and unified personalities. To counteract the individuating power of flesh-and-blood actors, Claudel introduces the hero's all-too-human antagonists as nameless crowds or in grotesque triplicates: "three guitar players" stand for the unimaginative populace mocking the visionary project of reaching the East through the West; "three creditors" for the egotistical greed motivating most of its supporters; "three wise men" for the Machiavellian pragmatism of King Ferdinand's court. Such vignettes easily blend with the four allegorical figures Envy, Ignorance, Vainglory, and Avarice, who preside over a Spanish square dance representing, we are told, the comings and goings on the "bureaucratic chessboards" of *all* governments (50–51/4). Ferdinand of Aragon and his courtiers thus exact what is Caesar's (while his saintly Queen Isabella presses God's claims) well beyond the confines of the play's stylized Hispanic and historical setting.

The kinds of *ethos* manifested, respectively, by a diabolic Cook and an angelic Messenger further defy any realistic notion of character. Claudel's most radical device of depsychologizing can be seen, however, in his doubling the representation of Columbus. Not only does he thereby contrast the seafarer's evolving life and the playwright's retrospective image of the essential meaning of that life as distinct dramatic projections of the same human substance. He also makes Columbus II (the one in the proscenium) emerge as the stage-bound protagonist's spiritual guide in moments of trans-historical significance. When the young man (Columbus I) needs encouragement to leave his family and his country, his essential self (Columbus II) provides it for him: "Leave, leave, leave your country! Like Abraham whom the Lord God called out of Ur in Chaldea. . . . Leave your family! Leave, leave your mother! The Will of God is your country! Everything that keeps you from leaving is your enemy" (59/9). And the reference to Abraham is not the only one designed to embed historical existence in atemporal biblical typology. Noah's dove returning to the ark with the green branch of hope, Moses and Peter crossing the sea unharmed, and the pilgrim apostle Santiago (James) are among the archetypal travelers whose missions call for reenactment by the namesake of Christopher, the legendary bearer of the reincarnated Christ Child across a river.

Two concepts of thought (*dianoia*) emerge from the *Poetics*, and both have played important roles in later criticism. The first, prevalent in Chapter 6, may be defined as the *explicit meaning* of uttered or utterable speeches; the second, expressly distinguished from the first in Chapter 19, has to do with the *thematic import* of performed or performable acts. Plays can, of course, express thought in both senses of *dianoia*. Yet to the extent that a playwright's message reaches us less through the diction of a mouthpiece character than through the interacting media of plot, character, diction, music, and spectacle, he or she avoids shortcircuiting implicit theme into explicit maxim, and the play's *dianoia* becomes discernible only through the totality of its *mythos, ethos, lexis, melos,* and *opsis.* Claudel's Reader, for example, is undoubtedly an "authorial" character like Shakespeare's Chorus in *Henry V,* Wilder's Stage Manager in *Our Town,* or Brecht's Singer in *The Caucasian Chalk*

Circle. The role assigned to him is, however, clearly not that of the author's fully reliable spokesman. He is, rather, the perplexed *explicateur* of a book displaying certain customary shortcomings of written documents. Some pages are stuck together, some names erased or simply missing (142–43/38); such is the textual evidence (containing, perhaps, nothing but the truth yet clearly not the whole truth of the implied author) on which "posterity" has to base its judgment, taking sides between the voyager's Accuser and his Defender, whose respective voices emerge from the same poorly informed posterity—from the midst of the Chorus.

Judgment is called for, above all, concerning the project of "unifying mankind," envisioned by Columbus and presumably accomplished in the wake of his voyages. The Reader puts his distanced view of the atrocities involved with the early stages of globalizing human civilization in logically balanced and historically circumspect sentences: "The savages, harshly treated, kept slaughtering the invaders, thus provoking hideous reprisals. In order to cultivate those unhealthy lands, slavery had to be reintroduced" (130/35). Columbus himself, when confronted with filmic images of the dire consequences of his voyages of discovery, cannot help recognizing: "I have sinned" (155/42). To be sure, he also offers rationalizations at both the economic and metaphysical levels: he found no gold yet had to pacify greedy creditors, hence his attempt to sell Indians as slaves in Seville; he had promised to "snatch" the world from darkness, not from suffering, hence his (anticipatory) acceptance of later slave trade as the apparently only means of "making Africa, too, necessary to mankind" (156/42). Such ethnocentric hubris may suffice to save him or latter-day descendants of explorers and colonizers from the sinister Cook's counsel of despair. But it cannot lift anyone above the self-assertion of a "fierce soul" (*coeur dur* or hardened heart [173/47]) to the realization of the primacy of justice over geopolitics—that is to say, to the view expressed to Columbus by the late Queen's Messenger that the Earth is but a plaything, a little ball, not worthy to be "enveloped by the wings of your spirit" (174/47). It seems that Columbus failed when he failed to hold the globe—that "apple in Paradise" (59/9)—merely between his fingers. He has tasted the forbidden fruit with carnal greed and spiritual pride. Only *sub specie aeternitatis* is his lifework vindicated. As Isabella rides toward the Paradise of Love on Christopher's mule (the repentant sinner's last earthly possession, offered to her on his deathbed), the Reader and the Chorus—they, too, in the transfigured lucidity of the Paradise of the Idea—explicate to her the anagogic meaning of the mystical union between sinner and saint, voyage and arrival, quest and peace: "The New World has been your gateway to the Eternal World, the sea that Christopher placed under your feet has been your gateway to the stars" (193/54).

The biblical significance of the mule as "bearer of Christ" into Jerusalem—the event celebrated on Palm Sunday—makes that lowly beast, too, a figurative precursor of Claudel's hero, whose earthly achievement carries Isabella into New Jerusalem to plead there for his salvation. This typological association, fully revealed through the "spectacle" of the final scene, is prepared at the plane of diction in the course of the dialogue. Columbus I protests against the innkeeper's plan to seize the mule in lieu of outstanding debts almost as if the threat were to his own person: "Only this poor brute is left to me, this loyal servant, this good companion who believes in me, who never quarrels and does everything I tell him to" (178/48). In the French original, he even refers to his "last friend," the mongrel, as "a poor old mule like myself" (179), thereby expressing his own sense of being a hybrid creature: sinner and visionary or, more generally, body and spirit compressed into a single human existence. Yet the important phrase is missing from Claudel's own English translation (48). Such—possibly accidental—differences between two equally "authorized versions" make it cumbersome to discuss certain details of the play's diction. In most instances, however, the deviations of the English text from the original *lexis* underscore the same principle governing word choice in both versions, namely, the principle of assimilating the represented action to its manifold biblical prefigurations. Indeed, a large number of lexical differences stem from Claudel's attempt to adjust the language of the play to the different linguistic expectations of French and Anglo-American audiences familiar with different translations of the Bible. Unless spontaneously perceived as such, the allusions to Genesis, the Song of Songs, the Book of Job, the Gospels, and Revelation would fail to reinforce the typological matrix of the play's plot and characters. Likewise, the intertextual reference to the bondage of God's chosen people in the psalm *De Profundis,* intoned by the hero and chanted by the Chorus as acoustic background to the conversation between Columbus and the Messenger, must be recognized if the scene titled "Christophe et Isabelle" in French and, more pointedly, "Love" in English is fully to reveal the spiritual dialectic of bondage and liberation.

But history, for Claudel, is not only the cyclical recurrence of certain types of events in the chronological space between Creation and the Last Judgment; it is also what happens to happen here and now. In 1927, therefore, he saw the fifteenth-century voyager's project of "unifying mankind" as having special implications for isolationist America, especially since his ambassadorship to Washington personally involved the playwright with latter-day attempts at such global integration. It was part of his congenial assignment to try to renegotiate the war debts (France's to the United States and Germany's to France) that were crippling the reconstruction of Europe's economic and social fabric and ultimately enabled Hitler's rise to power. The down-to-earth idiom used by the creditors of Columbus satirically contrasts with the language of his visionary offer of "all the gold of the setting sun" (70/14), but the laughable trio of greedy "money lenders" also displays early marks of the kind of practical wisdom that was needed for initiating the Marshall Plan some twenty years and another world war later. Realizing that Columbus cannot pay his debt now but may share the monetary exploits of his project in due course, the creditors are willing to risk some additional loans: "It is better to make a little effort" (in the sharper English version, "to accept squeezing") "than to lose everything" (71–72/14–15).

The deeper sense of "losing everything" eludes the money lenders, of course, just as the deeper sense of the seafarer's spiritual interpretation of his last name eludes the three guitar players mocking the Dove as if he were a pigeon. Nor does his narrow-minded Accuser really understand what Columbus and he himself are saying when the boastful but symbolic sentence "I always felt that I was a King and the Son of a King" is repudiated in words whose suggestiveness will not survive translation: "The truth is that he was the son of *un tisserand de Gênes*" (55–56/8)—not just "a weaver in Genoa" but also a weaver of Tortures, Constraints, Wants, financial and other kinds of Embarrassment. A deeper truth than the Accuser's is that the "beautiful harbor of Genoa" (*ce beau port de Gênes* [57/9]) harbors too many *gênes* to hold young Christopher back from his voyage to the "doors of eternity" (*les Portes Éternelles*, 198–99/57), which are, in the final scene, about to unclose. In Claudel's poetic diction *nomen est omen,* whether it is the hero's name or the name of his birthplace. This is why Columbus will leave behind *gênes* and forgo settling in a cozy home "like the pigeon beside his pigeonette" (69/14); having escaped what his detractors call his "pigeon house" (*pigeonnier* [75/16]), he may spread his wings among "numberless throbbing stars" described by Isabella in the last scene as "swarms of white doves" (196/56).

The stars approaching on the backdrop as "on astronomic charts" belong, of course, to spectacle rather than diction, and the same holds for the initial and final projected images of a dove spreading its wings over the turning globe. The symbolic spectacle of Claudel's *Book of Christopher Columbus* thus frames what is conveyed by the dialogue ostensibly derived from (or else commenting upon) the Book within the *Book.* Spectacle comes to the fore whenever spoken words would unduly verbalize mental or spiritual events. The dramatization of unspoken thought in nonverbal form is particularly well served by Claudel's early recourse to cinematography. For example, filmed images of Marco Polo's journey project what young Christopher is reading about but also duplicate those stage actions (his mother looking at him and his sister looking into the book over his shoulder) that happen to register in the reading man's consciousness (56/8). In contrast to such visual embodiments of lucid awareness, "a group of confused shadows" (157–58/43) on the screen accompany in a later scene the complaining voices of his "abandoned" mother and wife, as well as of his former and later selves. In this instance, too, a confluence of diction and spectacle—imagined speech and imaginary sights—project the mental events taking place as Columbus, chained to a mast, agonizes on his last return from the lands that he discovered but could not administer to the King's satisfaction.

Well beyond the realm of either sensory or hallucinatory perception, the mystic alliance in God between Columbus and the Queen is dramatized by the sole means of spectacle. In three consecutive scenes without spoken words, we first see "a whirlwind of doves" chase away Envy, Ignorance, Vainglory, and Avarice, the four allegorical figures of the courtly quadrille; in the atmosphere of thereby regained innocence, the child Isabella is then seen to take a dove out of a cage and pull a ring over the bird's leg before setting it free; finally the dove is shown flying across the sea. All this leads to the next scene, already discussed, in which Columbus receives his calling and at the end of which Isabella's dove, both on the screen and on stage, brings young Christopher the ring that will never leave his finger; his determination to leave his country "like Abraham whom the Lord God called out of Ur in Chaldea" thus becomes a mutually acknowledged covenant (54–61/5–10). And spectacle of an altogether different kind represents the spiritual powers attempting to press human and inanimate nature into service against the Christ-Bearer's mission.

The precolumbian "gods of blood and darkness," as the Reader calls them (97/23), are not about to give up without a good fight their "comfortable" existence in what one of them anachronistically calls "this beautiful America" (101/25). Claudel's Indian sun god especially bemoans the threatening cessation of human sacrifice at his altar. He exclaims in the graphic English version:

Alas! Alas! When Baal and Apollo went out of fashion in the old world, I had found such a nice, cozy place here in Mexico. Alas!

III

Alas! for the good meals of tender human flesh, for the good, warm
blood, the splendid Aztec caldron! That throbbing heart which the
High Priest drew for me out of a mountain of warm corpses, what a
fine morsel! I am through now with my diet of warm blood gushing
fresh from the wound! [102/25]

Failing to realize that, through the "sin" of Columbus and others,
human sacrifice of various sorts will continue to be offered, the
pagan gods attempt to stem the tide of religious history by inciting
mutiny among the sailors and by "churning the sea": an "immense
tug-of-war" develops across the stage, roughing the imaginary waters with a fiercely undulating rope being pulled and slacked back
and forth by the divided host of grotesquely hideous demons
(104/25–26). This highly "ethnocentric" spectacle, degrading
non-Christian deities into fiendish spirits, seems to belie Claudel's
own rather more cosmopolitan sense of the sacred—a sense expressed, for example, in his enthusiasm for the spiritual dimension
of the Oriental theater and in the decisively meta-Christian thrust of
his letter dated December 17, 1927, to Darius Milhaud: "Christopher Columbus is basically Prometheus. A man alone with all the
voices of sea, sky, and nature around him" (1972:74). In the context of the play, however, the unconditional rejection of tribal deities appealing to instincts of violence in their worshipers draws
justification from their approaching subduer's allegiance to a faith
that, in principle at least, proclaims the universal brotherhood and
sisterhood of all people and the sanctity of all human life.

When at the end of Part I the three ships are seen approaching
from the vantage point of a not yet reached New World, they do not
immediately reveal a motley crew of better-armed invaders, and we
are also spared the sight of curious or hostile crowds of no less
fallible natives. Christopher's flotilla carries what the scene's heading calls "The Redeemer" to a symbolic landscape teeming with
animal and plant life as well as crumbling, ferocious idols—a world
not necessarily hospitable to the human potential for being saved
from the manifold egotistical, divisive, and bloodthirsty powers

within. Here as elsewhere, the music is meant to accompany or counterpoint (rather than to drown) the play's plot, characters, thought, diction, and spectacle. According to the eloquent stage directions, we are first to hear "the murmur of America, executed by instruments and the Chorus, unspeakably gloomy and bitter" (the last word being *amer* in the original). But at the appearance of the "three sails of Christopher Columbus," the mingled "murmur of land, forest, and sea, swelling with a feeling of terror, anguish, and hope," begins to be mixed with the celebratory notes of the Te Deum sung in the distance until finally, in a more realistic and more sinister vein, cannon shots and the shouts of sailors, too, are heard "among" (as only the English version has it) "the howling of the gods" (127–28/32–33). Even as he describes for readers and spectators the acoustic component of proposed "stage business," Claudel thus attempts to fuse matter-of-fact suggestions for the theatrical representation of action with quasi-lyric enactment of the implied author's version: the choice of *amer* as a poetically apposite adjective qualifying America's murmur and the subtly ironic description of the warlike noise of the invaders as blending into the howling of their supposedly more aggressive antagonists are obvious cases in point.

His duties as a diplomat prevented Claudel from attending the 1930 Berlin production of Milhaud's operatic version, but his correspondence with the composer attests to his formative influence on their collaborative effort. His specific suggestions, as in the letter of May 18, 1928, tend to propose ways of ensuring the interplay of music with other aspects of the performance:

> When I was thinking of my—our—*Christophe Colomb,* as I often do, I had the following idea:
> After the brief shadow scene following the storm, the stage is completely blacked out. The chorus is lit only by a few candles, and only the basses are heard, beginning to croak the *De Profundis*. The stage lights are brought up gradually. The backcloth is of a cold unpleasant green like that from which the black plumes of cypresses

stand out in El Greco's paintings. Then a sudden *forte* as though a curtain were rising, and we see the procession emerge. A huge catafalque appears, flanked by golden statues veiled with crepe and plumed. It is escorted by masked warriors and cowled penitents carrying lighted tapers. During the whole scene, without interruption, a woman's voice, perhaps two? like a lament, or the bubbling of a stream or a madwoman. Then toward the end the character changes and the music takes on a grave tenderness while the woman's voice becomes full of love and consolation. I imagine also an instrument heard from time to time (perhaps a clarinet) which grips the heart. [1966:111/1972:75]

Claudel expressed his general approval of the spirit, if not necessarily all details, of Milhaud's score when he contrasted it, in a lecture delivered at Yale University shortly before the first Berlin performance, to Wagnerian opera. Rather than plunge the audience "by the magic of a great fusion of different sounds—particularly the brass—into a kind of narcotic atmosphere," Milhaud and Claudel "wanted to show how the soul gradually arrives at music, how the phrase springs from rhythm, the flame from fire, melody from speech, poetry from the coarsest reality." And the intention of showing music "in the process of its birth," as it comes "from within ourselves," was paralleled by the two friends' refusal to accept ready-made decor—the "inert matter" of a fixed set or unchanging backdrop.

> When a wave of music, poetry, and action sweeps along the spectator's soul, why confront him with a fake sky as shrill and trivial as a café wall? . . . Why not let the images suggested by poetry and sound be exhaled like smoke, settle for a moment on the screen, and gradually fade to make room for other dreams? In a word, why not use the cinema? . . . Why not use the screen as a magic mirror on which all sorts of hints and shadows, more or less clear or confused, pass, stir, mingle, and separate? Why not open the door of the cloudy world where ideas are born of sensations and the phantom of the future mingles with the shadow of the past? [1935:32–37/1972:87–89].

Needless to say, the cloudy, turbid, confused, or even troubled world of our minds—Claudel's phrase just quoted is *ce monde troublé*—is packed with moving images of history rather than inert archival records. Hence Claudel's purpose in adding a filmic dimension to stage spectacle was clearly not the quasi-documentary one of pretending to show the audience something like a miraculously preserved newsreel from the fifteenth century. Instead, he seems to have regarded the potential contribution of cinematic projections to historical drama as the visual equivalent of music. Such melodic *opsis* or optical *melos,* if you will, was to serve as a subtle means of enacting theatrical vision and of making us envision history in the shape of imaginable and imageable, but by no means fully visible, action.

The Past Envisioned Now

While the Renaissance attempt to unify mankind appears eternally justified in Claudel's "Paradise of the Idea" and "Paradise of Love," the play also connects the geopolitical "sin" of Columbus with the misdeeds committed by colonizers long after the fifteenth-century explorer's death. Similarly, albeit without a transcendental dimension, Brecht wants us to see the life of Galileo not simply as a self-contained, unalterable chapter in the history of science. The three versions of his *Life of Galileo* are versions of a chapter that must always be written in the light of present evidence as to the ongoing impact of a larger "life"—the evolving life of human knowledge and self-knowledge—on the future of mankind. And as a comparison of the three principal versions of Brecht's play suggests, what is written may have to be rewritten even within the span of a crucial decade.

To be sure, Galileo does not emerge as an admirable hero from any of the extant versions. Already in the first, written in Danish exile (1938–39) and performed at the Zürich Schauspielhaus (1943), he abjures the Copernican hypothesis of a heliocentric universe, which his astronomic observations have fully confirmed, out of sheer cowardice: he has just been shown the instruments of torture by the authorities who recently burned Giordano Bruno (1600) and Lucillio Vanini (1619) as unrepentant heretics. As for the received view that the cunning scientist gave in to the Inquisition in order to attain at least relative freedom for further major discoveries, Brecht makes Galileo himself invalidate that interpretation in the very first version of the play:

> No member of the scientific world is logically entitled to point to his own possible contributions to research if he has failed to honor his profession as such and to defend it against the use of force. . . . Science has no use for people who fail to stick up for reason. It must expel them in ignominy, because, however many truths science knows, it could have no future in a world of lies. [1972:294]

Yet the playwright's attitude toward Galileo became much more critical during his lengthy collaboration, beginning in 1944, with the English actor Charles Laughton on the second version of the play to be eventually performed near Los Angeles (Beverly Hills) and in New York (1947). As he stated in the preamble to this American version: "The 'atomic' age made its debut at Hiroshima in the middle of our work. Overnight the biography of the founder of the new system of physics read differently" (1972:224). This version, and even more the last one whose variants were performed in Cologne (1955), Nuremberg (1956), Vienna (1956) and, shortly after Brecht's death, by the playwright's own Berliner Ensemble (1957), shifted the original conflict between the "letter" and the "spirit" of science—that is, between the making of particular discoveries and the taking of a stand for the freedom of research—to a conflict between pure science and the social commitment of individual scientists. To quote from the American version, which in this respect was further amplified after Brecht's move to the German Democratic Republic:

GALILEO: I take it the intent of science is to ease human existence. If you give away to coercion, science can be crippled, and your new machines simply suggest new drudgeries. Should you then, in time, discover all there is to be discovered, your progress must become a progress away from the bulk of humanity. The gulf might even grow so wide that the sound of your cheering at some new achievement would be echoed by a universal howl of horror. [1972:463]

The passages quoted above from the first and second versions are in both instances spoken by Galileo to his former disciple Andrea, who, in the second and third versions, rejects Galileo's self-indictment as a far too "savage analysis." To be sure, Andrea himself unequivocally condemns Galileo's "treason" until he comes to realize that his former teacher has not capitulated to the point of actually giving up research and that, furthermore, he has been preparing a clandestine copy of his latest work, whose original had to be submitted to the Holy Office. But, in Brecht's final version, Andrea expresses his regained enthusiasm for Galileo in particularly pointed language: "This will be the foundation of a new physics. . . . You were hiding the truth. From the enemy. Even in the field of ethics you were centuries ahead of us" (1967, 3:1337/1972:91–92). Galileo's ironic response to this speech and his subsequent self-indictment do not deter Andrea from emulating what he takes to be his former teacher's courage; he decides to smuggle the manuscript of the *Discorsi* across the Italian border with a view to having it published in Protestant Holland. In Brecht's view, however, such acts of personal bravery cannot atone for the "original sin" of science, committed by Galileo and reenacted by Andrea and others for whom "science knows only one commandment: scientific contribution" (1339/93). The devotees of this kind of pure science will always permit a momentous "scandal" with social significance (such as the "discrediting" by the new astronomy of the Bible and of the authorities claiming to rely on it) to degenerate into a mere "dispute between experts" (1967, 17:1108/1972:225). Whether Brecht, in dramatizing what he called the original sin of science, believed that anything like the heated conversation between Galileo and Andrea actually took place is of course the wrong question to ask. He obviously didn't: historiographers know nothing of an Andrea Sarti, who in Brecht's play is the son of Galileo's housekeeper and, judging from the circumstance that Brecht's Galileo and Mrs. Sarti occasionally address each other with the intimate *du* instead of the more appropriate *Sie*, possibly Galileo's son as well. Even the question as to whether Brecht believed that the conversation concerning the social function of science could have taken place in the seventeenth century would miss the point. The right question to ask is *how* Brecht adopted Shaw's principle, discussed in Chapter 1, according to which the historical playwright's "veracity" may force upon him a "sacrifice of verisimilitude" when he represents his characters as saying what they "actually would have said if they had known what they were doing" (1971:52–53). To answer that question in detail, it will prove useful to discuss *Life of Galileo*, mainly in its final version, as another attempt by a twentieth-century playwright to dramatize history without subordinating five aspects of drama to a sixth, whether it be plot, character, thought, diction, music, or spectacle.

Brecht has repeatedly characterized *Life of Galileo* as a dramaturgically conservative work. Beyond doubt, the play's structure is less innovative than the structure of Claudel's *Book of Christopher Columbus* or that of Brecht's own dramatic works dating from the late twenties and early thirties. Yet a central principle of his previous program for the "epic theater" (cf. 1967, 17:1010/1964:37) remains observed: the reader's or spectator's attention is focused on the course (*Gang*) rather than the finish or outcome (*Ausgang*) of events. Brecht achieves this kind of audience response not only by fragmenting the plot of his play into fifteen well-rounded episodes, each containing its own thematic climax. More important, he punctuates the represented action with a battery of quasi-narrative interventions. Already in the first version of the play, each scene (like the chapters of some novels and the scenes of Claudel's play) was given a descriptive title. In the second version, these headings were replaced by versified narrative introductions. The final version, however, contains both the titles and Brecht's German version of the preambles (quoted here, as they were first published, in English translation). For example, Scene 1 is titled "Galileo Galilei, teacher of mathematics in Padua, sets out to demonstrate the new Copernican system" and is prefaced as follows:

> In the year sixteen hundred and nine
> Science' light began to shine.
> At Padua city, in a modest house
> Galileo Galilei set out to prove
> The sun is still, the earth is on the move.
>
> [1231/3]

The title and preamble of Scene 6 may also serve to illustrate how Brecht dramatizes his thematic vision of the rise and fall of Galileo in the narrative framework of envisioned action. Here, as in several other scenes, the events soon to be represented are first chronicled in the present tense characteristic of plot summaries and then in a mixture of tense appropriate to historiographic report (past) and commentary (present):

> 1616: The Collegium Romanum, the research institute of the Vatican, confirms Galileo's discoveries.

> Things take indeed a wondrous turn
> When learned men do stoop to learn.
> Clavius, we are pleased to say,
> Upheld Galileo Galilei.
>
> [1278/42]

In a few instances, the preamble is missing or relates to the mood rather than the action of the scene to come. But the invariably present titles suffice to give all scenes an air of the exemplary in both senses of the word: each dramatized episode is significant, but it is significant mainly as a sample of behavior to be examined with a view to finding out what, how, and why it exemplifies.

Now the titles are, in most performances, either projected on a screen or painted on a drop curtain or placard descending from the flies while the versified preambles are either recited by an actor or sung, with Hanns Eisler's 1947 music, by a chorus. It is also possible, however, to reverse that relationship between medium and message by presenting the titles through acoustic and the preambles through visual means of communication. In any event, spectacle and music (including the intentionally simplistic verbal music of the rhythms and rhymes of the chronicler's doggerel) will be used to undercut rather than heighten the suspense of plot and character development. Scene 10, of course, might have subordinated plot, character, thought, and perhaps even diction to music and spectacle. Brecht has therefore prefaced the ballad singer's song about "the horrendous doctrine and teaching of Mr. Galileo Galilei" and the carnivalesque mock celebration of "Galileo Galilei, the Bible-smasher" with a lengthy title: "In the course of the next ten years Galileo's doctrine is disseminated among the common people. Pamphleteers and ballad singers everywhere seize upon the new ideas. In the carnival of 1632 the guilds in many Italian cities take astronomy as the theme for their carnival processions" (1312/70). Invoking undramatized events of "the next ten years" and simultaneous occurrences "in many Italian cities," such a panoramic narrative preamble ties the scene's music and spectacle closely to the other aspects of drama as it suggests that this episode, too, must be seen as a sample—a negative sample of the popular impact that the emerging spirit of unprejudiced inquiry, owing to Galileo's readiness to compromise, failed to sustain.

The words "failed to sustain" come close to expressing the main theme of Brecht's play, which is predicated on the assumption that the uprising against unwarranted authority in science could and should have lent support to a comparable uprising against unwarranted authority in the social sphere. Galileo expressly associates the two very early in Scene 1. He has just shown the eleven-year-old Andrea an intricate model of the Ptolemaic system representing the earth at the center of eight crystal spheres. Delighted by the bright young boy's response—"That's pretty. But we are so incapsulated''—Galileo elaborates on it in the longest speech of the play:

> Yes, that's how I felt too when I saw the thing for the first time. . . . Walls and rings and immobility. For two thousand years men believed that the sun and all the stars of heaven were circling around them. The pope, the cardinals, princes, and scholars, the captains, merchants, fishwives, and schoolchildren, all thought they were sitting motionless inside this crystal sphere. But now we'll get out of it. Andrea, we are in full sail. Because the old times are gone, and this is a new age. . . . Where Faith was seated for a thousand years, now sits Doubt. . . . Everybody is saying: Yes, that's what is written in the books, but let's see it for ourselves. . . . This has stirred up a breeze that lifts even the gold-braided coats of princes and prelates, revealing stout and spindly legs, legs just like ours. . . . It was long taught that the stars are pinned to a crystal vault, which keeps them from falling down. Now we have mustered the courage to let them float free, with nothing to hold them, they are in full sail, just as our ships are in full sail. And the earth rolls merrily around the sun, and all the fishwives, merchants, princes, and cardinals, and even the pope, roll with it. Overnight, the universe has lost its center and now, in the morning, it has innumerable centers. So that everyone and no one can be seen as the center. Because, all of a sudden, there is a lot of room. [1232–34/4–6]

Conspicuously enough, this paean to the New Age is spoken by Galileo *not* as a representative of seventeenth-century astronomy. The rhetoric of the last sentences clearly relies on much more recent theories of relativity in physics as well as politics. It postulates a world in which no object is more in motion or more central, in which no human being (in George Orwell's ironic phrase critical of totalitarian communism) is more equal, than any other. Early on, therefore—and not only in the self-indictment of the penultimate scene, as some critics have argued—Galileo's diction contradicts his character, if by "character" we mean personality traits attributable to a stage figure's historical prototype. But if, on the basis of Galileo's overtly anachronistic diction, we conceive of Brecht's Galileo as manifesting an *ethos* that, in the playwright's view, characterizes the transhistorical archetype of the scientist who divorces the means of science from its end—increase in knowledge from service to humanity—then we can accept Galileo's words both at the beginning and toward the end of the play as spoken in, and according to, "character."

When Brecht referred to Galileo's crime as the "original sin" (*Erbsünde*) of the modern natural sciences he was careful to place the theological term between quotation marks (1967, 17:1109/1972:225). He would surely have winced at the metaphysical overtones of the term "archetype" just applied to his protagonist. After all, the implications of a character's transcending the interhuman historical world of "strict drama" fit in much more smoothly with the world view of a playwright of transcendence (e.g., Eliot, Claudel, Wilder) than with the world view of a playwright of immanence (e.g., Shaw, Brecht, Weiss). Yet, just as Shaw's concept of a "superpersonal" Evolutionary Appetite (1971:13–14) enables him to see Joan as the harbinger of such future ideas as nationalism and Protestantism, Brecht's Hegelian-Marxist view of history as ultimately reasonable enables him to see all actions of the past as unfolding a deeper level of dialectical truth than can be perceived within the ideological framework of the historical agents themselves. But are the retrospecting observers of past actions not limited by their own ideological frameworks? Aren't they, too, historical agents involved in actions, including the action of envisioning or making others envision past actions, rather than serene possessors of some ultimate truth? Of course they are, and Brecht would be the last person to deny this. Indeed, he is said to have repeatedly interrupted the 1956 East Berlin rehearsals after Galileo's words "My aim is not to prove that I have been right, but to find out whether or not I have been" (1311/69) in order to point out that, for a Marxist, this is "the most important sentence of the play" (cf. Hecht 1963:109).

In Brecht's opinion, Marxists should engage in unprejudiced, "scientific" study of social realities with a view to altering them; but they should not proceed in the self-congratulatory conviction of having entered, or almost entered, something like an earthly paradise—not to mention some "paradise of the idea" where, according to Claudel's *Explicateur,* "everything begins anew" in luminous, definitive explication. To the contrary, Galileo's very next sentence alludes to the inscription over the entrance to Dante's Inferno as a motto to be adapted to the self-understanding of empirical science: "I say: Abandon hope, all ye who enter upon observation." Even as he precipitously determines to resume his interdicted research into the motion of the stars—he had just heard that the old pope is about to die and that Cardinal Barberini, a mathematician, is likely to succeed to the papal throne—Galileo advises his disciples to exercise utmost critical caution in matters pertaining to science:

Yes, we shall put everything in question once again. . . . And what we find today we'll wipe from the blackboard tomorrow, and not write it down again until we find it a second time. And if there is something we wish to find, we'll regard it with particular distrust, should we actually find it. Accordingly, we'll approach our observations of the sun with a relentless resolve to prove that the earth *stands still.* Only after we have failed, after we have been totally and hopelessly defeated and are licking our wounds in utter dejection, only then shall we begin to ask whether we were not right after all about the movement of the earth! (*With a twinkle.*) But if every other assumption should go up in smoke, then no more mercy for those who have not explored, yet talk! [1311/69–70]

In certain respects, of course, Galileo himself is one of "those who have not explored, yet talk." Without much ado, he takes for granted that the new pope will be less "reactionary" than the old one under whom a first warning was issued to him. When Mrs. Sarti points out that "His Holiness isn't even dead yet," he brushes her observation aside in a most unscientific way: "Pretty close, pretty close!" Thus Mrs. Sarti is justified in complaining that blind faith wins out against Galileo's principle of carefully weighing all evidence when "something really suits his fancy" (*wenn es zu etwas kommt, was in seinen Kram passt* [1308/67]). It is, indeed, Galileo's "blind faith" in the efficacy of thought (*dianoia*) and the consistency of character (*ethos*) that makes him project a rational happy end for the plot (*mythos*) of his story. Yet the more complex plot of history does not bear out his assumptions: facts and figures will be brushed aside when they do not suit our fancy, and Barberini as pope no longer acts "in character" as Galileo's friendly admirer.

The limited power of reason is most imaginatively demonstrated in the last scene of the second version, for which the initial stage direction reads:

> *Before a little Italian customs house early in the morning. Andrea sits upon one of his traveling trunks at the barrier and reads Galileo's book. The window of a small house is still lit, and a big grotesque shadow, like an old witch and her cauldron, falls upon the house wall beyond. Barefoot children in rags see it and point to the little house.* [1972:465]

The somewhat implausible optics calls for a symbolic interpretation of the action taking place under the witchlike shadow. Indeed, the scene as a whole suggests a very gloomy picture, if not necessarily of incorrigible human nature, at least of the predicament of unprejudiced thought in a country from which, after Galileo's recantation, the fruits of his research must be smuggled out. Having outwitted the customs officers—"Anything dangerous in these books? . . . Oh, figures. No harm in figures" (465)—Andrea undertakes to prove to a bunch of children that the woman, whose grotesque shadow seems to indicate the contrary, is not a witch "stirring hell-broth" after all. He lifts up one of the boys, exactly as Galileo picked up young Andrea in

Scene 1 to demonstrate to him the revolution of the earth around the sun, and the boy now sees for himself through the window that Old Marina is "just an old girl cooking porridge" (466). Yet this lesson in empirical observation remains ineffectual, and the children continue to act—one is reminded of Plato's parable of the cave dwellers (*Republic,* 7:514a–517b)—on the basis of their deceptive interpretation of the grotesque witchlike shadow. The very boy who should know better kicks over Old Marina's milk jug and shouts after the departing Andrea: "She *is* a witch! She *is* a witch!" Thus the second version of the play about what should have been the dawn of a new, scientific age ends as its final scene began: stubbornly aggressive urchins are pressing the rudimentary mathematics of the first line of their teasing ditty into the service of deeply ingrained superstition:

> One, two, three, four, five six,
> Old Marina is a witch.
> At night, on a broomstick she sits
> And on the church steeple she spits.
> (*The customs officers laugh. Andrea goes.*)
> [467]

In an earlier scene titled "The Pope," Galileo's unexamined faith in character is rendered obsolete by spectacle (*opsis*) just as compelling as the deceptive Platonic shadow and by "music" (*melos*) just as suggestive as the final laughter of the customs officer. Here, too, the initial stage directions clearly indicate how the scene's diction (*lexis*) is to be counterpointed by nonverbal aspects of the performance: "*A room in the Vatican. Pope Urban VIII (formerly Cardinal Barberini) had received the Cardinal Inquisitor. During the audience the pope is being dressed. From outside the shuffling of many feet is heard*" (1321/78). The scene shows the transformation of Galileo's former supporter, who still considers him "the greatest physicist of this time, a beacon for Italy, and not some confused crank," into a clothes tree for the papal robes. Brecht's dialogue underplays the increasing personal antagonism,

attested by historiographers, between two individuals—Galileo Galilei and Maffeo Barberini. What interests him is the institutional
logic that connects the Vatican's spiritual attempt to keep science in
its place as the handmaiden of theology with the secular project of
strengthening the church's position both in the current international
power struggle of the Thirty-Year War and in the longer-range
struggle between social classes.

At the beginning of the scene the new pope exclaims: "No! No!
No! . . . I will not permit the multiplication tables to be broken."
But, as he is being dressed to receive "the doctors of all the fac-
ulties, the representatives of all the religious orders and of the entire
clergy," he must listen to the Inquisitor's plea: the faith of the
faithful in scriptural truth is not to be broken either. For the Inquisitor, the Galilei affair is not a matter of the multiplication tables.
It has to do, rather, with the "alarming unrest" that has come over
the world—an unrest in the minds of certain people anxious to
"transfer it to the immovable earth." And the Inquisitor spells out
some of the social implications of the new science:

> They cry out: the figures force our hands! But where do the figures
> come from? Everybody knows they come from doubt. These people
> doubt everything. Shall we build human society on doubt and no
> longer on faith? "You are my master but I wonder if that's a good
> arrangement." "This is your house and wife, but I wonder if they
> shouldn't be mine." . . . Why, one is tempted to ask, is this sudden
> interest in so recondite a science as astronomy? . . . . Where will it
> end if those weak in the flesh and inclined to all kinds of excess come
> to believe only in their own reason, which this madman [Galileo]
> declares to be the only court of appeal? [1322–23/78–79]

The acoustic background of the constant "shuffling of feet," and
perhaps not only of the feet of the faithful, makes Barberini increasingly nervous. He still wants to avoid "the condemning of
physical facts" and the exchanging of such battle cries as "For the
Church!" versus "For Reason!" Yet in the end, fully robed in

papal regalia, he gives up his opposition to the planned trial and merely insists that Galileo not be tortured. "At the very most, the instruments may be shown to him." The pragmatically minded Inquisitor is satisfied: "That will suffice, your Holiness. Mr. Galilei is well-versed in instruments" (1324–25/80–81). As Inquisitor and Pope now see eye to eye, the spokesman for the old institution and its new leader can confront the waiting multitude and the world at large in complete concord. Barberini has become The Pope; the logic of social function has prevailed over the idiosyncrasy of character.

In the Preface to *Saint Joan,* Shaw (somewhat unjustly) remarked that a "novice" could read Shakespeare's plays "without learning that the world is finally governed by forces expressing themselves in religions and laws which make epochs rather than by vulgarly ambitious individuals who make rows." According to Shaw, Shakespeare's characters are portrayed "as if they were beings in the air, without public responsibilities of any kind," and thus "seem natural to our middle classes, who are comfortable and irresponsible at other people's expense, and are neither ashamed of that condition nor even conscious of it" (1971:50–51). As a theorist and practitioner of *Verfremdungseffekte*—dramaturgical and staging devices of estrangement helping the audience to keep its distance—Brecht was of course eager to make whatever tends to seem natural appear strikingly unnatural from the vantage point of his view of man's historically changing nature. His portrayal of characters never stops, therefore, at the level of "vulgarly ambitious individuals who make rows." Instead, he prefers to dramatize the social forces "which make epochs." Hence his invention of such characters as Ludovico Marsili, the (class-consciously aristocratic) fiancé of Galileo's daughter; Vanni, the (progressively bourgeois) iron manufacturer, whose offer of assistance against the authorities Galileo haughtily declines; Federzoni, the even more progressive lens grinder, whose (proletarian) lack of Latin does not diminish his contributions to scientific experiments; and the "Little Monk" Fulganzio, whose personal wavering between scientific curiosity

127

and religious faith emerges as an internalized conflict between his peasant background and his place in the ruling church hierarchy.

Since Galileo, in his diction, exhibits very Brechtian attitudes toward these as well as other characters, his action of submitting to the authorities appears particularly shameful: it is premeditated treason not only in an intellectual but in a social sense as well. After all, Brecht's Galileo has always been conscious of the close connection between the "new thoughts" of science and the "people who work with their hands":

> Who else wants to find out the causes of things? Those who see bread only on their tables don't want to know how it was baked; that crowd will rather thank God than the baker. But the men who make the bread will understand that nothing moves unless something moves it. Your sister at the olive press, Fulganzio, won't be too amazed but probably laugh when she hears that the sun is not a gold escutcheon but a lever; the earth moves because the sun moves it. [1310/68–69]

In order to link the scientific impulse to understand the world and the desire of the underprivileged to change it, Brecht did not hesitate to exaggerate the historical Galileo's financial troubles to the point of making the physicist's housekeeper worry about how to pay the milkman. Nor did he care to temper Galileo's enthusiasm for the "high curiosity" of lowly seamen "who left our shores a hundred years ago without knowing what shores, if any, they might reach" (1270/36) with authorial hindsight into the ethics and the politics of maritime trade and colonization. As he states in the informative note titled "Praise or Condemnation of Galileo?" the playwright's main intention was to show "how society extorts from its individuals what it needs from them." And Brecht's concept of such "extortion" is almost as biological as it is social. He speaks of the "research drive" (*Forschungstrieb*) as a "social phenomenon hardly less pleasurable and compulsive than the drive to procreate" (*Zeugungstrieb*) and suggests that the researcher's private pleasure—whether he delights in old wines or new ideas—becomes reprehensible when research is pursued regardless of its transindividual purpose: "In the end, [Galileo] indulges his science like a vice, secretly and probably with pangs of conscience" (17:1109/1972: 225).

It is fair to say that the Galileo of the penultimate scene shares with the church and other authorities a profound mistrust of science pursued for its own sake—that is to say, for the sake of the scientist's private pleasure of uninhibited inquiry. Almost like a parent who has been applying a double standard of sexual conduct to his own and his children's generations, Galileo waxes particularly eloquent about his own vice of intellectual debauchery when he discovers its mirror image in Andrea's bent toward it. As discussed before, the young scholar is ready to forgive Galileo's treason against the spirit of science as soon as he beholds the secretly prepared copy of the *Discorsi*—a great contribution to its letter. Andrea even dramatizes his retrospective apologetics in a historical playlet Brecht has refused to write as his own version of how Galileo's conduct should be remembered: "With the man on the street we said: "He'll die, but he'll never recant.—You came back and said: I have recanted but I shall live.—Your hands are stained, we said.—You said: Better stained than empty." Galileo seems amused: "Better stained than empty. Sounds realistic. Sounds like me. A new science, a new ethics." Ultimately, however, he rejects Andrea's view of the recantation as a praiseworthy act of "hiding the truth," yet to be discovered, "from the enemy." For one thing, "there is no scientific work that only one man can write." For another, there is no merit in writing or reading books for the egotistical, quasi-sexual pleasure of doing so: "Welcome to the gutter, brother in science and cousin in treason! . . . Oh, irresistible sight of a book, that hallowed commodity. The mouth waters, the curses are drowned. The great Babylonian whore, the murderous beast, the scarlet woman, opens her thighs, and everything is different!" (1337–39/92–93).

The allusion to the biblical figure of the Great Whore (Revelation 17) couples the book—here the image of illicit, "pure" research, free of social commitment—with the apocalyptic image of illicit, "dirty" sexuality, devoid of biological purpose. *Forschungstrieb* and *Zeugungstrieb* without transindividual justification are thus equally renounced by the Galileo of this speech—just as they are equally renounced by the church. The parallel between Galileo's final rejection of "pure" science and the authoritarian attitude exhibited by the church is all the more striking since it is reinforced by Galileo's espousing, in the second and third versions of his self-indictment, the same concern that, in an earlier scene of those versions, the conservative Philosopher voiced with respect to unconstrained research:

PHILOSOPHER: I can only wonder what all this is supposed to lead to.
GALILEO: As scientists, I should think, we have no business asking what the truth may lead us to.
PHILOSOPHER (*wildly*): Mr. Galilei, the truth may lead us to all sorts of things! [1270/35]

In 1938–39, shortly after the disappearance or elimination of some of Brecht's friends in Stalinist Russia (cf. 1972:vii–ix), the Galileo of the first version retained throughout the entire play his radically liberal opposition to any attempt by a ruling philosophy to curb unprejudiced inquiry (cf. esp. 294). Under the mushroom clouds of the first nuclear bombs, Brecht's second version of the play replaced this "liberal" view of research by Galileo's warning, already quoted, that the scientists' cheering at some new discovery may become "echoed by a universal howl of horror" (463). In the final version, completed in the 1950s when scientists on both sides of the Iron Curtain were helping to produce ever new means of nuclear and biological warfare, Brecht further sharpened Galileo's indictment of scientists who fail to examine what their research (as the Philosopher put it) "may lead to": "Had I held out, scientists could have developed something like the physicians' Hippocratic oath, the vow to use their knowledge only for the good of mankind. As things stand now, the best we can hope for is a race of inventive dwarfs who can be hired to do anything" (1341/94).

It should be noted that the newly added reference to the Hippocratic oath makes Galileo's final view mediate between two equally objectionable concepts of science: one that demands unconditional freedom for scientific and technological progress and one that rejects such freedom in the name of a particular ideology, against which no appeal can be made—whether to scientific evidence or to the scientist's conscience. Much like Kant's categorical imperative, a generalized Hippocratic vow to use knowledge "only for the good of mankind" would not take from individual persons—whether they are physicians or physicists—the burden and privilege of empirical observation and moral choice. The thought expressed in the two sentences just quoted was thus needed lest Galileo's final speech, as well as the dialectical *dianoia* of the entire play, repudiate his initial commitment, retained in the first scene of all three versions, to the relentlessly critical spirit of a "new age." Rather than for preconceived notions as to where the truth may—or should be allowed to—"lead us," Galileo's amended speech pleads for a resolutely diagnostic approach to the not yet wholesome human condition. Brecht seems to have sketched the important addition in America (cf. 1972:304–5) but to have felt the need for working it into the play only when his personal circumstances became similar to the historical Galileo's situation: when he, too, was living in a social system whose basic principles he affirmed without condoning its authoritarian tendency to interfere with the right of people to diagnose and treat, to interpret and change, the world as they see fit.

Staging Action and Vision

Claudel's *Book of Christopher Columbus* and Brecht's *Life of Galileo* convey their tragicomic mood in a predominantly romantic and a predominantly satirical vein, respectively. We are to admire man's fortunate fall, exemplified by the earthly fate of Columbus, and to feel indignation over some men's unfortunate rise, exemplified by Galileo's "original sin" leading to the propagation of a bribable "race of inventive dwarfs." Yet both playwrights, in attempting to prompt us to change ourselves as well as to change the world, refuse to narrow the emotive response elicited by their protagonists. To invoke some of the moods mentioned in Chapter 2, Claudel seems particularly anxious to temper joy with awe as well as derision; Brecht, to alloy pity especially with scorn. This becomes conspicuous as one considers two crucial episodes in the lives of Columbus and Galilei that have *not* been dramatized: just as Claudel has declined to show the festive scene of his hero's first return to Spain, Brecht has eschewed the potentially melodramatic low point of his story—Galileo's recantation in the chambers of the Inquisition.

There is much grumbling among members of Claudel's chorus when it turns out that the expected "grand triumphal scene" of the voyager's first return to Spain is missing from the Book: such a scene would surely have included "a little ballet," perhaps a "mixture of fandango and belly dance," to supply what the show has been lacking so far, namely, "sex appeal" (*un peu de femmes* [140–41/37]). This challenge against the authority of the Book and its Reader characterizes the kind of all-too-human posterity for and by whom history keeps being envisioned and reenacted. Since, however, Claudel sees any triumph within history as far too temporary to deserve unrestrained celebration, he discredits our desire for unearned joy by associating it with a shallow posterity's voyeuristic demand, expressed by some members of the chorus, for outright burlesque.

Brecht in turn discredits our knee-jerk reaction of pity for the great scientist facing the threat of torture and death at the hands of his intellectual inferiors when he invokes the primal scene of scientific treason indirectly—through the disheartening effect of Galileo's recantation both on his disciples and on the life of generations to follow. The narrative heading for Scene 13, "On June 22, 1633, Galileo Galilei abjures his doctrine of the motion of the earth before the Inquisition," countervenes any possible suspense as to what is going to happen, while the lyric preamble anticipates the recantation's thematic significance:

> June twenty-second, sixteen thirty-three
> A momentous day for you and me.
> Of all the days that was the one
> An age of reason could have begun.
>
> [1325/81]

As the curtain rises, we see Galileo's timid daughter Virginia pray for a reconciliatory outcome—Galileo has by now been interrogated for almost a month—and hear the Little Monk, Federzoni, and Andrea express their hope that the prisoner will remain steadfast. Even as word comes from the authorities that the proceedings are about to conclude and that Galileo will soon return and "may need a bed," the worried physicists cannot quite believe the rest of the message: "Mr. Galilei is expected to recant at five o'clock before the plenary session of the Inquisition. The big bell of St. Mark's will be rung and the wording of the abjuration will be proclaimed publicly" (1327/83). Soon after the appointed time, the big bell indeed "begins to boom," and "from the street the announcer is heard reciting Galileo's recantation." Then darkness falls while the bell is still booming; for a few moments, the negative "spectacle" of a blackout and the deafening "music" of the church bell completely supersede "diction" in divulging "plot," "theme," and "character."

When the stage grows light again, "diction" reclaims its place with a vengeance in the theatrical representation of the "original sin" of science. After the upset disciples have turned first against and then away from the arriving Galileo, he counters Andrea's earlier remark "Unhappy the land that has no heroes!" with this smugly defiant curtain line: "No. Unhappy the land that needs a hero." At this point, however, a remarkable reading follows, in front of the curtain, from Galileo's *Discorsi:*

Is it not obvious that a horse falling from a height of three or four ells will break its legs, whereas a dog would not suffer any damage, nor would a cat from a height of eight or nine ells, or a cricket from a tower, or an ant even if it were to fall from the moon? And just as smaller animals are comparatively stronger than larger ones, so small plants too stand up better: an oak tree two hundred ells high cannot sustain its branches in the same proportion as a small oak tree, nor can nature let a horse grow as large as twenty horses or produce a giant ten times the size of man unless it changes all the proportions of the limbs and especially of the bones, which would have to be strengthened far beyond the size demanded by mere proportion.— The common assumption that large and small machines are equally durable is apparently erroneous. [1329–30/85]

In the context of the play, we are forced to perceive the lengthy recitation from the historical Galileo's last treatise not only in terms of the explicit meaning of the words. The physicist's direct presentation of theoretical vision emerges here as fraught with indirect significance concerning the play's dramatic action. Whether the quoted passage was actually written long before or (more likely) long after the recantation, we hear it spoken, in the theater, *just after* Galileo has shrugged off his responsibility to act like a hero. Whether it is presented by the same or by another actor, we cannot help perceiving the scientific text as Galileo's apologetic explanation of his own ''fall''—a rationalizing rather than rational attempt to describe an event as natural and inevitable which, according to the playwright, need and should not have occurred.

''How could I, this large eating-drinking-thinking machine, have withstood the devastating power of biological and social forces unleashed within and around me?'' Such is the possibly suppressed thought motivating Galileo's behavior in the undramatized scene of his recantation. Rather than force mental events, whether conscious or unconscious, into the rigid linguistic mold of a soliloquy, Brecht chose to render them obliquely as befits the nonverbal dimension of an action that the scene's narrative heading, lyric preamble, and dramatic dialogue make us envision without its being actually represented on the stage. And Brecht's deft use of direct quotation from a scientific work as a means of indirect dramatic characterization has far-reaching implications. It suggests that even natural laws or other kinds of universal truths will emerge from human discourse as being envisioned in particular historical contexts and that, therefore, all scientific or otherwise theoretical discourse not only thematically presents but also, in a quasi-lyric fashion, enacts vision.

Claudel and Brecht thus approach the dialectic of Action and Vision—the quintessentially temporal and the potentially timeless—in diametrically opposed yet complementary ways. Claudel treats a particular voyage across the Atlantic as revelatory of universal truth; Brecht treats the search for universal laws as motivated—and made relevant—by particular historical circumstances. The concepts of both revelation and relevance entail, however, the necessary existence of interpreters of what is revealed and of what is relevant. This is why all action and vision, as we can know them, remain bound up with the interpretive and imaginative human acts of envisioning and enactment. Whatever timeless essence history may unfold in the private, "lyric" awareness of individuals and the public, "dramatic" sphere of their interaction must be regathered, still within the historical domain, into particular "narrative" interpretations or generalized, "thematic" world views. The unfolding and regathering of essence can thus not be divorced from historical human existence. Narrative historiography and systematic philosophy are able to assert or to deny that this is so. But performed historical drama can do more because, in the theater, both particular interpretations (of an episode or of a character) and general overviews (of the whole plot or of the total human constellation of a play's dramatic figures) must be *enacted* by performers and *envisioned* by the audience in the literal sense of the two words. Each theater event is, therefore, a doubly "interpreting event"—an event, that is, of interpretation by performers and by spectators at the same time. In the next chapter I will have more to say about theater events in general from both a semiotic and a hermeneutic point of view. But since, of our twelve playwrights, Brecht has propounded the most extensive and most influential set of ideas as to the art and craft of staging, it seems appropriate to conclude the present chapter by exploring what light his much-discussed theory of the theater can shed on *Life of Galileo* and other instances of modern historical tragicomedy as eminently performable works of drama.

Brecht's theory of the theater evolved in manifest opposition to a widely held view of acting that had long been associated with Horace. In lines 102–3 of his "Ars Poetica," also known as "Epistle to the Piso Brothers," Horace suggests that poets need to follow what he takes to be a sound precept for any kind of role modeling: "Feel grief if you would have me weep" (si vis me flere, dolendum est / Primum ipsi tibi). Even though Horace's concern is with the poet's art, the context of the words just quoted supports the generally held opinion that he meant to give the same commonsensical advice to actors. The contrary view of acting, most sharply expressed in Denis Diderot's eighteenth-century dialogue "Paradoxe sur le comédien," is based on the recognition that the actor may not always be able to "feel grief" while portraying a pitiable character and that, furthermore, excessive emotion of any kind may interfere with effective acting. Diderot contrasts *l'homme sensible,* the sensitive man, whose tears "ascend from the heart," with *le comédien,* the actor, whose tears "descend from the brain." According to his deftly argued paradox, "extreme sensitivity" to a character's plight or joy makes for bad actors, mediocre sensitivity for mediocre actors, and "absolute lack" of such sensitivity for "sublime actors": c'est le manque absolu de sensibilité qui prépare les acteurs sublimes (1875:370/1957:20).

Somewhat less paradoxically, it seems fair to say that every great actor strikes a balance between the extremes of complete emotional identification with the part and complete critical distance from it. The kind of balance he strikes will be codetermined by his individual talent and by the part assigned to him on a particular occasion. But, to recall our previous consideration of two complementary strategies of desire, the relative degree of self-transcending empathy and self-assertive detachment manifested by the actor in a particular performance will also depend on the prevailing literary and theatrical expectations of his contemporaries. Around 1600, for example, Shakespeare made Hamlet counsel the Players: "In the very torrent, tempest, and as I may say, whirlwind of your passion, you must acquire and beget a temperance that may give it smoothness" (III.ii). Around 1900, William Archer spelled out in fanciful but psychologically illuminating terms how Hamlet's advice might be followed. In a sense refuting the disciples of both Horace and Diderot, Archer ascribed to the actor a "dual"—or rather multiple—consciousness. In his *Masks or Faces?* (1888), the distinguished Scottish critic, playwright, and translator of Ibsen's works came to the following conclusion:

> There are many "brownies," as Mr. Stevenson puts it, in the actor's brain, and one of them may be agonizing with Othello, while another is criticizing his every tone and gesture, a third restraining him from strangling Iago in good earnest, and a fourth wondering whether the play will be over in time to let him catch the last train. [1957:184]

This refutation of the two extreme theories is, to some extent, an unintended vindication of both: in order to "make us weep," Archer's actor should and should not "feel grief," should and should not "lack sensitivity," at the same time.

Needless to say, Horace, Hamlet, Diderot, and Archer were offering advice to the actors of their own times. Significant differences aside, most plays performed in the first century B.C. and the bulk of European drama between Shakespeare and Ibsen focused on lively interaction between human beings. The actor in a play of that nature could easily employ at least one "brownie" of his brain for the purpose of emotional identification with his part. Yet the situation was different between Horace (or rather Seneca) and Shakespeare. Particularly in the Middle Ages, the stage was largely a vehicle of religious celebration and didactic allegory. Any style of acting appropriate for the portrayal of Macbeth or even of his witch-es would have been inadequate to the task of impersonating Adam and Eve, Jesus Christ, Vice, Gluttony, or Good Works. Several trends of modern drama have likewise been moving away from those types of dialogue and characterization that Horace, Hamlet, Diderot, and Archer seem to have had in mind. With Anton Chekhov and the soulful method of acting Konstantin Stanislavski developed before the First World War for the staging of Ibsen's and Chekhov's plays, the theatrical portrayal of dramatic characters in interaction with each other and in apparent independence from the play's author and its audience reached a point from which further progress had to be sought in completely different stylistic directions.

In the realm of historical drama, movement in one such direction has been propelled by some playwrights' unabashed willingness to opt (in Shaw's already quoted words) for a "sacrifice of verisimilitude" in order to achieve "veracity." As the reader will recall, Shaw considered it "the business of the stage to make its figures more intelligible to themselves than they would be in real life; for by no other means can they be made intelligible to the audience" (1971:52–53). Of course, good playwrights have always tended to prefer an effective, intelligible story to accurate but obscure history; whenever necessary, they would readily adjust the available evidence to their preferred medium or message. But Shaw's *Saint Joan* and many other historical plays of the twentieth century deviate from the trodden paths of historical drama by virtue of the authors' overt refusal to adjust the presentation of what they consider the actual truth to the requirements of factual plausibility. When we read or view their plays, our point of intellectual orientation thus keeps shifting between what emerges as the author's stance and what we may construe as that of the historical figures. Such shifts of perspective are required because most characters considered in this study are neither mere projections of the authorial vision (that would make them caricatures or allegorical figures) nor ostensibly free verbal agents speaking what would strike us as the genuine language of their interpersonal action. When, for instance, Cau-

138

chon protests the "irregular" haste of the English taking Joan, just sentenced, to the stake, Shaw makes the Inquisitor shrewdly pacify him: "We have proceeded in perfect order. *If the English choose to put themselves in the wrong, it is not our business to put them in the right. A flaw in the procedure may be useful later on: one never knows.* And the sooner it is over, the better for that poor girl" (145). The sentences italicized for the present discussion express a thought that could hardly have occurred to an inquisitor of the fifteenth century. But even if it had, the incriminating words themselves would not have been uttered in the circumstances whether or not the historical inquisitor and Cauchon knew as fully as Shaw hoped to know "what they were really doing." Before and after the italicized words, the Inquisitor "speaks his mind." For the length of two sentences, he rather speaks the playwright's, who proposes to represent (and I quote again from Shaw's Preface) "not only the visible and human puppets but the Church, the Inquisition, the Feudal System" (51) as historical hindsight has taught him to perceive them.

What approach should actors and directors take to such a "split" character with his clearly divided allegiances to plot and theme, to dramatic action and authorial vision? This question may well have occurred to a German *Dramaturg*—one of several literary advisers contracted to Max Reinhardt's chain of theaters—as he attended the rehearsals for Reinhardt's 1924 Berlin production of *Saint Joan*. And since the ambitious young man by the name of Bertolt Brecht shared with the Irish playwright a marked preference for the bird's-eye view of social trends over a thoroughgoing psychological delineation of individual characters, he decided—or so it appears—to out-Shaw Shaw in two different ways. First, in his own plays written from this time on, he increasingly relied on spoken or sung choruses, monologues, asides, and other formal devices through which authorial vision may permeate the dramatic interaction of the characters. Second, in his theoretical and critical writings, he began to advocate a style of acting that suspends the spectator's illusion of witnessing a self-contained series of events so that the author's or

139

the director's point of view may noticeably interfere with the perspective inherent in the represented action.

My assumption of Shaw's influence on Brecht's theory of distanced staging is corroborated by some pertinent dates: before the first English and German productions of *Saint Joan* and the roughly simultaneous publication of the play with the substantial Preface (1924), Brecht wrote a biting review of Shaw's *Pygmalion* in 1920 (1967, 15:24–26). Yet in July 1926, he published two acclamatory newspaper articles on Shaw 96–101/1964:10–13); in the same month, Brecht was working on *Mann ist Mann,* a play with several formal devices for the breaking of theatrical illusion, and gave the interview in which, for the first time on a public occasion, he rejected the actor's and the spectator's empathy (*Einfühlung*) with a dramatic character (1964:14–16). For the purpose of this discussion, the issue of actual indebtedness may be left aside. What should concern us is that two central tenets of Brecht's theory of staging are clearly analogous to ideas expressed in Shaw's Preface to *Saint Joan.* The first is that the actor should overtly superimpose his understanding of the character he is playing on the character's supposed understanding of himself; both Brecht and Shaw assumed that the dramatic characters, without such outside help, would not be sufficiently "intelligible" to the audience. The second tenet is implied by the first and has to do with a tragicomic aspect of some works by both Shaw and Brecht. In the Preface to *Saint Joan,* Shaw called the burning of Joan a "pious murder," committed by "normally innocent people in the energy of their righteousness," and observed that "this contradiction at once brings an element of comedy into the tragedy: the angels may weep at the murder, but the gods laugh at the murderers" (1971:51–52). In the heyday of Expressionism, the angels' emotional involvement *with* individual suffering was unlikely to be ignored on the German stage. Brecht and his allies in the movement of "new objectivity" (*neue Sachlichkeit*) came therefore to stress the gods' (and the Marxists') analytical detachment *from* it. The style of staging Brecht became famous for advocating did not only reflect the assumption that the author had envisioned the vicissitudes of the characters from a point of view superior to their own. It also prescribed for the performers of serious plays an attitude closer to the clown's habitual detachment from his part than to the tragic actor's feigned or sincere involvement with his. Brecht trusted that the spectators, responding to this style of staging, would not empathize with the plight of a character so presented; rather, they would give some hard rational thought to the question of how the character's predicament could and should have been averted (cf. 1967, 16:546–58/1964:121–28).

It is clear that most butts of comedy have usually been presented (if not, indeed, caricatured) in such a spirit of detachment. This is how the spectator watching Shakespeare's Malvolio or Molière's Harpagon can be made to laugh, even in moments of their temporary triumphs, *at* those characters, not *with* them. The villains of melodrama and tragedy engage the emotions in a likewise adverse fashion; the actors and particularly the spectators tend to identify with the implied author's scorn or hatred for Richard III and Iago, not with Richard's and Iago's self-love or the scorn and hatred of those characters for the others. Thus Brecht's demand for distance is innovative mainly with regard to those characters who, unless they are played with detachment, would display tragic qualities and elicit empathetic concern from the audience.

There was, of course, a wholesome shift of emphasis in Brecht's views on this subject. In his sharply polemical statements around 1930, he rejected any kind of identification with dramatic figures. Instead of saying, "This man's suffering appals me because there is no way out for him. . . . I weep with those who weep and laugh with those who laugh," the spectator of Brecht's distanced "epic theater" was supposed to say as late as in 1936, "This man's suffering appals me because there would be a way out for him after all. . . . I laugh at him who weeps and weep over him who laughs" (1967, 15:265/1964:71). Around 1950, Brecht still argued for the primacy of detached observation in the theater of our "scientific age," but he now conceded that a moderate degree of emotional involvement with the character is permissible on the part of both the actor and the spectator (cf. 1967, 16:678, 683, 899–900/1964:190, 193, 270–71). As a result, the potentially tragic reality of human suffering could begin to receive in Brecht's and his disciples' East Berlin productions almost as much stress as the potentially comic insight into its avoidability. To use Shaw's metaphors of the weeping angels and laughing gods, the author (and very detached, severe judge) of Galileo and Mother Courage may have come to realize that man's road to divine comprehension leads through angelic compassion. Or, as one might say in the earthier terms of a stage director, Brecht finally decided to give the spectators a vivid enough inside view of the characters whom they should ultimately contemplate from without with critical detachment. Indeed, a certain degree of emotive empathy emerges from some of Brecht's posthumously published fragments about his reformed concept of "dialectical" (rather than one-sidedly "epic") theater as the necessary antithesis to rational distance (cf. esp. 1967, 16:701–3, 815–16/1964:248–49, 276–77).

From the late forties on, Brecht was thus applying something like William Archer's concept of the actor's dual consciousness to the audience; he now wished to manipulate the tension between different "brownies" in the spectator's brain. Yet Brecht never ceased to insist that the theater's chief means of precluding the spectator's excessive empathy with a character is the conspicuous absence of complete emotional identification between the actor and his part. Just like Horace and unlike Diderot, Brecht thus continued to assume that the actor's actual attitude toward the character will serve as a kind of role model for the spectators: they will identify with and emulate the detached actor just the same as they will identify with and emulate the actor playing his part with empathy. *Feel grief if you would have me weep,* said Horace to the actor. *Do not feel grief so that you can appear to do so and thus make me weep,* countered Diderot. *Do not feel grief so that you will not appear to do so and thus will not make me weep either,* runs the early Brechtian doctrine. It can be restated in a positive form that is strikingly Horatian, *Keep your distance if you would have me keep mine;* or, to do better justice to the last phase of Brecht's development, *Keep your distance to the extent that you would have me keep mine.*

These formulas (and the diagrams of Figure 1 based upon them) highlight some aspects of difference and similarity in the respective views of Horace, Diderot, and Brecht. Further reflection on Brecht's theory and practice of staging will reveal, however, that my graphic representation of Brecht's "system" corresponds far too closely to his own description of it. In his "Short Organum for the Theater" (1949), Brecht described the ideal Brechtian performance in a memorable phrase: "the acting Laughton does not disappear in the enacted Galileo" (or, in John Willett's more literal rendering of *der zeigende Laughton* and *in dem gezeigten Galilei,* "the showman Laughton does not disappear in the Galileo whom he is showing"). While Brecht characterized this peculiar situation by saying that "the actor appears on stage in a dual form," John Willett's (in this case less literal) translation of the words *in zweifacher Gestalt,* "in a double

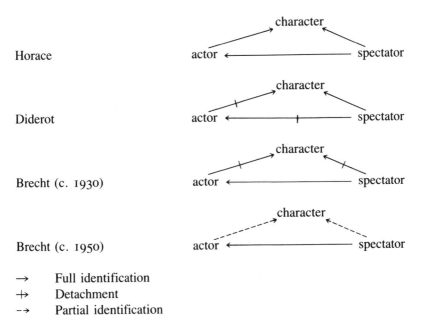

Horace

Diderot

Brecht (c. 1930)

Brecht (c. 1950)

→ Full identification
↛ Detachment
-→ Partial identification

Figure 1

role,'' may do better justice to what actually happens: Brecht in effect requires the actor to play two parts, "the acting Laughton" as well as "the enacted Galileo" (1967, 6:683–84/1964:194). Simultaneously or in an alternating fashion, the Brechtian actor must portray both the great scientist Galileo and the conscious (preferably also class-conscious) actor who shares Brecht's view that the great scientist, since he failed to stand up for his truth against the church, was also a great social criminal. Clearly, the latter part, that of the distancing actor, must be "studied" in advance and "played" night after night with just as much skill and care as the former, the part of Galileo. After all, Charles Laughton, the private citizen and member of the acting profession, is not exactly the same person as "the acting Laughton"—the actor playing Galileo in a certain way, on a particular occasion. Without the actor's success in evoking a persuasive image of himself as the showman on a specific job, even his most sincere distance from Galileo will either fail to be communicated to the audience or else prevent the stage image of the character he plays from being constituted.

My view of the Brechtian actor's double role, first presented in "The Actor's Face as the Author's Mask: On the Paradox of Brechtian Staging" (1976), has since been corroborated by at least one other critic. In *The Theater Event: Modern Theories of Performance,* Timothy Wiles speaks of the "superior knowledge" that Brecht's actor "feigns to possess" as "he plays the part of 'the Brechtian actor who knows,' along with playing a specific character" (1980:80–81). Brecht himself, however, eschewed the full exploration of the question of role playing and especially the question of playing a double role. Was he too naive or too shrewd to embark on such an exploration? I suspect the latter. Why should a spiritual second cousin of Jaroslav Hašek's *Good Soldier Schweik,* whose cunningly self-serving simplemindedness one of Brecht's plays transposed from the First to the Second World War, have provided a theory that such spectators of his own life as the Un-American Activities Committee or the East German authorities might have applied to the practice of his own "living theater" with

144

embarrassing results? Brecht and his East Berlin circle of friends and followers had especially good reason to repress any desire they may have had to probe into the possibility that, on the stage as well as in real life, one can appear to be a loyal party worker without actually being one. As the head of the rather controversial Berliner Ensemble, Brecht had little or no motivation to investigate whether his best disciples, the most convincing conveyors of the distancing, "scientific," "Marxian" attitude among the actors, were in fact (or should even try to be) the best disciples of the Stalinist ideologues of the German Democratic Republic as well.

For whatever reason, Brecht's theory remained quite Horatian indeed. Until about 1940, Brecht stated more or less explicitly that the appearance of critical distance results from the actor's genuinely detached attitude and that, therefore, the actor's genuine distance is needed if a similar attitude of distance is to be generated in the spectator. Around 1950, he softened his anti-emotional argument but, as far as I can see, continued to claim that the mostly detached attitude that the actors should appear to have and should try to awaken in the audience is practically identical with their actual frame of mind. According to Diderot's paradox, an actor who personally neither glorifies nor indicts Galileo would be best equipped to play the double role Brecht wants him to play. With William Archer's concept of dual consciousness in mind, we might say that one "brownie" in the actor's brain could, both intellectually and emotionally, endorse the non-Marxist Galileo while another one so endorses the Marxist actor playing Galileo. But the Brechtian doctrine prescribes a far less equal distribution of the actor's empathy between the two aspects of his double role. It requires that the part of Galileo be played with considerable detachment while the part of the detached actor is being played with complete identification; indeed, the spectators are expected to think that the actor *is* rather than *plays* this second part, namely, the part of the actor-playing-Galileo-with-detachment. The audience of a Brechtian performance is thus invited to see through only one of two layers of theatrical make-believe. Its attention is called to the fact that the distancing actor wears the features of Galileo only as a "mask." Yet it should ignore the no less important fact that the distancing actor's features—visible whenever the mask of Galileo is dropped—are features of another "mask," which may or may not resemble the actor's real "face." In other words, *Brecht wants us to accept the actor's second mask at face value.* But we need not do so; and to the extent that a spectator retains his disbelief concerning the identity between the "distancing actor" and the actual personality of the actor, he will also retain his own identity as the actual spectator who only temporarily wears the mask of the "distanced spectator"—the role assigned to him by a Brechtian playwright or director.

For the purpose of clarifying the psychological implications of Brecht's theory of staging, it may be useful to distinguish typographically between the actual ACTOR and SPECTATOR on the one hand and, on the other, the "actor" and "spectator" as roles played by the former two in a Brechtian production (see Figure 2). Whereas the actual ACTOR's feelings remain unexplored, he clearly appears to identify with the "actor" and to keep considerable but not complete distance from the character. The "actor" (who is played by the ACTOR and appears to be playing the character) keeps his critical distance from the character. The "spectator," deceived by the feigned identity between ACTOR and "actor," keeps considerable distance from the character through identification with the distancing "actor." Yet the SPECTATOR, who realizes that the AC-TOR and the "actor" are not identical, shares the ACTOR's apparently mixed attitude toward the character and probably evolves a similarly mixed attitude toward the one-sided "actor." The enlightened SPECTATOR will in fact end up identifying less with the "spectator" than with the ACTOR—that is, with the way of thinking and feeling he attributes to the ACTOR on the basis of the given performance. All this is, as Figure 2 indicates, fairly complicated, and a Brechtian production indeed presupposes sophisticated actors and audiences. Oddly enough, however, the psychological machinery involved may well enhance the aesthetic effect of certain plays. As Martin Esslin noted, the Brechtian actor (our ACTOR)

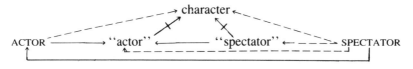

Figure 2

offers a most suggestive ''split image'' of man—''impelled by his emotions, critically yet helplessly aware of their irrationality''— whenever he shows ''the actions of the character and simultaneously presents'' (in the role of our ''actor'') ''the critical reasoning that might have stopped him from acting as he does'' (1971:263–64).

One great difficulty facing the Brechtian ACTOR as he plays his double role is that most of his lines have been written for the character ''impelled by his emotions'' and not for the ''actor'' who, just like the author and the director, should be ''aware of their irrationality.'' It is mainly through gestures, including the gestures of his voice, that the ''actor'' can intrude on the fictitious world in which the character he plays and the other characters exist. Yet Brecht managed to give most of his antiheroes certain speeches or (more frequently) songs that in fact only the detached ''actors'' playing them could be expected to utter. The following lines from Galileo's self-condemnation, other parts of which were quoted in the previous section of this chapter, may serve as an illustration:

> GALILEO: My dear Sarti, even in my present condition I can give you a few hints about the proper concerns of science. . . . It trades in knowledge, which is obtained through doubt. Providing everybody with knowledge of everything, science aims at making doubters of everybody. But princes, landlords, and priests keep the majority of the people in a pearly haze of superstition and outworn words to cover up their machinations. . . . Those selfseeking, violent men, who greedily exploited the fruits of science for their own ends, also felt the cold stare of science focused upon the millennial, yet artificial misery that mankind could obviously get rid of by getting rid of them. . . . The battle for measuring the sky has been won by

147

doubt; by credulity, the Roman housewife must keep losing her battle for milk. Science, Sarti, is involved in both battles. If mankind goes on stumbling in a pearly haze of superstition and outworn words and remains too ignorant for fully developing its own strength, it will never be able to deploy the forces of nature that science has discovered. . . . If scientists, intimidated by selfish rulers, confine themselves to accumulating knowledge for its own sake, science will be crippled and your new machines will only mean new afflictions. [1967, 3:1339–40/1972:93–94]

Along with other *Verfremdungseffekte*, such lines—properly spoken—will offer the spectator direct access to the author's vision, which in most other plays is conveyed by a chorus, certain asides and monologues, or the entire work, and *not* through conversations between the principal participants of the represented action.

To amplify the terms Shaw introduced in his Preface to *Saint Joan, dramatic* "verisimilitude" yields to *thematic* "veracity" when Galileo as he may have appeared to himself and to his contemporaries is suddenly replaced by Galileo as Brecht wants the "actor" and "spectator" to understand the character in the light of the historical consequences attributed by the playwright to his recantation. On such occasions, of course, the Brechtian "actor" will appear to identify with the author or the director at least as much as he appears to identify with himself as the ACTOR—the psychophysical substratum of the character he is playing. This, however, means a *shift* in emotional commitment, not the *absence* of it. Just as a class-conscious revolutionary or the loyal party worker will place the good of the community, usually determined by some "author" or "director" figure, above his own good, the Brechtian "actor" is expected to embrace a central, authorial and authoritative, interpretation of the entire story (*Fabel*) rather than one participant's thoughts and feelings about it. Such an attitude, when conspicuously displayed by the "actor," makes the ACTOR, too, appear to have resisted the self-transcending desire of "becoming" Galileo. But while the "actor" (as well as the ACTOR) appears to assert

148

his own self against the individual part, both give us the impression of having yielded to a self-transcending desire with respect to the collective production as a whole. The resulting interplay between each major performer's satirically self-assertive distance from his or her potentially tragic role and the same performer's romantically self-transcending empathy with the playwright or director as the guiding spirit of a potentially comic production can go a long way toward both entertaining and committing the audience of a Brechtian performance. The performers themselves, of course, remain painfully vulnerable to the self-willed martyr's tragicomic temptation, discussed in Chapter 2, to engage in a willfully self-serving surrender of the will to selfhood. This may well be one reason why Brecht's theory of staging, as well as Aristotle's comparable stress on plot rather than character in Chapter 6 of the *Poetics,* is more popular with playwrights and directors than with actors and actresses. In an important sense, however, the friendly and uncomplicated ghost of Horace hovers over Brecht's subtly partisan stage: the greater the distance between the ''actor'' and the character, the greater the empathy (or something very close to empathy) between the ''spectator'' and the ''actor'' as well as between the ''spectator'' and the author and/or director implied by the overall pattern of a given performance.

That the ''author'' implied by a literary work is not identical with the actual AUTHOR is a critical commonplace and should not require further elaboration. The parallel distinctions between implied ''actor'' and actual ACTOR and between implied ''director'' and actual DIRECTOR are, however, rarely invoked. Yet some of their implications clearly suggest useful lines of inquiry into such plays as Thornton Wilder's *The Skin of Our Teeth* and Peter Weiss's *Marat/Sade.* In the next chapter, I will indeed interpret the new use made by those plays of the old device called ''play within the play'' as an effort to write the complex psychology of ostensibly distanced staging into the very structure of a dramatic work.

5

The Face Value of the Actor's Mask:
The Skin of Our Teeth and
Marat/Sade

As the first character appearing on stage in Thornton Wilder's *Skin of Our Teeth* (1942), the maid Sabina offers a delightfully prattling sketch of the other members of the Antrobus household. First she describes them as a suburban foursome of commuter husband, homemaker wife, rough-and-ready son, and would-be homemaker daughter ("she'll make some good man a good wife some day, if he'll just come down off the movie screen and ask her"). But then she expands the social stereotype into the anthropological prototype of the upwardly mobile human family: "We've managed to survive for some time now, catch as catch can, the fat and the lean, and if the dinosaurs don't trample us to death, and if the grasshoppers don't eat up our garden, we'll all live to see better days, knock on wood" (1958:72).

As we already know, the situation of the Antrobuses is quite precarious. Before the curtain with a projection screen in the middle of it rose, a news broadcast had been heard about the alarming weather conditions: "There is a report that a wall of ice is moving southward across these counties. The disruption of communications by the cold wave now crossing the country has rendered exact information difficult, but little credence is given to the rumor that the ice had pushed the Cathedral of Montreal as far as St. Albans,

Vermont'' (70). In short, the Ice Age cometh. Small wonder that Sabina should worry ''whether the master will get home safely; whether he'll bring home anything to eat.'' But her attitude oscillates between premature despair and flippant resilience. When ''a portion of the wall above the door, right, flies up into the air and disappears,'' she continues in the undaunted spirit of *carpe diem:* ''. . . and my advice to you is not to inquire into why or whither but just enjoy your ice cream while it's on your plate,—that's my philosophy. Don't forget that a few years ago we came through the depression by the skin of our teeth! One more tight squeeze like that and where will we be?'' (72).

This speech, explicitly addressed to a 1942 New York audience still enjoying its ice cream amidst alarming news reports from overseas, is also intended to involve the spectators as members of a much more extended human family. After all, the cleaning crew, whose picture was projected on the screen also showing the front doors of the theater in which the audience has just gathered, had come across a lost article identified by the loudspeaker announcer as ''a wedding ring, inscribed: To Eva from Adam. Genesis II:18'' (70). Are we to infer that the rightful owner belongs to the cast or to last night's audience? In any event, the ring is one of the invisible stage props in Wilder's world theater, which draws no clear line between spectators and characters and does not maintain for very long the distinction between actors and characters either. When the last sentence of Sabina's speech ''One more tight squeeze like that and where will we be?'' elicits no response from her fellow actors, she nervously begins to repeat some of her previous lines until we hear a voice offstage: ''Make up something! Invent something!'' After a frustrated attempt to do so, she ''flings pretense to the winds and coming downstage says with indignation'':

I can't invent any words for this play, and I'm glad I can't. I hate this play and every word of it. As for me, I don't understand a single word of it, anyway,—all about the troubles the human race has gone through, there's a subject for you. Besides, the author hasn't made up his silly mind as to whether we're all living back in caves or in New Jersey today, and that's the way it is all the way through. Oh—why can't we have plays like we used to have—*Peg o' My Heart*, and *Smilin' Thru*, and *The Bat*—good entertainment with a message you can take home with you? [73]

Up to now, this aside to the audience could have been spoken by anyone—whether performer or spectator—who happens to dislike the play being produced. Yet the lines immediately following firmly anchor the entire speech in a new layer of theatrical make-believe:

SABINA: I took this hateful job because I had to. For two years I've sat up in my room living on a sandwich and a cup of tea a day, waiting for better times in the theatre. And look at me now: I—I who've played in *Rain* and *The Barretts of Wimpole Street* and *First Lady*—God in Heaven! (*The* STAGE MANAGER *puts his head out from the hole in the scenery.*)

MR. FITZPATRICK: Miss Sommerset! Miss Sommerset!

SABINA: Oh! Anyway!—nothing matters! It'll all be the same in a hundred years. [73]

The actress playing Sabina (Tallulah Bankhead in Elia Kazan's first New York production, Vivien Leigh in Laurence Olivier's 1945 London revival) now appears in the fictive part of a rather obscure, as well as obtuse, young American actress. When Mrs. Antrobus finally appears, her violent reproach—"Sabina, you have let the fire go out. . . . Here it is the coldest day of the year right in the middle of August, and you have let the fire go out" (73)—may thus be understood at a number of levels. The suburban housewife of New Jersey and a female troglodyte of the Ice Age speak the line, as if in unison, with audible overtones invoking the voice of Miss Sommerset's fellow actress, who has just missed her cue but is paradoxically allowed by the script to offer both direct comment on Sabina's negligence and indirect comment on Miss Sommerset's poor taste in drama as a reflection of her generally extinguished spirit: just like Sabina, Miss Sommerset has "let the fire go out."

The uttering of the sentences just quoted is clearly not a bit of naturalistic action where actor and character, the stage and the space it represents, the temporal progress of the performance and that of the performed action might stand in a simple one-to-one relationship of theatrical representation. Mrs. Antrobus' belated entrance helps instead to evoke an interconnected set of topical, archetypal, and self-referentially theatrical implications; and it helps to stress the simultaneous need for multiple interpretive perspectives.

Theater and Role Playing

The most conspicuous interpreters of a performed play are, of course, the performing artists. Although they are aided (if not guided or in some instances governed) by the director and such nonperforming members of the production staff as stage and costume designers, prop manufacturers, and the like, it is the actors and actresses who wear what appears to be their personal interpretations of a play's plot,theme, and (especially) characters on their sleeves. Whatever they do and say on stage amounts, in most productions, to the lion's share of the scenic representation of dramatized events. Since Wilder's dialogue and stage directions frequently refer to a performance to be imagined, even his silent reader is much more likely to visualize the characters as played by actors than to attend directly (as a reader, say, of *The Cherry Orchard* might) to the dramatized events. Peter Weiss's *Marat/Sade* likewise implants, as its full title indicates, one dramatic performance into another: *The Persecution and Assassination of Jean-Paul Marat as Performed by the Inmates of the Asylum of Charenton under the Direction of the Marquis de Sade* (1964). The potential of both plays for being enacted on stage must therefore inform the critical study of their texts to an even greater extent than is the case with many other works of drama. Yet an attempt to investigate the details of just a very few selected productions of the two plays would, besides being somewhat haphazard, require more space than seems to me warranted in the context of the present study. In principle, I will thus consider *The Skin of Our Teeth* and *Marat/Sade* in the way in which I have considered the other discussed plays, namely, as instances of eminently performable and often successfully performed drama (rather than mere sets of verbal cues for mounting diverse theatrical productions). Since, however, the question of role playing, both in the theater and in life, must figure prominently in any adequate approach to these two plays, my detailed discussion of them will benefit from being prefaced by some general remarks about the nature of theatrical communication and representation on and off the stage.

Every theater event is made up of what happens on the stage and in the auditorium. Minimally, such an event may be described as follows: actors perform while spectators watch and listen. Further reflection reveals, however, that the situation is more complex than that. Not only are the actors watching other actors and listening to them. Nor are the spectators, as in the case of catching laughter, being perceived and responded to by other spectators only. The actors, too, are watching and listening to the spectators, who thus participate actively in the theater event. Even by conspicuously displaying no indication of following the performance, the spectators can have a devastating impact on it. From the point of view of communication, theater events therefore consist of interacting stage events and auditorium events, whether or not a particular play or production takes explicit notice of the potential for two-way communication during every performance between actors and spectators.

Yet stage events and auditorium events presuppose each other not only with regard to the communicative processes involved in a theater event. They are just as complementary with regard to the evocative, representational dimension of every performance. Supported by props, decor, lighting, noise, music, and the like, the actors participate in stage events with a view to evoking dramatic events. They can do so either through the direct representation of enacted events or by enacting verbal accounts of offstage, reported events. The evocation of both kinds of dramatic events is, however, designed for the audience and requires its receptive participation. For example, the stage event of Laurence Olivier's pushing a dagger against a curtain, based on the actor's interpretation of Shakespeare's text, will not evoke the dramatic event of Hamlet's killing Polonius unless the spectators appropriately interpret both what they see the actor do and what they hear him and the other performers say. From the point of view of representation, theater events therefore consist of interpretive stage events and of the auditorium events of interpreting the stage events as dramatic events.

The art of theatrical communication and representation relies on the simultaneous presence of the principal senders and receivers of messages (namely, the performers and the spectators) as well as on the simultaneous presence of the principal signifiers and signifieds of images (namely, the bodies and voices of the performers and the physical actions and speech acts of the represented characters). The simultaneous presence of performers and spectators infuses the theater event with a much higher degree of continuous interaction between the "producers" and "consumers" of art than the degree characteristic of other types of artistic communication. (The same holds for partly improvised performances of music and of oral literature, which, of course, amount to theater events of a certain kind.) The simultaneous presence of performers and characters in turn privileges showing over telling or, in Nelson Goodman's more precise terminology, exemplification over denotation as a mode of reference, in the representational dimension of theatrical worldmaking (1968:52–67; 1978:63–70). Owing to the fact that the performers figure prominently in both the communicative and the mimetic or referential relationships just mentioned, their function of establishing contact between the other entities involved (namely, the spectators and the characters) has long been the focus of most discussions, whether formal or informal, of the nature of theatrical experience. Our very idea of the theater may, indeed, be seen as derived from, based upon, or at least emerging out of our idea of acting in the sense of the ubiquitous human activities of role modeling and role playing.

Toward the end of the last section of Chapter 4 I drew the distinction between ACTOR and "actor" with the analogous literary distinction in mind between the actual author of a text and the author implied by it. To be sure, there is a significant difference between the two sets of concepts: whereas the actual author is always concealed, so to speak, behind the text and its implied author, the actual ACTOR is seen and heard by the SPECTATOR whenever the "spectator"—the theatrical analogue to the reader implied by a text— sees and hears the "actor." Yet the ACTOR is analogous to the actual author and the "actor" is analogous to the implied author for the following reason. Strictly speaking (and phrased in semiotic terms), only the "actor" or the "actress" is a visible and audible sign that palpably functions—hence the rich complexity of the theater event—in all three modes of signification distinguished by Charles Sanders Peirce (cf. esp. 1955:98–119). As an icon, the "actor" or "actress" evokes qualities of the imagined character by dint of postulated resemblance between them. As an index, he or she indicates qualities of the ACTOR or ACTRESS by dint of the factual connection between the theatrical sign and its performing maker. As a symbol, he or she helps to convey the total thematic message of a performance by dint of conventional association between certain kinds of action and vision. Peirce realized, of course, that the iconic, indexical, and symbolic modes of signification almost always interact. Likewise, the "actor" (or "actress") signifies a character, an ACTOR (or ACTRESS), and an authorial/directorial message *predominantly rather than exclusively* on the respective grounds of imagined resemblance, factual connection, and conventional association. For example, as Jiří Veltruský (cf. esp. 1976) and other early semioticians of the Prague school have shown in great detail, conventional associations always accompany the quasi-natural resemblance between the costume, mask or makeup, and behavior of what I call the "actor" and the corresponding aspects of the represented character.

On the basis of Veltruský's references (1976, 1981) to Ottakar Zich's as yet untranslated *Esthetics of Dramatic Art* (1931), I am pleased to note that my tripartite distinction between ACTOR, "actor," and character, first presented in "The Actor's Face as the Author's Mask: On the Paradox of Brechtian Staging" (1976), was anticipated by the prominent Czech scholar when he introduced the concept of *stage figure* (much like my concept of the "actor") as distinguishable from both the *actor* (my ACTOR) and the *dramatis persona* (the represented character). I rather suspect, however, that an "actor" who steps out of his role in order to comment on it or otherwise communicate with the audience would have struck Zich as assuming an entirely different role within which a new distinction between stage figure and character must be made. Such a distinction is certainly useful for some purposes, just as a distinction between the ACTOR-as-artist and the ACTOR-as-person is useful for some others (cf. Wilshire 1982:xvi,267, *et passim*). Distinctions of these kinds would, for instance, allow us to align the theory of dramatic performance more closely with the theory of narrative fiction. The ACTOR-as-person would correspond to the actual author of a novel, the ACTOR-as-artist to its implied author, the "actor" as stage figure to the narrator, and the dramatic character (whose story in the theater is, of course, "told" in the very special way of enactment) to a particular character in the novel; an "actor" passing in and out of character would then be comparable to a quasi-autobiographical narrator like David Copperfield, whose perspective on the narrated events shifts back and forth between the evolving tale, in which young David is the main character, and the hindsight of the adult teller (cf. Stanzel 1984:216–18). In keeping with the purpose of the present discussion, however, I will continue to apply Occam's razor to conceptual entities other than the ACTOR, the "actor," and the character. In many instances, even these three are easier to distinguish in theory than in practice simply because the "actor," as explained above, signifies simultaneously in an iconic, indexical, and symbolic fashion. What we see on the stage or, for that matter, on the screen is (to give a concrete example) Olivier-as-Hamlet-in-a-particular-production-of-a-particular-play: an extremely complex interplay of present or filmed ACTOR, imaginatively experienced fictive character, and the latent thematic import that the play and the production as a whole make us associate with the manifest behavior of the "actor."

This is not to say, of course, that different kinds of staging or filming cannot make us focus on just one member of the trio AC-TOR/"actor"/character at the expense of the other two. Just how and why such predominance is frequently established may be learned from a recent study in which Bert O. States (1983) contrasts three combinable and, to some extent, always combined modes of acting as the "representational," the "self-expressive," and the "collaborative." The first mode (I would call it primarily iconic) is geared toward the world of the represented characters. The second (and primarily indexical) mode feeds on the actor's personality as a virtuoso performer. The third (and, in the Peircean sense, primarily symbolic) mode highlights the process of express communication from stage to auditorium. It is clear that predominantly representational acting (e.g., a production following Stanislavsky's "method") tends to conceal both the ACTOR and the "actor" behind the portrayed character. By contrast, predominantly self-expressive acting (e.g., the typical performance of an opera or the "operatic" production of any play) tends to conceal "actor" and character behind the actually performing ACTOR (or virtuoso SINGER, as the case may be). Finally, the collaborative mode of acting that prevails, for example, in comic asides, Brechtian songs, and other types of direct verbal or gestural appeal by a performer or chorus to the audience tends to conceal ACTOR and character behind the "actor" engaged in direct communication with the "spectators." None of the three kinds of concealment will become complete unless the SPECTATOR surrenders his or her personal identity and, so to speak, *becomes* the "spectator" implied by the particular mode of acting

158

that predominates in an entire production or certain segments of it. Typically, such complete surrender does not occur. Hence most SPECTATORS do not enter into an exclusive relationship with the represented characters, the self-expressive ACTORS, or the collaborative "actors." If they did, they would either believe, for example, that a man named Polonius was actually killed a few feet away from where they are sitting; or fall in love with, for example, Laurence Olivier; or else see the violent scene in the Queen's bedroom only as a persuasive demonstration of an encoded message— the suggestion, for example, that repressed oedipal feelings may lead to irrational and sociopathic behavior. Precisely because the three modes of acting and our response to their various ways of worldmaking are, at some level, always combined, critical reflection is required for distinguishing the respective contributions of the represented character, the self-expressive ACTOR, and the collaborative "actor" to the SPECTATOR's complete theatrical experience.

Nevertheless, plays within plays and especially performances within performances have long been problematizing the naive assumption of a simple, unmediated relationship between actors and characters. They have, in a sense, anticipated the complex psychology of Brechtian staging (as outlined in Figure 2) by assigning some ACTORS a double role: that of a character and that of an "actor" playing that character. A performance within the performance may, of course, be either overtly theatrical or cunningly manipulative. In the "mousetrap" scene of *Hamlet* (III.ii), for example, and in the artisans' presentation of "Pyramus and Thisby" in *Midsummer Night's Dream* (V.i), Shakespeare makes some ACTORS play characters who, as "actors" of the respective "plays" within the PLAYS— those microdramas within macrodramas—are seen in the roles of other characters. But in half a dozen other plays, including *The Merchant of Venice* and *Twelfth Night,* he makes female characters appear disguised as men. Through this reversal of the transsexual disguise mandated by Elizabethan theatrical conventions, the young male ACTORS playing Portia and Viola also become responsible for the impersonation, by those skillful "actresses" on the stage of their projected lives, of a male judge in one case and a shipwrecked young man in the other.

Whether in the manner of *Hamlet* (play within play) or in that of *Twelfth Night* (disguise upon disguise), such doubling of evocative projection directs attention to the significant parallel between play-acting and the role playing involved in what Erving Goffman called "the presentation of self in everyday life" (1959). That parallel had figured briefly but prominently in Georg Simmel's and Helmuth Plessner's respective contributions "toward the philosophy of the actor" (1923; cf. esp. 244–46) and "toward the anthropology of the actor" (1953; cf. esp. 186–87), and I merely wish to articulate it here in terms of the distinctions among ACTOR, "actor," and character suggested above. In the final section of the next chapter, I will address the question of the unity of an actor's or other human being's self—a unity despite, if not indeed due to, the multiplicity of roles he or she is capable of playing.

The actual person of the PRESIDENT of a corporation, university, or the United States may be distinguished from the "president" whose public utterances in the microdrama of his presidency are largely authored or co-authored by speech writers and whose public gestures (in both senses of the phrase) are often designed by media consultants. Those backstage writers and directors of public events know that the "president" must project a certain image of the president whether or not that image—comparable to the character to be projected by the "actor"—more or less closely resembles the PRESIDENT, who is, in the macrodrama of his total life, many other things as well (for example, FATHER, ACTOR, and MIDWESTERNER). They will advise the PRESIDENT as to how the "president" can best project an appropriate image of the president on the basis of their familiarity with the interpretive conventions according to which his various AUDIENCES will interpret the rhetorical events of "presidential" utterances and gestures as being indeed presidential. Just as the "actor" playing Hamlet, for example, can be distinguished from both the ACTOR and the character, the "president" projecting or not projecting a presidential image can thus be distinguished from both the actual person (the PRESIDENT) and the projected image (the president).

This last distinction is important not only as a useful tool for unmasking deceptive make-believe. It also suggests why the presidential role, if enacted in keeping with the exigencies of the public drama in which it interacts with roles played by other people, may prescribe actions that the PRESIDENT as a particular person would not care to undertake. In this regard, the economically and politically conservative Richard Nixon's imposing a freeze on wages and prices, as well as his rapprochement with the People's Republic of China, may serve as an illustration. A comparable independence of the public role from the private person playing it has often been observed with respect to the judicial performance of Supreme Court justices who before their appointment are known to have displayed attitudes and inclinations contrary to their eventual voting records. One may conclude that PRESIDENTS and JUSTICES should be chosen (as well as impeached) in accordance with their ability to enact, as "presidents" and "justices," the presidential and judicial roles provided by the historical script being written, in part by themselves, during their tenure of office.

The far less difficult and less consequential task of choosing ACTORS for dramatic characters is usually carried out on an analogous principle, and the pleasant or unpleasant surprises during rehearsal parallel those experienced with respect to public figures. Obviously enough, the ACTOR also has his speech writers and media consultants when, in cooperation with the director and other members of the nonperforming staff, he prepares to perform a dramatic role in his capacity as the "actor"—that is to say, as a participant in the stage events of a particular production designed to evoke the dramatic events of a play. Sympathetic friends and professional counsellors notwithstanding, we tend to receive far less help when, for example as PARENTS or JOB APPLICANTS, we wish to project an effective or even admirable image of the parts that life has called upon us to play. Yet our success or failure in this kind of performance will largely depend on just how well we manage to perform

as "parents" or "job applicants" for our respective "audiences"—that is to say, on just how well we can anticipate the
interpretive acts of our CHILDREN and PROSPECTIVE EMPLOYERS in
their particular roles—for they, too, have many others—as our
"children" and "prospective employers." Likewise, the ACTOR
must gear the gestures of the "actor" to the interpretive conventions he and the director attribute to the SPECTATORS as "spectators" of the stage events. In this respect, the distinction between
SPECTATORS and "spectators" is important for the following reason.
The ACTOR's gesture of pushing a dagger against a curtain may or
may not be interpreted as a criminal act depending on whether the
SPECTATORS observe it as "spectators" of stage events or as "spectators" of an incident about which they can be required to give
sworn courtroom testimony. In the latter case, of course, each sub-
poenaed SPECTATOR is expected to assume the role of eyewitness in
one of those often theatrical happenings known as jury trials.

There is always some difference between the interpretive conventions applicable to stage events evoking dramatic events and those
applicable to the (less obviously "staged") events of the SPEC-
TATOR's life. That difference is not completely eliminated by even
the most naturalistic style of acting. But it is palpably accented
whenever, as in medieval liturgical drama or in the Japanese Nō
theater, a conspicuous set of nonrealistic stage conventions prevails
and whenever, even in the overall context of more or less realistic
methods of acting, the stage events call attention to themselves as
stage events (cf. Elam 1980:90–91). They obviously do so in the
productions of *The Skin of Our Teeth, Marat/Sade,* and many earlier plays that contain plays within plays to be enacted as performances within performances (cf. Nelson 1958). The presence of a
stage "audience" at the "performance" of the bungling artisans for
the court of Theseus, for example, underscores the function assigned to the AUDIENCE of any PERFORMANCE of *Midsummer
Night's Dream*—the function of interpreting stage events as dramatic events. Just as the "spectators" in Shakespeare's legendary Athens, the SPECTATORS of every theater event must imaginatively sup-

plement the stage events because, as Theseus tells Hippolyta, "the best of this kind are but shadows: and the worst no worse, if imagination amend them" (V.i.211–12).

Taking Play Seriously

Perhaps the most consistent doubling of the basic theatrical situation occurs in Ludwig Tieck's lightheartedly profound *Puss in Boots* (*Der gestiefelte Kater*, 1797). Here the "author" and some "spectators" repeatedly engage in discussions of the "play" being performed. The PLAY's relationship to the world outside it, the fact that it was written by an AUTHOR and is now being performed by ACTORS for SPECTATORS, thus becomes one of its major themes. Tieck's exquisite tour de force, almost certainly known to Weiss and quite possibly known to Wilder—who based *The Merchant of Yonkers* (1939), later retitled *The Matchmaker,* on Johann Nestroy's *Einen Jux will er sich machen* (1842)—amplifies the usual formula (Figure 3) into an analogous but larger network of relationships (Figure 4). A particularly tongue-in-cheek version of what Lionel Abel called "metatheatre" (1963) results: Tieck's PLAY, containing a

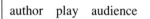

author	play	audience

Figure 3

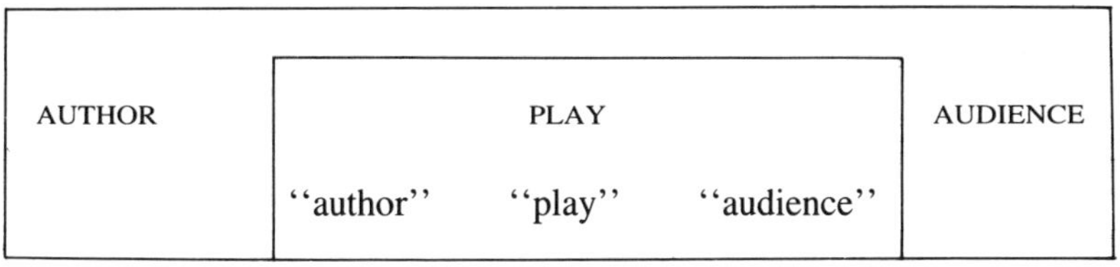

AUTHOR	PLAY			AUDIENCE
	"author"	"play"	"audience"	

Figure 4

163

"play" within itself, points to its own playfulness, reveals its AU-THOR's emotional detachment from his work, and invites similar detachment as the proper attitude to the work on the part of the AUDIENCE (whether it consists of SPECTATORS or READERS). On those relatively rare occasions when *Puss in Boots* is performed rather than read, it sheds particularly instructive light on the structure of theatrical make-believe. ACTORS and SPECTATORS share the AUTHOR's implied knowledge that the "author," the "actors," and the "spectators," including a "critic," must be played by ACTORS just the same as Hinze (the Puss) and his master Gottlieb are. At the same time, the "author," the "actors," and the "spectators" appear to believe that only the characters of the dramatized fairy tale are played by ACTORS.

Just like the brief comparable scenes of *Hamlet* and *Midsummer Night's Dream,* Tieck's entire text calls for two different *styles* of acting (not necessarily based on the predominance of any two of the three *modes* discussed above) so that two different levels of theatrical evocation may become operative. Yet empathy between performer and performed role is no more likely to occur in the case of the ACTORS playing supposedly real people (e.g., the "author," the "stage mechanic," the "prompter," the "critic," and other members of the "audience") than it is likely to occur in the case of the ACTORS who as "actors" are playing Hinze, Gottlieb, the King, the Princess, and other characters of the "play." That the ACTOR playing the "actor" playing the Puss in Boots will not empathize with that nominal hero of both the "play" and the PLAY goes without saying. Nor will he generate empathy between the SPECTATORS on the one hand and, on the other, the talkative tomcat, the "actor" playing the cat, or the ACTOR playing the "actor" playing the cat. Yet the implied author's "romantic irony"—an attitude of detachment from his avowedly fictive, playful work—will be shared by all ACTORS and SPECTATORS as "actors" and "spectators" of the PLAY. Joining the ironic conspiracy, they will, as it were, laugh or at least smile at the expense of both the characters of the "play" and its supposed ACTORS and SPECTATORS, who as "actors" and "spectators'' of the ''play'' participate in the stage events evoking those characters.

In most productions of *A Midsummer Night's Dream,* the artisans' performance of their ''play'' within Shakespeare's PLAY is staged and received in a similarly detached spirit. But can the same be said about the two playlets in *Hamlet*—the introductory ''dumb show'' and its tempestuously interrupted sequel? Typically, I believe, our emotional involvement is heightened rather than reduced while we watch Hamlet watch Claudius watch those ''plays'' within the PLAY. Here the added level of theatrical evocation tends to enhance the empathetic appeal of the primary one. While the ACTORS playing Hamlet and Claudius and the ACTOR playing the ''actor''-playing-Duke-Gonzago tend to disappear behind their respective single or double roles, the SPECTATORS tend to take the dramatic events at Elsinore—the staging and watching of events that take place in Vienna—very seriously indeed. One might say that AUTHOR and ACTORS exchange conspiratorial glances with the SPECTATORS if the theatrical situation is doubled within the overall framework of a comic plot but not if it is doubled within a tragic plot. In this respect as well as in some others, *The Skin of Our Teeth* is closer to romantic comedy and *Marat/Sade* is closer to tragic satire: while Weiss's SPECTATORS are likely to take both the ''play'' and (especially) the PLAY quite seriously, what Wilder's SPECTATORS are invited to take seriously is, above all, the PERFORMERS' play with the PLAY and with the ''play'' within the PLAY. Yet both plays, as we shall see, convey a sufficiently large number of generic moods to be considered tragicomic. Indeed, both playwrights tend to superimpose the stage events of their respective PLAYS on those of their respective ''plays'' with a view to eliciting contrasting moods from the ''actors'' and ''spectators'' of the ''plays'' on the one hand and from the ''actors'' and ''spectators'' of the PLAYS on the other.

A good example in Wilder's ''play'' is the burlesque scene in which scantily clad Miss Lily Fairweather, having just won first prize in an Atlantic City beauty contest, sets out to seduce Mr.

165

George Antrobus, the newly elected president of the conventioneer-ing "Ancient and Honorable Order of Mammals, Subdivision Hu-mans." All of a sudden, the "actress" playing the part—the same Miss Sommerset who played Sabina in the preceding act—switches from the "play" to the PLAY: "Just a moment, I have something I wish to say to the audience.—Ladies and Gentlemen. I'm not going to play this particular scene tonight. It's just a short scene and we're going to skip it. But I'll tell you what takes place and then we can continue the play from there on" (108). The "actor" playing Mr. Antrobus, too, is forced now to shift from the sexual indulgence afforded him by the "play" to the professional indignation de-manded of him by the PLAY. He summons Mr. Fitzpatrick, the stage manager of the "play," from the wings, but Miss Sommerset re-fuses to be disciplined and to return to the part of Lily Fairweather just yet. As she explains to a group of perplexed colleagues (several "actors" have by now come forward to the stage):

> Well, if you must know I have a personal guest in the audience tonight. Her life hasn't been exactly a happy one. I wouldn't let my friend hear some of these lines for the whole world. I don't suppose it occurred to the author that some other women might have gone through the experience of losing their husbands like this. Wild horses wouldn't drag from me the details of my friend's life . . . well, they'd been married twenty years, and before he got rich, why, she'd done the washing and everything.

The farcical clash between the "play" and the PLAY, compounded by the self-perpetuated satire against the cruel kindness of the ulti-mately most inconsiderate Miss Sommerset, is thus giving way to the reported events of a (presumably real-life) soap opera. Quite properly, some productions even reinforce the shift in mood by a "stage event" occurring in the auditorium; a female "spectator" may be made to leave her seat and rush out in tears while Miss Sommerset goes on with her unintended self-parody: "Nothing, nothing will make me say some of those lines . . . about 'a man outgrows a wife every seven years' . . . and that one about 'the Mohammedans being the only people who looked the subject square in the face.' Nothing'' (109). Gradually, the performance of the PLAY *about* a particular performance of the "play" once again merges *with* the latter performance. Through the seesaw between two levels of dramatic evocation, however, Lily's role as a particular homebreaker has been lifted out of its concrete particularity and received archetypal resonance invoking the spirit of countless manifestations of the great seductress all the way back to Lilith, the apocryphal Other Woman in Adam's life. Her subsequent words even point beyond the context of egocentric sexuality to all acts and attitudes of tragicomic "self-fulfillment" that lead to devastating frustration in other human beings:

Listen, George: *other* people haven't got feelings. Not in the same way that we have,—we who are presidents like you and prize winners like me. Listen, other people haven't got feelings; they just imagine they have. Within two weeks they go back to playing bridge and going to the movies. Listen, dear; everybody in the world except a few people like you and me are just people of straw. Most people have no insides at all. Now that you're president you'll see that. Listen, darling, there's a kind of secret society at the top of the world,—like you and me,—that knows this. [110]

Lily's no longer very secret society of supermen and superwomen is predicated on her view that "except for two things, pleasure and power,'' life is "boredom" and "foolishness." The larger human community postulated by Wilder's scheme of things is, however, based on a better guarded secret: Mrs. Antrobus flings the invisible bottle containing it into the ocean "far over the heads of the audience to the back of the auditorium.'' This secret—"all the things that a woman knows'' although "it's never been told to any man and it's never been told to any woman'' (114)—seems to underlie the propagation and survival of the human species in more or less extended, always fragile, but (in some form or another) always restored families. Indeed, Mrs. Antrobus' watchword for the year, "Save the Family," prevails over President Antrobus' inaugural watchword, "Enjoy Yourselves" (97–98), as soon as the beachside weather signal indicates that "the biggest storm in the whole world" (111) is coming to the endangered world of the stage. To escape from this reoccurring disaster of the mythical past, the Antrobuses embark together on a "boat at the end of the pier," herding along all sorts of invisible animals ("two of a kind, male and female") through the aisle into the as yet unflooded world of the auditorium. No longer tempted by the "serpentine dance" of the doomed but merrymaking conveners, Lily begs her way "back to the kitchen" of the extended family of Act I: "Mrs. Antrobus, take me. Don't you remember me? I'll work. I'll help. Don't leave me here!" In Wilder's latter-day version of the biblical story, "there's a lot of work to be done" after the deluge; so Lily-Sabina, once "raped home" by Mr. Antrobus from the Sabine hills of early Roman history (75), is allowed to be saved perhaps because, as Mrs. Antrobus says of all women as bearers of life's secret:

> We're not what books and plays say we are. We're not what adver-
> tisements say we are. We're not in the movies and we're not on the
> radio. We're not what you're all told and what you think we are.
> We're ourselves. And if any man can find one of us he'll learn why
> the whole universe was set in motion. [114]

Just as significantly, Antrobus, Jr., will also be saved, although, as we heard in Act I, he had caused the death of his brother and, in Act II, he is wanted by the Atlantic City police for having hit with a stone "one of those colored men that push the chairs." Mrs. Antrobus refuses to embark without him, and when her missing prodigal son does not respond to her calling him by his official name (Henry says later: "I didn't think you wanted me"), she bursts out in desperation," "Cain! Cain!"—thus reaffirming family ties one might wish to sever (117). The implication is clear: the Ice Age and the Flood will claim their victims but it is not for other members of the human family to decide who the victims shall be. All "refugees" of Act I had to be given food and shelter, not only those with obvious pragmatic or educational value to the Antrobuses (a doctor, Judge Moses, the Muses, and Homer); faced with the Flood, too, each man is his brother's keeper, whether or not that brother has been living up to the principle of such universal brotherhood.

Act III further illustrates the paradox that "strong unreconciled evil" (130) is an integral part of the ultimately redeemable human condition. After Act I exemplified natural scarcity through the Ice Age and Act II portrayed the high tide of the individual libido as bringing on a quasi-biblical flood, the final act explores the social disaster of war as another recurring predicament of the globally conceived human family. The camp follower Sabina brings the good news to the destroyed New Jersey home that Mrs. Antrobus and Gladys with her baby (no father is mentioned, but then the world has been militarized for years) may leave their underground hiding place. Mr. Antrobus is a bit delayed: the inventor in Act I of the wheel and the alphabet is still "thinking up new things," such as a recipe for "grass soup that doesn't give you the diarrhea" (125). Thus Henry, who "rose from corporal to captain, to major, to general" and turns out to have been "the enemy," returns before his father, still vowing to kill him: "I have spent seven years trying to find him; the others I killed were just substitutes" (126).

But distraught Henry's "complex" is oedipal in a social rather than a strictly Freudian sense. When Mr. Antrobus arrives and, nobly but somewhat condescendingly, proposes "trying to build up a peacetime with you in the middle of it," Henry protests:

I'm not going to be part of any peacetime of yours. . . . Try what? Living *here?*—Speaking polite downtown to all the old men like you? Standing like a sheep at the street corner until the red light turns to green? Being a good boy and a good sheep, like all the stinking ideas you get out of your books? Oh, no. I'll make a world, and I'll show you. [130]

169

Within the "play," the father outargues the son:

> How can you make a world for people to live in, unless you've first
> put order in yourself? Mark my words: I shall continue fighting you
> until my last breath as long as you mix up your idea of liberty with
> your idea of hogging everything for yourself. . . . You and I want the
> same thing; but until you think of it as something that everyone has a
> right to, you are my deadly enemy and I will destroy you. [130–31]

Yet, when the son makes for the father's throat, Miss Sommerset
interrupts the "play." For several minutes the PLAY takes over and,
by placing Henry's antisocial role in a different frame of reference,
highlights the palimpsest quality of human actions: Cain's bloody
rebellion against what he perceived as the unwarranted preferential
treatment of Abel's offering recurs not only in the Henry of the
"play" but also in the "actor" playing Henry.

> SABINA: Stop! Stop! Don't play this scene. You know what happened
>   last night. Stop the play! (*The men fall back, panting,* HENRY
>   *covers his face with his hands*). Last night you almost strangled
>   him. You became a regular savage. Stop it!
> HENRY: It's true. I'm sorry. I don't know what comes over me. I
>   have nothing against him personally. I respect him very much . . .
>   I . . . I admire him. But something comes over me. It's like I
>   become fifteen years old again. I . . . I . . . listen: my own father
>   used to whip me and lock me up every Saturday night. I never had
>   enough to eat. He never let me have enough money to buy decent
>   clothes. I was ashamed to go downtown. I never could go to the
>   dances. My father and my uncle put rules in the way of everything
>   I wanted to do. They tried to prevent my living at all. [131–32]

The "actress" playing Sabina claims to have known her colleague's
family and disputes the charges. The question as to who is right
remains moot, of course. But the fact remains that the scene to be
played reminds the young "actor" of his adolescence:

It's like I had some big emptiness inside me,—the emptiness of being hated and blocked at every turn. And the emptiness fills up with the one thought that you have to strike and fight and kill. Listen, it's as though you have to kill somebody else so as not to end up killing yourself. [132]

To be sure, Henry's attitude exemplifies both Adlerian "over-compensation" for actual or perceived powerlessness and Freud's revised view of aggressivity (as summarized in the thirty-second of his *New Introductory Lectures on Psychoanalysis*): "It really seems as though it is necessary for us to destroy some other thing or person in order not to destroy ourselves, in order to save ourselves from the disposition toward self-destruction" (1967:112/1965:105). Yet matters do not come to rest on this note—a combination of Alfred Adler's theory of the "inferiority complex" (1964:96–116) with his former master's eventual linking of aggressive human impulse to a postulated "death drive" or *Todestrieb* (cf. Freud 1967:114–15/1965:107–8). When the "actor" playing Mr. Antrobus joins the group therapy session of the PLAY, we begin to leave the Freudian sphere, whether orthodox or revisionist, altogether for an area of concern better explored in postwar psychology—the effect of "workaholic" behavior on one's psyche and human environment:

Wait a minute. I have something to say, too. It's not wholly his fault that he wants to strangle me in this scene. It's my fault, too. He wouldn't feel that way unless there were something in me that re-minded him of all that. He talks about an emptiness. Well, there is an emptiness in me, too. Yes,—work, work, work,—that's all I do. I have ceased to *live*. No wonder he feels that anger coming over him.

Before the PLAY yields the stage back to the "play," the "actor" playing Henry makes peace with the "actor" playing Mr. Antro-bus: "Thanks. Thanks for what you said. I'll be all right tomorrow. I won't lose control in that place. I promise" (132). But the AU-DIENCE is likely to realize that tonight's psychoanalysis of the son's patently rebellious and the father's latently oppressive mode of existence, enacted in the context of the "play" as well as in that of the PLAY, will have to be reenacted—with repeated reference to last night's near disaster—in tomorrow's and the next day's performance. That is to say, we are shown that therapeutic "diction" cannot permanently redeem existential "plot" and "character." Placed by nature between the always threatening Ice Age of scarcity and the always threatening Deluge of the libido, human beings must also contend with the potentially devastating consequences of the power gap that their cultural coexistence with each other continues to open up between individuals, generations, classes, nations, and other groups engaged in hot or cold warfare within the extended Antrobus family.

Do both the "play" and the PLAY convey an image, then, of human history as the eternal return of the same predicaments from which, with a great deal of luck, humankind can escape again and again "through the skin of our teeth?" Certainly, such an interpretation seems to be authorized by the cyclical pattern within which, at the end of Act III, Sabina begins to recite her opening lines from Act I: "Oh, oh, oh. Six o'clock and the master not home yet. Pray God nothing serious has happened to him crossing the Hudson River" (137; cf. 71). Soon enough, however, she comes to the footlights and addresses the audience: "This is where you came in. We have to go on for ages and ages yet." Sabina's "we" clearly refers not only to the characters of the "play" and the "actors" of the PLAY but to the SPECTATORS as well. And it refers to the SPECTATORS not only as "spectators" of the "play" and of the PLAY because she continues: "You go home. The end of this play isn't written yet." Having left the theater, the SPECTATORS will no longer remain "spectators." They cannot avoid turning into "actors" playing as yet undelineated characters on future "stages"—in future stages—of human development. They will have to *choose,* from their shared past experience, the voices that guide them, as Wilder makes Spinoza, Aristotle, Plato, and the Bible guide Mr. and Mrs. Antrobus, in their next attempt to build a new world.

What is being said through such voices is by no means tied to the particular brain cells contingently required for formulating and interpreting past experience for present and future application. This, I believe, is the meaning of Wilder's lifting the four short speeches from the "play" to the level of the PLAY and beyond by means of a pronouncedly accidental offstage event reported to the SPECTATORS. The ACTORS cast to recite the appropriate passages had dinner together and became afflicted with serious food poisoning; fortunately, however, four "splendid volunteers" (121) happen to have watched the rehearsals and have consented to speak the lines from the three philosophers and Genesis. The most purple passages of the "play" are thus being delivered by an usher, a wardrobe mistress, and the like but the words spoken are thereby elevated rather than lowered; they are shown to possess universal human significance. Has a playwright finally managed, then, to envelope a "play" within a PLAY in such a way as to allow the actor's mask to display its face value without any remnant of theatrical mediation between "actor," ACTOR, and character—between the stage, the world around the stage, and the world evoked by the stage? Certainly not. As the audience fully well knows, ACTORS are playing the volunteering "nonactors" in the two brief scenes involved: humankind's guiding ideas will not be effectively voiced without the rhetorical skill required for presenting them. But the ideas are there, and new ones are likely to arise, for everyone prepared to help perpetuate them through private and public acts of interpretation. In this respect, too, the end of the play about the Antrobuses "isn't written yet": even if all past human action and vision should exhibit certain patterns of cyclical recurrence according to their now prevailing interpretations, new interpretations can and probably will place old ones into different patterns of action and vision. The playfully open-ended, romantically ironic conclusion of Wilder's tragicomedy thus relates many of the moods distinguished in Chapter 2 to its primary "key" of serene acquiescence into our always limited and often changing comprehension of a perpetually interpretable pluriverse.

173

Dispersing Authority

While preparing their book *A Skeleton Key to "Finnegans Wake"* (1944), Joseph Campbell and Henry Morton Robinson reviewed (1942) the first production of *The Skin of Our Teeth* as though the play were indeed little more than an "interpretation" of certain aspects of James Joyce's last and extremely complex work. Their complaint about Wilder's failure to acknowledge the immediate source of many details of the play was certainly justified in a literal sense. It also revealed, however, a somewhat literal-minded understanding of the age-old intertextual tradition from which mythopoetic works such as Joyce's and Wilder's emerge and into which they are fully intended to merge. As Campbell and Robinson themselves pointed out in a follow-up article after the publication of the play, "Wilder not only vigorously adapted *Finnegans Wake* to the Broadway temper, but also intended that someone, somewhere, someday should recognize his deed for what it is" (1943:16). As a matter of fact, Wilder's "deed" of authoring one version among many of the myth of human survival "through the skin of our teeth" was not to be disguised; it was merely to be submerged in subsequent readings and performances rather than explicitly reflected upon by the playwright. Only one oblique reference, already quoted, to the "silly author" occurs in the PLAY, whose subject matter, after all, is not the writing of the "play" by a post-Joycean author but its performance by a post-Depression American company.

In contrast, Peter Weiss's play parallels the structure of Tieck's *Puss in Boots* more closely when it makes the Marquis de Sade not only direct and stage-manage but also author the "play," performed in 1808 by inmates of the Charenton insane asylum, about Charlotte Corday's 1793 assassination of Jean-Paul Marat. In addition to dramatizing a particular set of the acts of communication and representation that are involved in every theater event, Weiss has thereby dramatized a particular set of the communicative and representational acts involved in all writings of texts that are designed for or become subject to interpretation by persons other than their author. Furthermore, Weiss's play invites (while Wilder's play only permits) readers and spectators to engage in the deconstructive explanation of an author's manifest thematic intention and imaginative worldmaking in terms of the biographical and historical circumstances whose traces have "seeped into" the work without the author's conscious awareness.

In principle, every text is open to three fundamentally different kinds of interpretation. We may want to

(a) *explicate* it as a *message* signaled to us by its implied author;
(b) *explore* it as the *image* of a world in which we live or might have lived or would wish to live; and
(c) *explain* it as the symptomatic *seepage* that reveals the actual author's partly unconscious motivation for writing, as well as other factual conditions under which the text was produced.

The first kind is much like the translator's reconstructive interpretation of a discourse originally uttered or written in a different language; the second, much like the performer's participatory interpretation of a congenial role; the third, much like the detective's or the jury member's inferential interpretation of a potential piece of evidence in the light of what is taken to be the relevant set of circumstances. Ideally, of course, our reading of a text (and this applies also to our "reading" of a dramatic performance) should result in simultaneous transcoding, enactment, and detection. Yet, as I have argued elsewhere (1981b:111–12), our best realistic hope lies in the reciprocal fine-tuning of our successive acts of explication, exploration, and explanation through well-timed shifts of our hermeneutic focus between a text's communicative message, experienced image, and informative seepage.

Beyond doubt, the need for just such shifts is impressed upon thoughtful readers and spectators by the complex dramatic structure of *Marat/Sade*. Historians of the Napoleonic era tell us that Sade produced plays among the inmates of the Charenton asylum, some of whom, like the Marquis himself, were confined there for political rather than medical reasons. Weiss makes us imagine him writing and directing one in 1808 about Jean-Paul Marat, the middle-aged radical stabbed to death in a bathtub by the young and radically liberal Charlotte Corday in 1793. Sade's "play" is, however, not only about the assassination and the events directly leading up to it. Against the background of the violent revolutionary turmoil, enacted by the occasionally obstreperous inmates beyond the call of their theatrical duties, Sade also places Marat's life and death in the context of the conceptual turmoil of revolutionary ideas. Collectivist Marat's proto-Marxian plea for what seems to be the ruthless dictatorship of the proletariat is flanked by contrasting versions of radical individualism: the Girondist ideal of pure enlightened democracy and Sade's own program of complete instinctual liberation.

As the author of the "play," Sade has written some of the longest and, from his point of view, most persuasive speeches for himself. As director, too, he has stacked the cards by playing himself while assigning the other parts in such a way as to either overemphasize or ironically undercut the relationship between the respective "actors" and characters. Marat, constantly raving about clandestine enemies of the revolution, is played by a paranoiac patient; the role of the Judith-like heroine, Charlotte Corday, is given to a lethargic woman in constant need of prompting and goading; and a hard-to-restrain erotomaniac is to impersonate the Girondist deputy Duperret, who is Corday's idealistic lover and argues against her plan of eliminating, by way of assassination, Marat's increasingly dictatorial influence on public policy making. Furthermore, most participating inmates are "cast" in the nameless roles that make up the highly agitated Parisian masses of 1793. Under such circumstances, the performance of the "play" cannot fail to result in a chaotic experience for "actors," "spectators," and SPECTATORS alike.

Sade's authorial and directorial intentions thereby clash with those of Coulmier, the director of the asylum. While Coulmier intends the production of the "play" as a soothing therapeutic device, the PLAY often shows Sade as a voyeuristic spectator glee-

176

fully and triumphantly watching the "performance" excite rather than calm both the inmates and the onstage audience (consisting of Coulmier, his wife, and his daughter). The PLAY thus superimposes a conflict between Sade and Coulmier as representatives of two opposed authorial projects—that of raising and that of erasing consciousness by the respective means of thrill and gratification—on the central conflict of the "play" between Sade and Marat. The ultimate targets of both Sade's and Coulmier's theatrical objectives are, however, the SPECTATORS. At what appears to be the dress rehearsal of the "play," Coulmier's opening speech, possibly co-authored by Sade, is clearly addressed to them as temporary substitutes for the guests who will be invited to watch later performances:

Als Direktor der Heilanstalt Charenton
heisse ich Sie willkommen in diesem Salon

. . .

Wir bitten Sie uns Ihre Aufmerksamkeit zu gönnen
denn alle spielen so gut sie können

. . .

Als moderne und aufgeklärte Leute
sind wir dafür dass bei uns heute
die Patienten der Irrenanstalt
nicht mehr darben unter Gewalt
sondern sich in Bildung und Kunst betätigen

[1967:11−12]

As Director of the Clinic of Charenton
I would like to welcome you to this salon

. . .

We ask your kindly indulgence for
a cast never on stage before

. . .

We're modern enlightened and we don't agree
with locking up patients We prefer therapy
through education and especially art

[1965:4]

177

Interpreting Events

Throughout the play, Coulmier insists on the calming, therapeutic
use to which he is determined to put Sade's "play." Meaningfully
enough, it is being staged in the asylum's bathhouse—the place for
the occasional "hydrotherapy" of cold showers even during the
performance—so that the "actors" awaiting their cues cannot fail
to remember their original identities as PATIENTS. And Coulmier has
even exercised some preliminary censorship whose final authority
is, however, challenged whenever the Marquis refuses to serve as a
mere speech writer for someone else's ulterior authorial motives.
This is conspicuously the case with Sade's anticlerical speech. Before it is halted by Coulmier, Sade has linked the religious consolation of the deprived masses to their acquiescence into social oppression:

COULMIER:
Herr de Sade
Gegen dieses Treiben muss ich mich wenden,
wir einigten uns hier auf Streichung

.   .   .

Von einer Unterdrückung kann überhaupt keine Rede sein
Im Gegenteil da wird alles getan um die Not zu lindern
mit Kleidersammlung Krankenhilfe und Suppenverteilung
[42]

COULMIER:
Monsieur de Sade
I must interrupt this argument
We agreed to make some cuts in this passage

.   .   .

There is no question of anyone being oppressed
Quite on the contrary everything's done to relieve suffering
with clothing collections medical aid and soup kitchens
[29]

Since such interruptions of the "play" have been expected by Sade,
he has written into it certain lines by means of which the official

178

crier acting as Sade's master of ceremonies ostensibly distances the dramatized events from the world of the audience of both the "play" and the PLAY:

> AUSRUFER (*hebt den Zeigestab hoch*):
> Sollte jemand im Publikum sich getroffen fühlen
> so bitten wir denselben seinen Ärger abzukühlen
> und in Freundlichkeit zu bedenken
> dass wir den Blick in die Vergangenheit lenken
> in der alles anders war als heute
> Heute sind wir natürlich gottesfürchtige Leute
> (*schlägt ein Kreuzzeichen*)
>
> [42–43]

> HERALD (*raising his staff*):
> If our performance causes aggravation
> we hope you'll swallow down your indignation
> and please remember that we show
> only those things which happened long ago
> Remember things were very different then
> of course today we're all God-fearing men
> (*makes the sign of the cross*)
>
> [30]

Yet Sade and Weiss are obviously far from believing that "clothing collections medical aid and soup kitchens" or the like have made much difference between "long ago" and "today." In his controversy with Marat, who insists that generally higher standards of living will not make people equal, Sade only argues that equality could not make them happy. As is well known, the Marquis had been imprisoned for thirteen years for sexual aberrations before the revolution of 1789 freed and honored the unconventional aristocrat. While he was X-raying his mind in the Bastille (and promptly turning the diagnosis into still X-ratable novels, plays, and meditations), he learned that "this is a world of bodies" whose orifices are there "so one may hook and twine oneself in them." Clearly, Sade rebels against sexual repression and not (like Marat) against social oppression:

> diese Gefängnisse des Innern
> sind schlimmer als die tiefsten steinernen Verliese
> und solange sie nicht geöffnet werden
> bleibt all euer Aufruhr
> nur eine Gefängnisrevolte
> die niedergeschlagen wird
> von bestochenen Mitgefangenen
>
> [123–24]

> these cells of the inner self
> are worse than the deepest stone dungeon
> and as long as they are locked
> all your Revolution remains
> only a prison mutiny
> to be put down
> by corrupted fellow-prisoners
>
> [93]

The chorus of aroused inmates, accompanied by the corresponding pantomime, keeps repeating Sade's conclusion: "For what's the point of this revolution / without general copulation" (*Denn was wäre schon diese Revolution / ohne eine allgemeine Kopulation*). Yet it is clearly Sade's "play" rather than the PLAY by Weiss that thereby suggests the primacy of sexual over economic and political liberation. Just as significantly, it is the imagery of Sade's "play" that equates the vision of social justice with the revolutionary itch about which Marat complains, confined by his incurable skin disease to a bathtub for the entire length of his dramatized life: "my head's on fire / I can't breathe / . . . I am the Revolution" (27/16).

It is likewise Sade, not Weiss, who makes, and enjoys watching, a soporific patient perform Charlotte Corday's assassination of Marat as a quasi-sexual act. Swaying her body closer and closer to her helpless victim, she holds the dagger concealed under her neckcloth with her right hand, while her face is wildly distorted "by a mixed expression of hate and lust" and her left hand is "stretched out as if to caress." Having fondled Marat's chest, shoulders, and neck, Corday finally "pulls the dagger from her neckcloth" and, holding it with both hands, "raises her arms high to strike" (126–27/94–95). But Sade once again delays the consummation of her aggressive desire. Before the rape of the revolutionary spirit by an idealistic virgin, a lengthy scene (Weiss calls it "interruptus" in the Latin of sex manuals) brings the audience of 1808 up to date: the four singers chronicle the historical events from Marat's death to the consolidation of Napoleon's power. Only after this daydream-like junket into the future is Sade ready to end the foreplay and to watch (according to an untranslated stage direction: "triumphantly, shaking with silent laughter") the climactic event of his "play." Sade's directorial hand in that climax is made especially obvious by the original stage directions, once again incompletely translated in the English version of the play. Not only does murdered Marat strike the pose, familiar from Jacques Louis David's painting, of lying in the bathtub with a pen in his lifelessly fallen right hand and a sheet of paper in his left. The historical tableau is supplemented by the "author" and "director" of the "play" when the four singers, clearly nonhistorical creatures of Sade's imagination, grab Charlotte Corday from behind and "pull her arms backwards so that her neckcloth rips and her breasts are uncovered"; she is even made to "hand the dagger over to Sade" (130–31)—the prevailing "author"/"director," victorious character, and titillated "actor"/"spectator" of the "play."

Seeing Sade in all those capacities and especially in the last one mentioned is a crucial aspect of the complex experience elicited by Weiss's PLAY from responsive READERS and SPECTATORS. It makes them recognize their own existential complicity in the theater event. Their status as willing and interested "audience" allies rather than contrasts them with both Sade and Coulmier, who are, each in his own way, closely watching the show. Each SPECTATOR is meant to ask: Would I not, as an invited "spectator" of the "play," share

Coulmier's pompous concern with "therapy through education and especially art" and even condone his occasional use of drastic measures against the menacing crowd of refractory inmates? Do I not, as a "spectator" of the PLAY, share Sade's voyeuristic indulgence in acts of sexual and other kinds of violence and even condone his reliance on Coulmier's ruthless staff for keeping the show from prematurely collapsing into chaos? In more general terms, is my own response to both the "play" and the PLAY not analogous to the response of Coulmier and Sade in that all SPECTATORS perceive and influence stage events according to the roles they play and the characters they are in the overarching framework of their own private and public lives? By prompting such queries, the PLAY and its congenial productions (such as Peter Brook's stage and film versions) elicit simultaneous empathy with and distance from not only the characters, "actors," and ACTORS as such; they make the SPECTATORS react with the same mixture of attitudes to themselves. Indeed, much of the overpowering impact of the PLAY seems to me to stem from its capacity to split each of us into a SPECTATOR and a "spectator" with sustained potential awareness of that very split. The resulting enlightened uneasiness may be described in the psychological terms associated in Chapter 2 with certain rather undignified products of show business: introspecting READERS and especially SPECTATORS of *Marat/Sade* tend to come face to face with those layers of their personalities which make them—as "readers" and "spectators" of both the "play" and the PLAY—easy targets for any socially acceptable appeal to sadistic, masochistic, voyeuristic, or *schadenfroh* impulses in the human psyche. More than any other play being considered in the present study, *Marat/Sade* thus manages both to exploit and to repudiate some of the least sublimated strategies of desire involved with the erotics of retrospection.

But even if we disregard the unsavory roles modeled for us by the spectator function of Sade and Coulmier and limit our response to that odd couple of authorial/directorial characters in terms of the stage events for which they are directly responsible, we need not short-circuit the electrifying play's current into a simple set of thematic assertions such as the following: (1) Weiss shows what kind of egotistical, relentlessly pleasure-seeking person would write Sade's "play." (2) As a result, the Marquis's dismissal of Marat's way of thinking as a hopelessly absurd attempt to make his life meaningful is in turn dismissed. (3) Marat's project to pit the human-made meaning of revolutionary violence against the absurd, indifferent universe thus emerges as an admirable response to the human condition:

> Gegen das Schweigen der Natur
> stelle ich eine Tätigkeit
> In der grossen Gleichgültigkeit
> erfinde ich einen Sinn
> Anstatt reglos zuzusehn
> greife ich ein
> und ernenne gewisse Dinge für falsch
> und arbeite daran sie zu verändern und zu verbessern
> Es kommt drauf an
> sich am eigenen Haar in die Höhe zu ziehn
> sich selbst von innen nach aussen zu stülpen
> und alles mit neuen Augen zu sehen
>
> [38–39]

> Against Nature's silence I use action
> In the vast indifference I invent meaning
> I don't watch unmoved I intervene
> and say that this and this are wrong
> and I work to alter them and improve them
> The important thing
> is to pull yourselves up by your own hair
> to turn yourself inside out
> and see the whole world with fresh eyes
>
> [26–27]

There is, of course, nothing wrong with such an interpretation as long as one recognizes that it is partial in both senses of the word.

183

The repudiation of Marat by the biased "author" and "director" of the "play" does seem to be repudiated by the supposedly unbiased AUTHOR of the PLAY. But the strategy of the two repudiations is strikingly similar, and that similarity suggests how vulnerable every message, as well as every image, is to being interpreted as symptomatic seepage once a distancing hermeneutic attitude of what Wayne Booth has called "overstanding" (in contrast to empathetic understanding) has been adopted (1979:236, 242, *et passim*). For Sade, Marat's message is a symptom to be diagnosed rather than a signal to be heeded: inventing revolutionary meaning is just a form of scratching one's incurably itching skin until the bathtub—or is it the world?—becomes increasingly bloodstained. Weiss deconstructs Sade's message in an analogous manner: the universe will forever appear inalterably absurd if it is viewed through the egotistically pleasure-seeking eyes of alienated individualism. While Weiss's message thus "places" Sade's image of Marat as evoked by the tendentious author of "The Persecution and Assassination of Jean-Paul Marat," his own image of Sade also lends itself to readings and performances that radicalize its own deconstructive momentum. From such readings and performances, not only the "play" but the PLAY itself will emerge as tendentious and in need of further placing (with or without explicit reference to the AUTHOR's psyche and to his playing of certain public roles) in the dialectical hermeneutic process that is the self-placing of the human species through all interpretations and reinterpretations of history.

Owing to its perspective on Sade's "play" from without, Weiss's message (as I have tried to explicate it in the three numbered sentences above) carries with it greater potential for conveying the moods associated with certain forms of comedy and satire (triumph, derision, scorn, and concern). The play's total image of various worlds condemned to remain enclosed within their respective sets of biases and limitations may in turn elicit pity, grief, horror, and fear—the moods associated with certain forms of incipient tragedy. Indeed, some productions by Peter Brook and others have succeeded in exploring the PLAY's tragic aspects, thereby pointing beyond the AUTHOR's radical political message to the more radical hermeneutic critique—implied through the PLAY's pluralistic image of the world and history—of any single-minded radicalism.

Far from engaging the SPECTATOR's critical distance at the level of the "play" and his affirmative empathy at the level of the critical PLAY only, these productions force us constantly to oscillate between the two attitudes with respect to both sets of dramatic events. They thus build on such instances of Weiss's own fusion of the two worlds as the discussion between the Marat of 1793 and the Sade of 1808 or the remarkable rebel-rousing speeches of straight-jacketed Jacques Roux. Described in the list of characters as "former priest and radical socialist," Roux is not unequivocally assigned to either Sade's "play" or Weiss's PLAY: without consulting history books, we cannot be sure whether Roux is only a character in Sade's script, only an inmate in Coulmier's asylum, or both. Yet the "actor" playing this ambiguous part is very clearly the prime target of the stage acts of oppressive violence repeatedly performed by the male nurses and some nuns played by male ACTORS. What is far less clear from the text and need not be made clear in performance either is whether Roux's restrainers are primarily agents of Coulmier's soothing, Sade's sadistic, or Weiss's voyeuristic dramaturgy.

By such instances of blurred lines of demarcation between its various spheres of evoked historical existence, the PLAY as a whole suggests that we are by no means twice removed from the dramatized events of 1793. Rather, we are twice implicated in them as we lend imaginative substance to their reenactment by "actors" and for "spectators" of 1808, whose respective roles are obviously played by ACTORS and for SPECTATORS of our own time. On the perplexing evidence of our reluctantly empathetic assumption of the role assigned to us as "spectators" in 1964 (the date of the first production of *Marat/Sade*) or in the mid-1980s, we are likely to conclude that multiple and intertwined levels of authority, role playing, and spectatorial awareness constitute human relationships both in and outside the theater. Our scripts are censored, but all internal and external

185

censorship may be challenged by words or deeds. Our performances, in and out of prescribed roles, are directed and can be interrupted by others, but their performances are also directed and can be interrupted by us. As spectators or other kinds of interpreters we may take pleasure or displeasure, may find meaning or absurdity, in what we experience. But we cannot legitimately claim autonomous authority with respect to any of that. To the extent that we exist in certain social contexts and historical traditions of role playing, our way of experiencing life is being scripted, directed, watched, and interpreted by the Sades, Coulmiers, Weisses, and other authors, directors, and spectators, whose ubiquitous presence the PLAY has taught us to discern within ourselves and without.

6

History in the Making:
Caligula and *Amadeus*

FIRST PATRICIAN: Still no news.
THE OLD PATRICIAN: None last night, none this morning.
SECOND PATRICIAN: Three days without news. Strange indeed!
THE OLD PATRICIAN: Our messengers go out, our messengers return.
    And always they shake their heads and say: "Nothing." [1958:3]

This rendition by Stuart Gilbert of the opening lines of Albert
Camus's *Caligula* (1944; final version 1958) provides a dramaturgically effective "exposition" as it highlights the particular situation of the Emperor's perplexed subjects: young Caligula has
slipped out of the palace and cannot be found. A production based
on this translation may, of course, exploit our familiarity with such
plays as Samuel Beckett's *Waiting for Godot* (1952) and suggest the
existential significance of being reduced to the passive yet anxious
condition of waiting. The original text, however, evokes that condition more vividly and without restricting it to just some people in a
specific place and time. It plunges right away into a more univer-
sally predicated existential void where the first words spoken, *toujours rien,* may as well be taken literally ("always nothing") rather
than idiomatically ("still nothing"). With that almost oxymoric
description of unmitigated absurdity, followed by many more instances of *rien* in the first scene, the play clearly opens in a style
anticipating Beckett, Ionesco, and other representatives of what

187

Martin Esslin called "the theatre of the absurd" (1961). Esslin has persuasively linked the flourishing of absurdist drama in the 1950s to the world view adumbrated in Camus's *Myth of Sisyphus* (1942) and Sartre's *Being and Nothingness* (1943). But even in the realm of dramatic diction no subsequent play has surpassed the stark lucidity with which the first few lines of *Caligula* evoke the human predicament of always craving for meaningful existence in a universe devoid of inherent significance:

PREMIER PATRICIEN: Toujours rien.
LE VIEUX PATRICIEN: Rien le matin, rien le soir.
DEUXIÈME PATRICIEN: Rien depuis trois jours.
LE VIEUX PATRICIEN: Les courriers partent, les courriers reviennent.
    Ils secouent la tête et disent: "Rien." [1962:7]

The playwright frequently revised the text, and Roger Quilliot's annotated Pléiade edition of Camus's *Théâtre, récits, nouvelles* (1962) documents many changes from the first two manuscripts of 1938–39, through the published versions of 1944, 1947, and 1958 (Gilbert's rather free translation is principally based on the 1947 French version), up to the script prepared by Camus for a 1958 Paris production. But the splendid lines just quoted from Quilliot's text, which follows the last published version, remained unchanged from 1944 onward. It is indeed hard to imagine how they could be improved. In a natural yet highly symbolic fashion, they make us perceive perceivers of the monotonous cycle of mornings and evenings, which is embedded here in the quasi-mythical stretch of three days but offers no hope, after Caligula's harrowing of hell, for a divinely ordained, redemptive resurrection.

The Lunacy of Narcissism

Caligula's temporary absence is an especially fitting emblem of the more permanent void in the play's universe since he, too, was hurled into existential depression by "having nothing":

188

THE OLD PATRICIAN: I saw him leave the palace. He looked strange.
FIRST PATRICIAN: I was there too, and I asked him what was the
  matter [*ce qu'il avait*].
SECOND PATRICIAN: Did he respond?
FIRST PATRICIAN: A single word: "Nothing." [7–8/3]

But even Cherea and Scipio, whose respective responses to the
world's absurdity will turn out to be so different from Caligula's
response, first enter the stage by echoing, each in his turn, the
play's initial nihilistic finding: "*Toujours rien*" (9/4)—"*Encore
rien*" (11/5). In short, we are shown no alternative to the absurdist
view of the state of human affairs. Only the question remains: What
to do about it?—a question that a less historically conscious and,
perhaps for that very reason, more resolutely absurdist playwright
would have been proud of not asking.

Distraught, his legs and garments all smeared with mud, Caligula
returns from his three days in the wilderness fully convinced of the
absence of meaning in a universe where, according to the "truth"
he claims to have just discovered, "men die, and they are not
happy" (16/8). This prophet of absurdity is, however, especially
upset to find that men come to terms with their predicament by
means of self-deception—be it through engulfment in petty everyday pleasures, be it through the subtler lies of *littérateurs* who
"attribute importance to beings and things" (24–25/14). As self-
appointed "professor who knows what he is talking about," Caligula vows to use his power "to make people live in truth" (16/9).
Throughout the play, we see him raise the consciousness of his
subjects by meting out death and unhappiness just a little more
capriciously than famine, disease, and war do. This is how Camus's
"philosopher-king"—Plato's utopian state is ruled here by a nihilistic thinker—attempts to carry the absurd to its logical conclusion.

But why should Caligula wish to do so? He invokes freedom as
his justification: "This world has no importance; if you realize that,
you win your freedom" (25/14). Since the kind of freedom he has
in mind can be had only "at someone else's expense" (46/28), he

can freely admit to having self-serving motives for his endeavor to "teach" the logic of absurdity: he wants to stage his life as "the most beautiful of spectacles." And since the world for Caligula is both a dressing room and a stage, Camus's stage directions require only two props as essential for the performance: a mirror, in front of which Caligula keeps posturing from his first entrance to the last, and a gong, which he bangs furiously to indicate the beginning of his grand spectacle, the "universal trial" of the world. Rather than pupils, this most theatrical professor of the absurd needs "judges, witnesses, defendants, all condemned in advance"; but he also needs—and here lies the trouble—a willing and interested audience (*mon public* [28/17]). More or less reduced to the status of objects—whether docile subjects or raped bodies and spirits—unfree men and women cannot signal to Caligula that he is indeed free; and when the rebels against his reign of radicalized absurdity take his life, they set an end to his freedom as well. This is why he must recognize at the end: "I haven't taken the road I should have, I have achieved nothing. My freedom isn't the right one" (108/73). As Camus noted in the Preface to the 1958 American edition of his plays:

> if [Caligula's] truth is to rebel against fate, his error lies in negating human beings [*les hommes*]. One cannot destroy everything without destroying oneself. . . . Unfaithful to man through fidelity to himself, Caligula accepts death because he has understood that no one can save himself all alone and that one cannot be free *against* other people. [1729/30/vi; italics added]

The Preface does not tell the whole story of the play, of course. However insistently he may deny this, Caligula came to "rebel against fate"—the human condition—on the basis of a deeply emotional experience rather than detached philosophizing. The realization that "men die, and they are not happy" was brought home to him, just before the play begins, by the death of his sister Drusilla, whom he had cherished with far more than brotherly affection. That the memory of their relationship haunts Caligula is subtly suggested by Camus's use of the moon and the mirror as master images of the play for Caligula's special kind of lunacy and narcissism. From his first entrance on, Caligula associates his project of defying fate, of having the freedom and power to do the impossible, with the desire to "have the moon" (14/7 *et passim*). To be sure, the Old Patrician's diagnosis of Caligula's strange behavior ("He is impotent" [32/20]) must be taken in a broader sense than it is intended by the diagnostician's one-track mind: Caligula desperately tries to disprove his powerlessness not as a male but as a human being. Yet the exigencies of the French language force him to make each of his many references to the moon as a grammatical subject or direct object by using the feminine noun *la lune* or the pronouns "she" (*elle*) and "her" (*la*): as if he were speaking about a woman. The most elaborate set of such references to the moon occurs in Caligula's wishfully poetic account, later revoked, of how he "had her thoroughly." Here the quasi-heterosexual aspect of his craving for the impossible is clearly indicated even in Gilbert's somewhat free but congenial translation:

It was a cloudless August night. . . . She was coy, to begin with. I'd gone to bed. First she was blood-red, low on the horizon. Then she began rising, quicker and quicker, growing brighter and brighter all the while. And the higher she climbed, the paler she grew, till she was like a milky pool in a dark wood rustling with stars. Slowly, shyly she approached through the warm night air, soft, light as gossamer, naked in beauty. She crossed the threshold of my room, glided to my bed, poured herself into it, and flooded me with her smiles and sheen. [71/46]

There can be little doubt that Caligula's thoroughly feminine moon owes its indirect light to a sun that has set forever just before the play begins. After Drusilla's death, Caligula may return to his old mistress, Caesonia, who seems genuinely attracted to him, and he may force himself on other women (as he does, during the banquet scene of Act II, on the wife of one of the patricians present). But he can no longer come as close as he could, with Drusilla alive, to what is both socially and individually "impossible." Through Drusilla's death, nature has radically deprived him of the opportunity to defy his culture's (if not all cultures') prohibition against physical incest and to indulge in what might be called the spiritual incest of loving one's own, sexually transformed, self in another, but almost identical, human being. For the gratifying thrill of that simultaneously self-assertive and self-transcending experience nothing will provide Caligula with a genuine substitute: not his attempt at transgressing the limits both of his sex and of his humanity by impersonating Venus in the grotesque spectacle of Act III, and not even his constant posturing in front of the mirror with which, whether he sees his own or Drusilla's image in it, he can conduct only a one-sided dialogue. This is perhaps why, at the end of Act I, he "frenetically effaces a reflection" on the mirror; and this is certainly why, at the end of the final act, he shatters the mirror just as he realizes that he has chosen the wrong path to freedom. His lonesome meanderings, both in the scorching sunlight of his sister-mistress and under the unattainably distant moon of the impossible, have kept him from truly encountering Others. At the climax of his narcissistic lunacy—a madness with system, to be sure—he is confronted not even with his true self (which would have to be a constantly evolving self among selves) but with an insubstantial mirror image (the momentarily frozen "self" as it is perceived by, while aping, itself).

To that spurious self, the only one he knows, Caligula cries out in the end: "I stretch out my hands, and it is you I find, always just you over against me, and I hate you" (107–8/73). Almost immediately after this outburst, "a clash of arms and whisperings are heard in the wings." But Caligula has no thought of attending to external dangers. Rather, he picks up a stool and hurls it against the mirror, which breaks, according to the last stage direction of the play, "in the same moment" as the armed conspirators enter from all sides. Clearly, his fellow human beings—those long-ignored yet significant Others—have only come to execute a death sentence that Caligula, having provoked their rebellion and having willfully disregarded all reports about it, has been drafting all along and has, by breaking the mirror, symbolically signed. His story, as Camus remarks in the Preface already quoted, is "the story of a superior suicide" (1730/vi). It is, in other words, a death-bound history of Caligula's own making.

For his *Caligula,* Camus borrowed many motifs from Suetonius' account of the monstrous emperor's life:

When the moon shone full and bright he always invited the Moongoddess to his bed. [1957:160]

. . . It was his habit to commit incest with each of his sisters in turn. . . . They say that he ravished his sister Drusilla before he came of age. . . . Later he took Drusilla from her husband . . . quite unashamedly treating her as his wife. At her death he . . . was so crazed with grief that he suddenly rushed from home by night, drove through Campania, took ship to Sicily, and returned just as impetuously without having shaved or cut his hair in the meantime. . . . He showed no such extreme love or respect for the two surviving sisters, and often, indeed, let his favorites sleep with them. [161]

. . . More than once he closed down the granaries and let the people go hungry. [163]

. . . Caligula seemed interested only in doing the apparently impossible. [168]

. . . He worked hard to make his naturally uncouth face even more repulsive, by practising fearful grimaces in front of a mirror. [173–74]

. . . Caligula paid no attention to tradition or current fashions in his dress; ignoring male conventions and even the human decencies. . . . He even dressed up as Venus. [175]

The above quotations from Robert Graves's translation of the Roman historian's *Twelve Caesars* fall short of indicating the full extent of parallelisms between the play and its principal source. But it was by no means an antiquarian interest in the distant past that made Camus write the play and cast himself in the role of Caligula for a planned production of the little theater he had organized in Algiers. In his hands, the play's reinterpreted history came to "illustrate" the suicidal frenzy and ravages that the "passion for the impossible" wreaks (1730/vi) by also reflecting, in the converse mirror of the much-revised play, Camus's own intellectual history: his increasingly successful integration of a philosophy of the absurd (Camus never consented to being classified as an existentialist thinker in the technical sense of the word) with the impassioned humanism of his later years. The first, highly lyrical version of 1938–39 centered on Caligula, who, at the time of becoming emperor, was twenty-five years old—almost exactly the age of the aspiring playwright-philosopher. It seems clear that, by supplying a quasi-existentialist motivation for one of the best-known self-defeating tyrants of history, Camus was chastising that aspect of his own thinking that might push anyone, through a "tragedy of the intelligence" (1730/vi), to the inhuman yearning for the "real" solitude, which came to be associated by Sartre with the "being-in-itself" of objects without consciousness, and which is ascribed by Caligula to the "silence and throbbing of a tree" (59/37).

Nonetheless, the Caligula of the extant manuscripts and of the two 1944 editions may not only be seen as emotionally more mature than the budding poet Scipio, whose love of a naively humanized nature he seems to have shared before learning to reject it as "anemic" (*manque de sangue* [58/36]). In Gérard Philipe's empathetic portrayal of the part, he could also strike the audiences of 1944 as intellectually more honest than the coolheaded Cherea, who, in the face of acknowledged absurdity, continues to "plead for this world" (25/14) and refuses to "push the absurd" (or anything else) "to all of its consequences." In a crucial confrontation with Caligula, Cherea expounds his philosophy of "illogical" compromise:

I am just like everyone else. Sometimes, to feel free of them, I wish that the people I love were dead, and I covet women whom, according to the laws of family and friendship, I shouldn't covet. To be logical, I would have to kill or copulate on such occasions. But I consider those vague urges of no importance. If everybody scrambled to realize them, we couldn't live, nor could we be happy. And, to repeat, that's what really matters to me. [78/51–52]

Cherea's "healthy" (*sain*) subordination of Caligula's inhuman logic of unrestrained freedom to the humane censorship of what, with Freud, might be called the Reality Principle also appears in the 1947 and 1958 versions. By 1947, however, the playwright's experience as an active member of the French Resistance against Hitler, and probably also his increasingly strong reluctance to "understand" (and thus condone) Stalin's differently motivated logic of totalitarianism, found its way into the play, especially through a newly added conversation between Scipio and Cherea at the beginning of Act IV.

This conversation highlights the fact that more is at stake in the human "rebellion against fate" than the establishing of a psychologically or ideologically well-adjusted relationship between the individual and his or her world. It is not enough to see the Scipio of the later versions as Caligula describes him in Act II: "You are pure in goodness, while I am pure in evil" (58/36); he is above all a deplorable dropout from the struggle against all forms of enslavement and oppression. The Scipio of 1947 and 1958 is unable to join the ranks of those planning to kill Caligula because he has become convinced that he must "suffer with" and "understand" him, even though the tyrant had the young man's father killed and will on occasion mock his poetry (83–84/55–56). Nor does it suffice any longer to oppose Caligula, as Cherea opposes him in the third act of all published versions, without hatred or scorn against "that aspect of oneself one is trying to keep concealed" (77/50–51). In and after 1947, such an attitude is but a preliminary phase in Cherea's development. Already in 1947, his attitude of the upright rebel, who is willing to risk his own life before he is prepared to take another, is sharply contrasted to the attitude of the scheming Old Patrician, who in a newly introduced scene offers Caligula a list of those

195

conspiring against him (72–75/47–49). In the final version of 1958, Cherea is the only man stabbing Caligula face to face (*en pleine figure*) while the Old Patrician—not only a counterrevolutionary representative of the ancien régime but also a spineless servant of any present or future powers that be—attacks him from behind (108/73).

The new Cherea emerging from the 1947 and 1958 editions is, however, not simply the boldest rebel, as well as the smartest strategist of the play, who manages to persuade the conspirators to delay action until the time is ripe. He must himself work up sufficient righteous indignation, beyond his deep personal aversion to the nihilistic philosophy that Caligula has been "transforming into corpses" (35/21), before he is actually ready to kill another, however monstrous, human being. According to his final confrontation with Scipio, added in 1947, Caligula's excesses against the petty and self-indulgent patricians do not strike Cherea as sufficiently objectionable; he has learned really to hate Caligula for his having managed to drive Scipio into incapacitating despair (*il t'a désespéré*). This one "crime" alone against the future freedom of a "young soul"—a crime "surpassing all that he has committed so far"—would suffice, Cherea says, to make him kill Caligula "with passion" (*avec emportement* [84/56]). An important theme from Camus's postwar writings—his rejection of capital punishment and other forms of calculated homicide, whether they are committed in the name of law and order or in the name of the historical necessity of revolutionary action—is dramatized here in a perhaps excessively allusive but, for the thoughtful reader and spectator, most illuminating fashion.

More enigmatic still is the entire role of the only person who, in the 1958 version of this deathful play, dies for rather than through Caligula: his freed slave and loyal confidant, Helicon. This character first appears in the second manuscript (mostly typescript) and becomes more and more important in each subsequent revision. It seems to me, however, that Camus's premature death in a 1960 car accident prevented him from making Helicon's increasingly significant function in Caligula's world fully intelligible. Yet Helicon is, in a sense, the play's most original character. In Suetonius' account of Caligula's reign we can read about Cherea and Caesonia, as well as the historical prototypes of all victims of Caligula's dramatized atrocities. Even the young poet Scipio seems to have been modeled, in a Bowdlerized fashion to be sure, after one of the emperor's boyfriends, whose second name is clearly associated with poetry: "a young man of consular family, Valerius Catullus" is reported to have "revealed publicly that he had enjoyed the Emperor" and to have also said, as is true about Camus's Caligula and Scipio in a more "Platonic" sense, "that they quite wore one another out in the process" (1957:167). But there is no mention in Suetonius of Helicon, nor does he or any other source tell us about a person whom Caligula expects to fetch the moon for him or about a loyal follower whose fate could have served as Camus's model for making Helicon, in the last version of the play, be stabbed by one of the conspirators just as he rushes in to warn Caligula against them.

Whether or not they were aware of the brief reference in Philo Judaeus, cited by Walter Strauss, to "an accursed and infamous slave" by the name of Helicon, who "attended upon and courted [Caligula], never leaving him for a moment" (1951:163), most critics have rightly ignored Helicon's tenuous historicity and, rather, puzzled over the circumstance that his name directs attention to Mount Helicon, the supposed dwelling place of the Muses. Could Camus, by retaining a name so much more conspicuously mythological than historical, have wished to make his Helicon represent, as Germaine Brée suggests at least concerning the pre-1958 versions of the play, "the artistic vision incarnate, detached from human passions, indifferent to human suffering" (1959:166)? I find it impossible to think so. Both Scipio and Cherea, as well as Caligula himself, have much more to do with literature and the arts than Caligula's freed slave, the coarsely cynical Helicon. The relationship between Caligula and Helicon, who all too willingly pretends to help his "liberating" master in the impossible effort to bring the moon from the heavens down to earth, seems to me to reveal a danger to which Camus devoted many pages of *The Rebel:* the renewed dehumanizing enslavement of former rebellious slaves through the "Caesarian revolution" (1951:307/1973:216) and its sequel, the "state terrorism" that proposes to assist the logic of history in bringing paradise from the sky of utopia down to earth (233–309/156–218). If Helicon is to be associated with one of the Muses, it should thus be with Clio, the Muse of History, whose name could easily be *mistaken* for an anagrammatic version of his. After all, it is by making—or is it, rather, faking?—history that Caligula has hoped to exchange the absurd world of his contemporaries for a perhaps more meaningful existence in the memory of those coming hereafter. Near the climax of the play, he proposes to share this "beautiful thought" with his court:

> Up to now my reign has been too happy. No universal plague, no religious persecution, not even a *coup d'état;* in short, nothing that could make us enter posterity. This is partly why, you see, I am trying to compensate for the parsimony of fate. . . . Well, I am just filling in for the plague. [93–94/62]

Seen in this light, human-made history cannot, of course, transcend the limits set by humanity-making nature; Caligula will at best "equal" (*s'égaler*) the gods by duplicating their cruelty (67/43). Just before breaking the mirror, he must therefore realize that not only his notions of freedom and of the self were misguided. In the final version of the play, where Caligula exclaims, "Helicon will not come" (rather than, as in the 1947 version, "has not come"), the renunciation of the project he has associated with Helicon is indeed categorical rather than contingent. The Helicon of whom Caligula's frenzied imagination expected the impossible will never come to illuminate the moonless, sultry night of human guilt and suffering: "Hélicon! Hélicon! Rien! rien encore. Oh! cette nuit est lourde! Hélicon ne viendra pas: nous serons coupables à jamais. Cette nuit est lourde comme la douleur humaine." The Helicon who does come to warn him ("Take heed, Caius! Take heed!") is emphatically not a miracle-working angel of history in the guise, as it were, of the liberated proletariat. He is simply a loyal henchman of Caligula's "Caesarian revolution," marching one step ahead of his leader from life through death into that realm of remembered existence whither Caligula urges himself to go in the penultimate line of the play, "À l'histoire, Caligula, à l'histoire."

The stabbed emperor's very last words ("I am still alive!") Camus could quote directly from Suetonius. In more than one sense, therefore, those words reach us, as the dying Caligula's demonic laughter turns into gasps, from the realm of history. In the intertextual context of historytelling we perceive the utterance as one of many events of the past re-presented by historiographers and historical playwrights. But in the theater event, where stage events are being interpreted by each spectator against the horizon of his or her own historical existence, the same utterance also makes us perceive the "actor" playing Caligula as an image of the history we live and, by living, make. We are not only permitted to know history-making Caligula *through* the narrated or dramatized versions of his story; we are also forced to recognize him *in* the world surrounding us, contemporary readers and spectators of Camus's play. In both realms of history, the logical and ethical nihilist— passionately in love with the impossible yet, until the very end, worshiping only his own alienated self at the mirror-altar of deified History—confronts us with the dying Caesar's perennially surviving claim, corroborated by the living presence of the ACTOR on the stage, "I am still alive" (108/73–74).

Legends of Ordinary Life

Or is it myth rather than history that is "still alive" in Camus's *Caligula?* One scholar surveying the critical reception of the play's French productions called Gérard Philipe's congenial enactment of the title character "an unforgettable creation, half-angel, half-demon" (Coombs 1968:76). Indeed, it is not difficult to transpose

Caligula's self-love from a Greco-Roman into a Judeo-Christian key and to align him less with Narcissus than with an Adversary or Fallen Angel—Satan *manqué* in a world without God—while Cherea assumes the role of the "title character" in this much revised and politically ever more enlightened dramatization of the playwright's *Myth of Sisyphus*. Just like that prototype of Camus's "absurd hero" (1942:162/1969:120), Cherea is "superior to his fate" and "stronger than his rock" (163/121) because he is "convinced of the wholly human origin of all that is human" (166/123); he, too, engages in the ultimately "futile and hopeless labor" of human existence with "scorn of the gods," "hatred of death," and "passion for life" (162/120); he, too, knows the "night" (165/123) but pits himself against it with "lucidity" (164/121) and a hard-earned capacity for "silent joy" (165/123) and "happiness" (165/122). After each lost uphill battle against the human condition, its symbol—the rock of Sisyphus—rushes back down to the great plains of absurdity. But for Camus's Cherea and Sisyphus, "the struggle itself toward the heights is enough to fill a man's heart" (166/123). On such a reading, the true hero of *Caligula* is Cherea. In and through him, Caligula's "tragedy of the intelligence" is superseded by the tragicomic recognition that "happiness and the absurd are two sons of the same earth" (165/122). The reincarnation, as it were, of the ancient Greek hero first in Camus's Sisyphus and then in his Cherea suggests this: the incongruence between desire and reality—the lonely predicament in Homer's Hades of both Tantalus and Sisyphus (cf. *Odyssey*, XI.582–600)—holds those incapable of sharing and moderation captive in an everlasting state of frustration, while Cherea and human beings like him can turn their shared predicament into shared, fulfilling rebellion against both absurd fate and history's absurdly logical tyrants.

The incongruence between desire and reality motivates a different kind of lonely rebellion in Peter Shaffer's *Amadeus* (1979, revised version 1980). The very structure of the play makes us focus on the tragicomic fulfillment of the frustrated Antonio Salieri. This "fallen angel," ever conscious of his darkness being the shadow of divine light, is the almost always present onstage teller of his and Mozart's tale. Hence, what readers and spectators of *Amadeus* are made to perceive is the Devil's perception of his victory on earth over his "eternal enemies"—God and God's favored son.

At first sight, Salieri's rebellion is far less cosmic than Satan's. How could it involve anything like the large-scale battle for world supremacy between Milton's diabolic and angelic hosts? The once admired but mediocre composer's lifelong ambition is simply fame through music. Yet he has always wanted to *earn* that fame instead of "being called 'Distinguished' by people incapable of distinguishing" (93). And he has wanted to earn it *through music* because he considers music "God's art," in which every note is "either right or wrong *absolutely*. Not even time can alter that" (7). Thus when he is forced to recognize that Mozart's genius is incomparably superior to his own average talent, he comes to feel that his own music is *"absolutely worthless"* (93). In vain does he wish to be "owned—ordered—exhausted by an *Absolute*. Music." His complaint, "This was denied me, and with it all meaning" (95), expresses therefore the same bitter sense of cosmic disillusionment that has prompted Cain's as well as Satan's archetypal insurrection against what all three, each in his own way, perceive as God's unwarranted preference for their henceforth hated, and to be eliminated, rival. In each instance, evil is born out of wounded pride, and the wound is felt to have been inflicted by divine injustice.

Mozart and Salieri (1830), Pushkin's comparable dramatization in quasi-Miltonic terms of the relationship between the two musicians, remained in the Romantic vein associated with Blake's, Shelley's, and Byron's apparent attitude toward Satan and the Satanic. In Robert Louis Jackson's words, the Russian playwright's diabolic Salieri is "precisely an example of the union, albeit perverse, of extraordinary talent and—villainy. . . . Evil here is the result, in part at least, of the most earnest efforts to arrive at the secrets of his art, a result of an excess of sensibility for the beautiful" (1976:266). By contrast, Shaffer's Salieri is an ambitious but clearly mediocre man, whose means and ends rather well exemplify what Hannah Arendt (in the different context of her report about the Eichmann trial) called the "banality of evil." Already at the age of sixteen, and long before he has had occasion to develop feelings of resentment, young Antonio Salieri set out to realize the desire of his early childhood, which was "to join all the composers who had celebrated His glory through the long Italian past," in a rather peculiar fashion. As the aged composer reports in one of his direct addresses to the twentieth-century audience—"Ghosts of the Future! Shades of time to come!" (6)—he proposed a bargain to the image of God the Father "painted on the flaking wall" of his hometown church. Impersonating both his former self and the responding voice perceived by the fervent adolescent, Salieri leaves his wheelchair to reenact his consequential encounter with the "old candle-smoked God in a mulberry robe" who, because "tradesmen had put him up there," was "staring at the world with dealer's eyes":

> Those eyes made bargains, real and irreversible. (*He kneels.*) The night before I left Legnago forever, I went to see Him, and made a bargain with Him myself. I was a sober sixteen, filled with a desperate sense of right. I knelt before the God of Bargains, and I prayed through the mouldering plaster with all my soul. . . . "*Signore,* let me be a composer. Grant me sufficient fame to enjoy it. In return, I will live with virtue. I will strive to better the lot of my fellows. And I will honor You with much music all the days of my life!" As I said *Amen,* I saw His eyes flare. (*As* "*God.*") "*Bene.* Go forth Antonio. Serve Me and mankind, and you will be blessed!" . . . "*Grazie!*" I called back. "I am Your servant for life!" . . . The very next day, a family friend suddenly appeared—out of the blue—took me off to Vienna and paid for me to study music! Shortly afterward, I met the Emperor, who favored me. Clearly my bargain had been accepted! [8]

Or so Salieri thought; hence his grave disappointment when his virtue and exertions appear to be mocked by God, who, by Salieri's light, has failed to honor his end of the bargain. The apparent breach of promise is driven home to Salieri on what he later calls "that dreadful Night of the Manuscripts" (49): his first reading, in 1781 or thereabouts, of young Mozart's fully mature scores. The days are long gone when Mozart's musician father could profitably parade the child prodigy through the courts and cities of Europe. The manuscripts have in fact been brought to Salieri by Mozart's wife, Constanze, in the hope of improving the sorry state of her and her husband's finances through a favorable recommendation by the influential Herr Court Composer. But her project backfires because the crushing exposure to some of Mozart's masterpieces turns Salieri into Mozart's—and God's—lifelong enemy. As he pages through the Twenty-ninth Symphony in A major, the Sinfonia Concertante for Violin and Viola, the Concerto for Flute and Harp, and the C Minor Mass, some passages of those works become audible to the audience as well—not in their actual acoustic glory, to be sure, but in a slightly distorted way that should suggest that "the sublime work of genius" is being "experienced by another musician's increasingly agonized mind" (xiv). Just as Salieri expresses his belief that he is "staring through the cage of those meticulous ink strokes at—an Absolute Beauty," the following stage direction describes the highest (or lowest) moments of his agony:

A faint thundery sound is heard accumulating, like a distant sea. . . . And out of the thundery roar writhes and rises the clear sound of a soprano, singing the Kyrie from the C Minor Mass. The accretion of noise around her voice falls away—it is suddenly clear and bright— then clearer and brighter. The light grows bright: too bright: burning white, then scalding white! Salieri rises in the downpour of it, and in the flood of music, which is growing ever louder—filling the theater—as the soprano yields to the full chorus, fortissimo, singing its massive counterpoint. [45–46]

This acoustically and visually suggested "opening of heaven" brings to mind Book VII, lines 205–8, of Milton's Paradise Lost ("Heav'n op'n'd wide/Her everduring Gates, Harmonious sound/On golden Hinges moving, to let forth / The King of Glory''). By way of contrast, it is also reminiscent of the Gospel account of the epiphany immediately following John's baptism of Jesus in the Jordan River (Matt. 3:16, Mark 1:10, Luke 3:21): Salieri, six years Mozart's senior and already an established ''prophet'' in Vienna, is clearly not the man to assume the role of a John the Baptist. Far from being content to play second fiddle in God's musical universe, he cannot joyfully recognize that ''after me comes a man who ranks before me'' (John 1:29), bear public witness that ''this is the Son of God'' (John 1:34), and ''prepare the way of the Lord, make his path straight'' (Luke 3:4). Rather, this would-be ''first Arch-Angel, great in Power, in favor and preëminence,'' becomes ''fraught with envy against the Son of God'' (*Paradise Lost,* V. 660–62). With the manuscripts in his hand, Salieri staggers toward the spectators ''like a man caught in a tumbling and violent sea.'' Then he ''drops the portfolio'' and ''falls senseless to the ground.'' Finally, he emerges from the crushing epiphany with this embittered address to God:

> *Capisco!* I know my fate. . . . Tonight at an inn somewhere in this city stands a giggling child who can put on paper, without actually setting down his billiard cue, casual notes which turn my most considered ones into lifeless scratches. *Grazie, Signore!* . . . Until this day I have pursued virtue with rigor. I have labored long hours to relieve my fellow men. I have worked and worked the talent You allowed me. . . . Solely that in the end, in the practice of the art which alone makes the world comprehensible to me, I might hear Your Voice! And now I do hear it—and it says only one name: MOZART! . . . Spiteful, sniggering, conceited, infantine Mozart. . . . *Him* You have chosen to be Your sole conduct! And *my* only reward—my sublime privilege—is to be the sole man alive in this time who shall clearly recognize Your Incarnation! [46–47]

Instead of accepting a role in which he could ''straighten the path'' for God's emissary on earth, Salieri claims to take the side of ''mocked'' Man in the ensuing battle against *Dio ingiusto,* the ''unjust God'' not rewarding virtue, whom he also calls *''Nemico*

Eterno"—the name traditionally reserved for Satan as God's and Man's "eternal enemy." With all the blasphemous pathos of the diabolic villain in an Italian tragic opera, he goes on to swear: "To my last breath I shall *block* You on earth, as far as I am able!" After this most dramatic of the many flashbacks from 1823 to the last decade of Mozart's life (1756–91), he then dismisses the audience for a brief intermission. "When I return," he says, "I'll tell you about the war I fought with God through His preferred Creature— Mozart, named Amadeus. In the waging of which, of course, the Creature had to be destroyed" (47).

The view afforded to the spectators of "spiteful, sniggering, conceited, infantine Mozart" is, to be sure, continually mediated by Salieri's narratives and "playlets" within the PLAY. Yet most episodes narrated or dramatized by Salieri are in no substantial disagreement with the documentary and anecdotal evidence concerning the all too human characteristics of musical Absolute's "sole conduct" and "Incarnation" in the latter part of the eighteenth century. Divine sound-become-flesh appears to have become just that; not only in *Amadeus* but in many of his extant letters, Mozart can be seen exhibiting the marks of an unchecked, playfully lascivious beastliness. It should not unduly shock us, therefore, that "Miaouw! . . . Miaouw! . . . Miaouw!" are the first "words" uttered on stage by the twenty-five-year-old genius. He is chasing his girlfriend, Constanze, in a cat-and-mouse game that will land both of them on the floor of an aristocrat's library, right between the fortepiano and a high-backed wing chair from which Salieri is forced to eavesdrop unobserved:

> SALIERI: (*To audience.*) Before I could rise, it had become difficult to do so.
> MOZART: I am going to bite you in half with my fang-wangs! My little Stanzerl-wanzerl-banzerl!
>   (*She laughs delightedly, lying prone beneath him.*)
> You're trembling! . . . I think you're frightened of puss-wuss! I think you're scared to death! (*Intimately.*) I think you're going to shit yourself!

205

Before the Majordomo stalks in on the exuberant couple to summon them to the concert to be given next door, we hear Mozart imitate the noise of a fart and declare to the "not really shocked" Constanze: "I'd want everything backwards once I was married. I'd want to lick my wife's arse instead of her face" (15–17). On a later and similar occasion, Salieri overhears Constanze complain to Mozart, now her husband, that he "had . . . every single female pupil," and that perhaps Salieri has so many more pupils than Mozart because "he doesn't drag them into bed." Mozart replies: "Of course he doesn't! He can't get it up, that's why! . . . Have you ever heard his music? That's the sound of someone who *can't get it up!* At least *I* can do *that.* . . . (*Shouting.*) No one ever said I couldn't do *that!*" (36–37).

Throughout the play, Mozart's speeches abound with indecorous puns and indecent references to bodily functions even if the topic of conversation is "God's art"—music. For example, he justifies his rejection of operas based on "boring legends" about gods or mythological heroes and his enthusiasm for the down-to-earth libretto of *The Marriage of Figaro* (1786) as follows:

MOZART: I want to do a piece about real people, Baron! And I want to set it in a real place! A *boudoir!* Because that to me is the most exciting place on earth! Underclothes on the floor! Sheets still warm from a woman's body! Even a pisspot brimming under the bed!

. . .

VAN SWIETEN: I had assumed, now that you had joined our Brotherhood of Masons, you would choose more elevated themes.
MOZART: (*Impatiently.*) Oh, elevated! Elevated! . . . The only thing a man should elevate is his doodle. [56]

But these (and some more) irreverent remarks in the pompous presence of Baron Gottfried Van Swieten, Prefect of the Imperial Library, Count Johann Kilian von Strack, Groom of the Imperial Chamber, and Court Composer Antonio Salieri lead up to Mozart's

hand begins feebly to beat out drum measures from the music."
Mozart no longer hears what Constanze is saying to him and,
eventually, *"the drum strokes get slower, and stop."* Yet even as "
*she becomes aware that Mozart is dead," "the great chord of the
'Amen' does not resolve itself, but lingers on in intense reverbera-
tion"* (90–91). Since the stage directions indicating the musical
dimension of the PLAY are not part of Salieri's "play," we may
assume that the contrast between the gradually fading "drum
strokes" and the reverberating dissonance does not indicate simply
that Mozart's heart has stopped before he could complete his last
piece of music. The unresolved dramatic dissonance between the
stopping heart and the unfinished yet continuing music may also
signal the beginning of Mozart's as yet unfinished ascension, within
human memory, from the realm of the "son" (a man *made by*
history's natural and social processes) to that of the "father" (a
maker of cultural history through artistic creativity).

It is instructive to contrast the complex image of Mozart emerging from *Amadeus* with the rather flat image of Shakespeare—
another prime hero of our culture—as it is delineated in Edward
Bond's *Bingo: Scenes of Money and Death* (1974). Having taken
the oppressors' side in the class struggle, Bond's Shakespeare is
ruthlessly reduced to a doomed creature (rather than gifted creator)
of history: he is seen committing physical suicide while his intellectual and moral demise appears to have occurred long before the
beginning of the play. This "overstanding" treatment of his tower-
ing precursor by an author whose own best play to date may well be
a genuinely powerful adaptation of *Lear* (1972) calls for a deconstructive interpretation along the lines, perhaps, of Harold
Bloom's inquiries into "the anxiety of influence" (1973) among
British and American poets. At the very least, it is tempting to see
Bingo in psychoanalytical terms as the abreaction of a less potent
playwright's quasi-sexual envy of a mightier pen. By contrast,
Shaffer succeeds in projecting whatever oedipal spite he or his
performers and audiences may harbor against Mozart as a founding
father of our cultural tradition onto Salieri, whose witnessed re-

bellion against being inferior preempts our own need to be satirically indignant when it is more rewarding romantically to admire.

It would, of course, be wrong to interpret Shaffer's polyphonic symbolism of fatherhood in a homophonically positive, let alone literally Christian, manner. Other than to Salieri, God the Father does not "speak" in the play. And Salieri's perception of Him as a God who shows not even "one drop" of pity (70), "does not help," and "does not love" because "He can only *use*" (88) suggests a strange mixture of impersonal deism and deliberately oppositional Satanism. The latter comes to the fore when Salieri celebrates what can only be described as a diabolic black mass: he "tears off a corner" of a page from Mozart's Requiem, "elevates it in the manner of the Communion Service, places it on his tongue and eats it." He even declares in pain: "I eat what God gives me. Dose after dose. For all of life. His poison. We are both poisoned, Amadeus. I with you: you with me" (88). Such a view of God— and nothing *verbal* in the play contradicts it—leaves ordinary human beings at the banal mercy of a self-love that knows itself to be undeserved. As Salieri tells the twentieth-century audience at the end of the play:

Now I go to become a ghost myself. I will stand in the shadows when you come here to this earth in your turns. And when you feel the dreadful bite of your failures—and hear the taunting of unachievable, uncaring God—I will whisper my name to you: "Salieri: Patron Saint of Mediocrities!" And in the depth of your downcastness you can pray to me. And I will forgive you. . . . Mediocrities everywhere—now and to come—I absolve you all. Amen! (*He extends his arms upward and outward to embrace the assembled audience in a wide gesture of benediction—finally folding his arms high across his own breast in a gesture of self-sanctification.*) [95–97]

At this final point of the performance, however, "*the lights fade completely*" and, according to the very last stage direction, "*the last four chords of the Masonic Funeral Music of AMADEUS MOZART sound throughout the theater.*" Thus the music of

Ama-deus, who loves God and/or is loved by God, outlasts Salieri's "play." More important still: in the ears of the departing spectators, Mozart's music outlasts the PLAY as well.

To be sure, what the audience is made to hear at the end, just like what it was made to hear throughout the performance, is not the "Absolute Beauty" supposedly enclosed in the "cage" of Mozart's "meticulous ink strokes." What is now (and can ever be) *heard* is but a particular performance of a particular piece of music; and each "hearing" of any music—whether it is triggered by actual sound or by the reading of a score—further relativizes the Absolute. By making *melos* an integral part of his play, by making it and the play's *mythos, ethos, dianoia, lexis,* and *opsis* constantly comment upon one another, Shaffer makes it especially clear that Mozart's music enters the theater event, as it were, between relativizing quotation marks. In the conceptual framework of Chapter 5 one might say that the performed "music" we hear (just like any "actor" we watch) is a sign that functions in all three Peircean modes of signification: it is an *index* of Mozart's MUSIC; an *icon* of the absolute music that we are invited to imagine as one of the entities being represented on the stage; and a *symbol* of the play's tragicomic theme—the necessarily frustrating or otherwise flawed reception of the Absolute in the human sphere of the Relative. Even the music cannot, therefore, be considered as a simple, massive, unmediated presence of the past in each present or future performance of Salieri's "play" or Shaffer's PLAY. It, too, partakes of the complex dialectic of all future-bound representation of the past that was discussed in Chapter I and about which more will be said in the concluding section of this chapter. Especially in the scenes dramatizing one or more than one listener's response to music, the playwright makes us perceive perceivers: not only Salieri but also, for example, the yawning Emperor Joseph II and members of his court or the somewhat unruly music-hall crowd watching and listening to *The Magic Flute.* We may distance our perception of the music from theirs without thereby becoming able to distance it from ours. And our perception of the music is, of course, just another historical, relativizing medium for the Absolute Message.

213

Has that message ever been fully revealed even to a musical genius of Mozart's stature? Shaffer's Mozart seems to doubt that it has when he pleads with the Masked Figure, whom he takes to be God's emissary, for more time so that he may "write a real piece of music": "I know I've boasted I've written hundreds, but it's not true. I've written nothing finally good!" (87). But if the Absolute (like Caligula's Moon) can only be approximated and aspired to, if it will not be attained through either art or history, then the "pain" and "need" that Salieri hears in Mozart's music and, tentatively, attributes to God—"Is it *Your* need? Can it be Yours?"—may well be the quintessentially human pain and need of self-conscious insufficiency. That need is, indeed, "forever unfulfillable, yet fulfilling him who hears it, utterly" (19). We "hear" that need when we painfully, rather than glibly, realize that the history we make or write falls short of being (if there is such a thing) His story, and that the art we create, interpret, and appreciate must always remain, by comparison with the incomparable Absolute, impaired dys-art. This is, perhaps, what is suggested by the remarkable name of the un-fulfilled lover of Greek art, Dr. Dysart, in Shaffer's *Equus* (cf. Klein 1979:128). And the limitation of all art by dint of the historicity of all artists is forcefully implied by an early speech of Salieri, who believes that he is merely extolling, in words addressed to a latter-day audience, the mission of eighteenth-century musicians:

> You, when you come, will be told that we musicians of the eighteenth century were no better than servants: the willing slaves of the well-to-do. This is quite true. It is also quite false. . . . We took unremarkable men—usual bankers, run-of-the-mill priests, ordinary soldiers and statesmen and wives—and sacramentalized their mediocrity. . . . The savor of their days remains behind because of *us,* our music still remembered while their politics are long forgotten. . . . Tell me, before you call us servants, who served whom? And who, I wonder, in your generations, will immortalize *you?* [11]

Being forced to "sacramentalize mediocrity" and to "immortalize" deficient lives and times in the very process of attempting to

214

transcend or at least to illuminate them makes artists at once masters and servants of history. And the interpreters of art—whether they actively perform or merely hear, view, read, and then think or write about it—are subject to the same dialectic of mastery and servitude. Our acts of public or private interpretation can only expand those public and private horizons that, even expanded, will have forever confined our fields of action and vision.

Recapitulation: The Future of the Past

And yet: one should beware of absolutizing the relative as though it were more than what it is, namely, a horizon. The liar's para-dox—does he tell the truth when he says, "I am lying?"—applies to skeptics and relativists who ignore the self-consuming implica-tions of skepticism and relativism and thus mistake their horizon for just what that horizon keeps them from seeing. Such a charge of deluded naiveté cannot be leveled against most plays discussed in this study. They articulate (rather than pretend to eliminate) the paradox involved; and they do so through highlighting (rather than trying to conceal) what Hans-Georg Gadamer has called the her-meneutic "fusion of horizons" (1972:284–95/1975:267–78). By stressing both the fusion of the historyteller's present perspective with the past events of his or her tale and the fusion of the play-wright's or director's authorial vision with the characters' repre-sented actions, modern historical tragicomedy denies the indepen-dent absolute validity of either present vision or past actions only to affirm with greater vigor a relative future for both.

This future emerges as part of the continuing hermeneutic process of humankind's placing itself—between the *arche* of causes and origins and the *telos* of purposes and ends—through the mythmak-ing interpretations and reinterpretations of history. Whether they live in entirely or predominantly oral, literate, or postliterate (elec-tronic) cultures, the men and women in charge of generating and managing information about the shared past of a particular community have considerable impact on the community's present and future as well. To a significant degree, they help devise the ways in which members of their communities understand themselves as players of historically rooted roles in the public dramas of life—that is to say, the ways in which human beings interact *as* spouses, parents, siblings, offspring, employers, employees, co-workers, experts, patients, political or spiritual leaders and followers, and the like. But they also influence the ways in which each of us feels that we are more than the sum of our public roles. After all, our introspective or empathetic sense of selfhood—the assumption that there is a private face behind every public mask—is based largely on the historical (as well as the mythical and literary) reports that our culture has made us receive and assimilate about significant instances of role playing in exemplary situations. As Erving Goffman put it in the different but related context of his *Frame Analysis: An Essay on the Organization of Experience* (1974):

> Just as the current situation prescribes the official guise behind which we will conceal ourselves, so it provides for where and how we will show through, the culture itself prescribing what sort of entity we must believe ourselves to be in order to have something to show through in this manner. [573–74]

It is clear that we respond to narrated events *as actions* and to described states of affairs *as situations* by an imaginative projection of our own hopes and fears into the represented fulfillments and frustrations of others. It is equally clear that we learn (or think we learn) a great deal about ourselves by interpreting other people's interpretations of what it must have been and must have felt like to be Adam and Eve, Sisyphus and Cherea, Satan and Salieri, Joan of Arc, Don Quixote, Napoleon, or Romeo and Juliet. And this kind of learning has an existential, formative impact on the learner. I am no longer the same when I have learned who I am; and once I have learned (or think I have learned) who I am, there is a whole new me to learn about. Hence the need for "the admission to self by self of the unfinishability of the individuation of itself" (Wilshire 1982: 227). On such a view, of course, the self is hardly something that can be objectified (*the* self) and possessed (*my* self, *your* self) or even quantified and multiplied (our *several respective* selves, her *other* self). Nor is "my self" simply the totality of my roles (including the one of publicly puzzling, as the implied author of this paragraph, about what is so very private: myself). It may be more appropriate to say this: In and through all the roles I have ever played and will ever play, as well as in and through the kind and degree of endorsement and distance with which I am playing each, *selfing occurs to me.* It occurs to me simultaneously in both senses of "occurs": selfing happens to me as I am becoming aware of selfing, and I become aware of selfing as selfing is happening to me. In short, the self *is not* but, as Freud once said of the *Ich,* "should become" in the historical process of cultivation or "cultural labor" (*Kulturarbeit*), which he likened to "the draining of the Zuider Zee" (1967:86/1965:80).

The translation of Freud's *Ich* as "ego" in the Standard Edition of his works is perhaps the most significant one of the numerous misrenderings recently chastised by Bruno Bettelheim (1983). Some of the others are "superego" for *Überich,* "parapraxis" for *Fehlleistung,* "instinct" for *Trieb,* "psyche" for *Seele,* and "id" for *Es.* Each of those terms signals the translators' (not necessarily conscious) effort to expurgate from Freud's language all traces of the compassionate humanist's general appeal to a lay public and thus to promote psychoanalysis as a detached, perhaps esoteric, and certainly profitable speciality of medical science. Consider the id and the ego as supposed equivalents of Freud's key concepts of *das Es* and *das Ich* (1967:76–86/1965:69–80). These nouns, based on two of the most familiar pronouns in any language, "it" and "I," lose their natural affiliation with the darkly impersonal and the lucidly responsive and responsible aspects of my soul—and of *your* soul when you say *I*—if they are forced into the pseudoscientifically

Latinate garb of "the id" and "the ego." Moreover, "the ego" conjures up connotations of egotism that are altogether alien to Freud's notion of *das Ich* as the maturing soul's "realistic" defense against the unrestrained, infantile, truly egotistical Pleasure Principle of *das Es*. Worse still, the sentence to which I was alluding from Freud's *New Introductory Lectures on Psychoanalysis* (1933) appears in the English translation as "Where id was, there ego shall be" (1965:80). This half-English, half-Latin string of words is even more misleading than Bettelheim had the patience to point out in explicit detail (cf. esp. 1983:61–62, 106). What Freud really wrote concerning the purpose of psychoanalysis is: "Wo Es war, soll Ich werden" (1967:86)—that is to say, "Where It was, I should *become*" (italics added).

That sentence does not read like a medical prescription. In the context of Freud's work it is clearly the good doctor's secular prophecy of becoming well by becoming conscious of and responsible to both myself and a communally shared Principle of Reality. From the six simple words mental health emerges as self-propelled spiritual growth. They assign to agents (rather than patients) the task (*soll*) of becoming (*werden*) what each of us has the potential of being through appropriating more and more of the impersonal space (*wo*) of impulse-driven thingness (*Es*) that preexists (*war*) the dawning of personal identity (*Ich*). The carefully chosen words are, however, applicable not only to the emergence of the self from the chaotic *Es*—our fragmented manifold of unconscious private impulses. They strike me as applying also to the emergence of the self from the fragmented manifold of externally imposed public roles— that realm of the soul or psyche to which Freud, among other things, refers when he speaks of *das Überich*. In this respect, too, the self is not objectively *given,* nor will it be willfully *taken,* but it *should always become*. In the continual "cultural labor" of conscious or preconscious giving and taking, no "I" can be identified and objectified as that which has, once and for all, managed to come out from under the roles imposed on it by the script of circumstances and by the exacting stage management of that internalized tyrant, the Above-I. But in this respect, too, selfing can occur to each person who, without denying that even *persona* originally meant "role" and "mask," is capable of insisting: I should become.

Such becoming cannot occur to an individual person in supposedly splendid isolation from others. I see it as resulting, when it does occur, from the potentially always global *Kulturarbeit* of understanding: the reciprocal fitting of parts and wholes in the increasingly profound interpretation of our various roles in the quasi-dramatic contexts of our lives. Now, as Hans-Georg Gadamer insists, all understanding involves an exchange of questions and answers with one's tradition: a dialogue that a still present past and an already passing present do not so much enter into as, indeed, emerge from (1972:351–69/1975:325–41). As part of that dialogue, historytelling is not a matter of correlating two preexisting spheres of existence in which, respectively, *they were* and *I am*. It is, rather, what speech act theoreticians (cf. Austin 1975:6 *et passim*) might well call a "performative" enactment of that which, thereby, *we will have become*. Thus what appears to be a historiographer's or historical playwright's superimposition of a retrospective understanding on another person's or period's prospective understanding of a re-presented sequence of past events is, in fact, just one phase in the interminable worldmaking through humankind's interpretive appropriation of itself.

Quantitatively speaking, this process evolves through the constant replacement of every ostensibly definitive hermeneutic context by a larger one. Qualitatively, however, each such re-placement means the superimposition of a detached view from without on what turns out to have been an engaged, biased view from within. While the perspective from without carries with it greater potential for comedy, the realization that one's detached view of the limitations of others in turn results from another limited way of seeing may engender a sense of tragedy. The playwrights' dramatized insight into the complementary nature of the two modes of vision makes all plays discussed here particularly apt vehicles of that tragicomic mood which, I think, emanates from the perpetual re-visions of history by historiography.

That the past may find its meaning or justification through future retrospection is not a new idea, of course. "The gods did this, and spun the destruction of peoples for the sake of the singing of men hereafter" (*Odyssey,* VIII.579–80 in Richmond Lattimore's translation). Homer does not tell us whether the Phaiakian king's words managed to console Odysseus, who had been bewailing the bard's account of the Trojan war. But the implications of Alkinoös' statement are far-reaching. If the singing of men hereafter can justify even the destruction of peoples, then the gods "spin" history for the sake of historiography, and all Action is but raw, very raw, material for retrospective Vision. "Resourceful" Odysseus seems to draw an appropriate conclusion when he immediately assumes the role of narrator and, in the course of the next four books, makes ample use of the ontological primacy (or is it mere tactical advantage?) of the teller over the tale. Listeners and readers have not ceased to wonder whether he is telling the truth about his journeys to Hades and other elusively distant parts. One thing is certain, however. If he has not told his hosts How It Really Was, he has surely impressed upon them How It Should Be Remembered, and Odysseus receives praise and rewards for his story, which, whether or not it *was* history, certainly *made* some. *Within* the world of the *Odyssey,* the story secures the wherewithal for the hero's eventual homecoming and for his becoming what the great wanderer felt he could not become except in Ithaca—himself. In the world evolving *around* the poem, the same quasi-autobiographical narrative has prompted innumerable imitations and interpretations, including the rudimentary interpretation of the motivation for its telling suggested in the present paragraph.

Since every historyteller of consequence "makes" history both within and around the textual sphere of his or her discourse, Thornton Wilder's Sabina can address the audience—the extended family of Mr. and Mrs. Antrobus—at the final return to the beginning in

The Skin of Our Teeth: "This is where you came in. We have to go on for ages and ages yet. . . . The end of this play isn't written yet" (1958:137). Whether or not Marat can pull himself up by his own hair; whether or not Caligula is still alive; whether or not Salieri is right in praising artists for sacramentalizing mediocrity: theatergoers as well as other actors and spectators of the serious plays of history always bear reminding that there is more to come. More of the same, of course: more Action, and more Vision, and more imaginative interpretation of both Action and Vision.

Works Cited

Abel, Lionel. *Metatheatre: A New View of Dramatic Form*. New York: Hill & Wang, 1963.

Adler, Alfred. *Social Interest: A Challenge to Mankind*. Trans. John Litton and Richard Vaughan. New York: Capricorn, 1964.

Anouilh, Jean. *L'Alouette*. Paris: La Table ronde, 1953.

———. *The Lark*. Trans. Christopher Fry. New York: Oxford University Press, 1956.

Archer, William. *Masks or Faces?* See Denis Diderot, *The Paradox of Acting*.

Arendt, Hannah. *Eichmann in Jerusalem: A Report on the Banality of Evil*. New York: Viking Press, 1963.

Aristotle. *Poetics*. Trans. Leon Golden. Commentary by O. B. Hardison, Jr. Englewood Cliffs, N.J.: Prentice-Hall, 1968.

Austin, J. L. *How to Do Things with Words*, 2d ed. Cambridge: Harvard University Press, 1975.

Barthes, Roland. *Mythologies*. Paris: Editions du Seuil, 1957.

———. *Mythologies*. Trans. Annette Lavers. New York: Hill & Wang, 1972.

Bentley, Eric. *The Life of the Drama*. New York: Atheneum, 1964.

Bergson, Henri. "Laughter." In *Comedy*, with Introduction and Appendix by Wylie Sypher. Garden City, N.Y.: Doubleday, 1956.

Bettelheim, Bruno. *Freud and Man's Soul*. New York: Knopf, 1983.

Bloom, Harold. *The Anxiety of Influence: A Theory of Poetry*. New York: Oxford University Press, 1973.

Booth, Wayne C. *Critical Understanding: The Powers and Limits of Pluralism*. Chicago: University of Chicago Press, 1979.

Brecht, Bertolt. *Brecht on Theatre*. Ed. John Willett. New York: Hill & Wang, 1964.

———. *Gesammelte Werke*. 20 vols. Frankfurt: Suhrkamp, 1967. Vol. 3 includes *Leben des Galilei* (pp. 1229–1345); vol. 15 includes articles on Shaw (pp. 24–26 and 96–101) and "Vergnügungstheater oder Lehrtheater?" (pp. 262–72); vol. 16 includes "Die Strassenszene: Grundmodel einer Szene des epischen

Theaters'' (pp. 546–58), ''Kleines Organon für das Theater'' (pp. 661–708), ''Katzgraben-Notate'' (pp. 772–840), and ''Die Dialektik auf dem Theater'' (pp. 867–941); vol. 17 includes notes about *Aufstieg und Fall der Stadt Mahagonny* (pp. 1004–16) and about *Leben des Galilei* (pp. 1103–33).

————. *Collected Plays*, vol. 5. In *Plays, Poetry, and Prose*, ed. Ralph Manheim and John Willett. New York: Vintage, 1972. Includes the final version of *Life of Galileo*, trans. Wolfgang Sauerlander and Ralph Manheim (pp. 1–98), ''Notes and Variants'' to the play (pp. 213–305), and Charles Laughton's American version (pp. 402–67).

Brée, Germaine. *Camus*. New Brunswick, N.J.: Rutgers University Press, 1959.

Burke, Edmund. *Philosophical Inquiry into the Origin of Our Ideas of the Sublime and the Beautiful*. Ed. J. T. Boulton. New York: Columbia University Press, 1958.

Campbell, Joseph, and Henry Morton Robinson. ''The Skin of Whose Teeth?'' *Saturday Review of Literature*, 25 (December 19, 1942), 3–4, and 26 (February 13, 1943), 16–19.

Camus, Albert. *Caligula and Three Other Plays*. Trans. Stuart Gilbert. With a preface by the author, trans. Justin O'Brien. New York: Vintage, 1958. Includes *Caligula* (pp. 1–74).

————. *L'Homme révolté*. Paris: Gallimard, 1951.

————. *Le Mythe de Sisyphe: Essai sur l'absurde*. Paris: Gallimard, 1942.

————. *The Myth of Sisyphus and Other Essays*. Trans. Justin O'Brien. New York: Knopf, 1969.

————. *The Rebel*. Trans. Anthony Bower (1953). Harmondsworth: Penguin, 1973.

————. *Théâtre, récits, nouvelles*. Ed. Roger Quilliot. Paris: Gallimard, 1962. Includes *Caligula* (pp. 3–108) and prefaces, notes, and variants to the play (pp. 1729–87).

Claudel, Paul. *Claudel on the Theatre*. Ed. Jacques Petit and Jean-Pierre Kempf. Trans. Christine Trollope. Coral Gables, Fla.: University of Miami Press, 1972.

————. *The Book of Christopher Columbus*. Decorations by Jean Charlot. New Haven: Yale University Press, 1930.

————. *Le Livre de Christophe Colomb*. Paris: Gallimard, 1935. Includes ''Le Drame et la musique,'' a lecture delivered at Yale University in 1930 (pp. 9–37).

————. *Mes Idées sur le théâtre*. Ed. Jacques Petit and Jean-Pierre Kempf. Paris: Gallimard, 1966.

Coombs, Ilona. *Camus, homme de théâtre*. Paris: Nizet, 1968.

Danto, Arthur C. *Analytical Philosophy of History*. Cambridge: Cambridge University Press, 1968.

Derrida, Jacques. ''The Law of Genre.'' Trans. Avital Ronell. In *On Narrative*, ed. W. J. T. Mitchell, pp. 51–77. Chicago: University of Chicago Press, 1981.

Diderot, Denis. *Oeuvres complètes*. 20 vols. Ed. J. Assézat. Paris: Garnier, 1875–77. Vol. 8 (1875) includes ''Paradoxe sur le comédien'' (pp. 361–423).

————. *The Paradox of Acting*, trans. Walter Herries Pollock, and *Masks or Faces?* by William Archer. New York: Hill & Wang, 1957.

Dryden, John. *Essay of Dramatic Poesie*. In *The Works of John Dryden*, ed. Samuel Holt Monk, 17:3–81. Berkeley: University of California Press, 1971.

Dürrenmatt, Friedrich. *Four Plays*. New York: Grove Press, 1965[a]. Gerhard Nellhaus' translation of *Romulus the Great* (pp. 41–119) is based on the second version (1957) of the play.

————. *Komödien*. 7th ed. Zürich: Arche, 1965[b]. Includes *Romulus der Grosse*, "new version 1964" (pp. 7–79).

Elam, Keir. *The Semiotics of Theatre and Drama*. London: Methuen, 1980.

Eliade, Mircea. *Myth and Reality*. Trans. Willard R. Trask. New York: Harper & Row, 1963.

Eliot, T. S. *Murder in the Cathedral*. [4th ed., 1938.] New York: Harcourt, Brace & World, 1963.

————. *The Three Voices of Poetry*. New York: Cambridge University Press, 1954.

Esslin, Martin. *Brecht: The Man and His Work*. New rev. ed. Garden City, N.Y.: Doubleday, 1971.

————. *The Theatre of the Absurd*. New York: Doubleday, 1961.

Freud, Sigmund. *Neue Folge der Vorlesungen zur Einführung in die Psychoanalyse* (1933). In *Gesammelte Werke*, vol. 15. 4th reprint. Frankfurt: S. Fischer, 1967.

————. *New Introductory Lectures on Psychoanalysis*. Newly trans. and ed. James Strachey. New York: Norton, 1965. First published as vol. 22 of *The Standard Edition of the Complete Psychological Works of Sigmund Freud*. London: Hogarth Press, 1964.

Frisch, Max. *Die chinesische Mauer: Eine Farce*. [Neue Fassung, 1955.] Edition Suhrkamp no. 65. Frankfurt: Suhrkamp, 1967.

————. *Die chinesische Mauer: Eine Farce*. Version für Paris, 1972. Edition Suhrkamp no. 65. 12th reprint. Frankfurt: Suhrkamp, 1977.

————. *Four Plays*. Trans. Michael Bullock. London: Methuen, 1969. *The Great Wall of China* (pp. 1–84) is based on the German version of 1955.

Frye, Northrop. *Anatomy of Criticism*. Princeton: Princeton University Press, 1957.

Gadamer, Hans-Georg. *Truth and Method*. Translation ed. Garrett Barden and John Cumming from 2d German ed. (1965). New York: Seabury, 1975.

————. *Wahrheit und Methode: Grundzüge einer philosophischen Hermeneutik* (1960). 3d expanded ed. Tübingen: J. C. B. Mohr (Paul Siebeck), 1972.

Goethe, Johann Wolfgang. *Faust*. Trans. Walter Arndt. Ed. Cyrus Hamlin. New York: Norton, 1976.

————. *Goethe's Faust*. Trans. Walter Kaufmann. Garden City, N.Y.: Doubleday, 1961.

Goffman, Erving. *Frame Analysis: An Essay on the Organization of Experience*. Cambridge: Harvard University Press, 1974.

Works Cited

——. *The Presentation of Self in Everyday Life.* Garden City, N.Y.: Doubleday Anchor Books, 1959.

Goodman, Nelson. *Languages of Art: An Approach to a Theory of Symbols.* Indianapolis: Bobbs-Merrill, 1968.

——. *Ways of Worldmaking.* Indianapolis: Hackett, 1978.

Guthke, Karl S. *Modern Tragicomedy.* New York: Random House, 1966.

Habermas, Jürgen. *Knowledge and Human Interests.* Trans. Jeremy J. Shapiro. Boston: Beacon, 1971.

Hecht, Werner, ed. *Materialien zu Brechts "Leben des Galilei."* Edition Suhrkamp no. 44. Frankfurt: Suhrkamp, 1963.

Hernadi, Paul. "The Actor's Face as the Author's Mask: On the Paradox of Brechtian Staging." In *Literary Criticism and Psychology,* vol. 7 of *Yearbook of Comparative Criticism,* ed. Joseph P. Strelka, pp. 125–36. University Park: Pennsylvania State University Press, 1976[d].

——. *Beyond Genre: New Directions in Literary Classification.* Ithaca: Cornell University Press, 1972.

——. "Clio's Cousins: Historiography as Translation, Fiction, and Criticism." *New Literary History,* 7 (1976[a]), 247–57.

——. "Entertaining Commitments: A Reception Theory of Literary Genres." *Poetics,* 10 (1981[a]), 195–211.

——. "The Erotics of Retrospection: Historytelling, Audience Response, and the Strategies of Desire." *New Literary History,* 12 (1981[c]), 243–52.

——. "Literary Theory." In *Introduction to Scholarship in Modern Languages and Literatures,* ed. Joseph Gibaldi, pp. 98–115. New York: Modern Language Association, 1981[b].

——. "Literary Theory: A Compass for Critics." *Critical Inquiry,* 3 (1976[b]), 369–86.

——. "On the How, What, and Why of Narrative." *Critical Inquiry,* 7 (1980), 201–3. Reprinted in *On Narrative,* ed. W. J. T. Mitchell, pp. 197–99. Chicago: University of Chicago Press, 1981.

——. "Pseudohistorische Gestalten in der Nachkriegsdramatik." Ph.D. dissertation. University of Vienna, 1963.

——. "Re-presenting the Past: A Note on Narrative Historiography and Historical Drama." *History and Theory,* 15 (1976[c]), 45–51.

——. "So What? How So? and the Form That Matters." In *Interpretation of Narrative,* ed. Mario J. Valdés and Owen J. Miller, pp. 167–73. Toronto: University of Toronto Press, 1978[a].

——, ed. *What Is Criticism?* Bloomington: Indiana University Press, 1981[d]. Introduction.

——, ed. *What Is Literature?* Bloomington: Indiana University Press, 1978[b]. Introduction.

Holtz, William. "Thermodynamics and the Comic and Tragic Modes." *Western Humanities Review,* 25 (1971), 203–16.

Hugo, Victor. *Théâtre complet.* Paris: Gallimard, 1963.

Iser, Wolfgang. *The Act of Reading: A Theory of Aesthetic Response*. Baltimore: Johns Hopkins University Press, 1978.

Jackson, Robert Louis. "Miltonic Imagery and Design in Puškin's *Mozart and Salieri*." In *American Contributions to the Seventh International Congress of Slavists* (Warsaw, August 21–27, 1973). The Hague: Mouton, 1973.

Jaspers, Karl. *Tragedy Is Not Enough*. Trans. Harold A. T. Reiche et al. Boston: Beacon, 1952. [Translation of a section of *Von der Wahrheit*. (Munich Piper, 1947).]

Jauss, Hans Robert. *Toward an Aesthetic of Reception*. Trans. Timothy Bahti. Minneapolis: University of Minnesota Press, 1982.

Joyce, James. *A Portrait of the Artist as a Young Man*. London: Egoist, 1916.

Klein, Dennis A. *Peter Shaffer*. Boston: Twayne, 1979.

Koestler, Arthur. *The Act of Creation* (1964). 2d Danube ed. London: Hutchinson, 1976.

———. *The Yogi and the Commissar and Other Essays*. New York: Macmillan, 1945.

Labriolle, Jacqueline de. *Les "Christophe Colomb" de Paul Claudel*. Paris: C. Klincksieck, 1972.

Langer, Susanne K. *Feeling and Form*. New York: Scribner, 1953.

Lévi-Strauss, Claude. *The Savage Mind*. Trans. copyright by George Weidenfeld and Nicolson, Ltd., London. Chicago: University of Chicago Press, 1966.

Lindenberger, Herbert. *Historical Drama: The Relation of Literature and Reality*. Chicago: University of Chicago Press, 1975.

McCall, Dorothy. *The Theatre of Jean-Paul Sartre*. New York: Columbia University Press, 1969.

Nelson, Robert J. *Play within a Play: The Dramatist's Conception of His Art: Shakespeare to Anouilh*. New Haven: Yale University Press, 1958.

Pascal, Blaise. *Oeuvres*. 14 vols. Ed. Léon Brunschviecg, Pierre Boutroux, and Félix Gazier. Paris: Hachette, 1904–14. Vol. 13 (1904), ed. Léon Brunschviecg.

Peirce, Charles Sanders. *The Philosophy of Peirce: Selected Writings*. Ed. Justus Buchler (1940). Rpt. New York: Dover, 1955.

Plessner, Helmuth. *Zwischen Philosophie und Gesellschaft*. Bern: Francke, 1953. Includes "Zur Anthropologie des Schauspielers" (1948), pp. 180–92.

Plutchik, Robert. *The Emotions: Facts, Theories, and a New Model*. New York: Random House, 1962.

Ranke, Leopold von. *The Theory and Practice of History*. Ed. Georg G. Iggers and Konrad von Moltke. Indianapolis: Bobbs-Merrill, 1973. Includes the Preface (1824) to Ranke's *Geschichte der romanischen und germanischen Völker von 1494 bis 1535*.

Richter, Jean Paul. *Vorschule der Ästhetik*. Ed. Norbert Miller. Munich: Hanser, 1963.

Sartre, Jean-Paul. *Being and Nothingness: An Essay on Phenomenological Ontology*. Trans. Hazel E. Barnes. New York: Philosophical Library, 1956.

Works Cited

———. *The Devil and the Good Lord and Two Other Plays*. New York: Vintage Books, A Division of Random House, 1960. *The Devil and the Good Lord* is translated by Kitty Black.

———. *Le Diable et le bon dieu*. Paris: Gallimard, 1951.

———. *L'Être et le néant: Essai d'ontologie phénoménologique* (1943). 23d ed. Paris: Gallimard, 1949.

———. *Un Théâtre de situations*. Ed. Michel Contat and Michel Rybalka. Paris: Gallimard, 1973.

Schadewaldt, Wolfgang. "Furcht und Mitleid?: Zu Lessings Deutung des Aristotelischen Tragödiensatzes." *Hermes*, 83 (1955), 129–71.

Schiller, [Johann Christoph] Friedrich. *On Naive and Sentimental Poetry and On the Sublime*. Trans. Julius A. Elias. New York: Ungar, 1966.

———. *Schillers Werke: Nationalausgabe*. Ed. Lieselotte Blumenthal and Benno von Wiese. Vol. 20, ed. Benno von Wiese (Weimar: Hermann Böhlaus Nachfolger, 1962) includes "Über naive und sentimentalische Dichtung" (pp. 413–503).

Schlegel, Friedrich. *Charakteristiken und Kritiken I (1796–1801)*. Ed. Hans Eichner. Vol. 2 of *Kritische Friedrich-Schlegel-Ausgabe*, ed. Ernst Behler et al. (Paderborn: Schöningh, 1967) includes "Athenäums-Fragmente" (pp. 165–255).

Shaffer, Peter. *Amadeus*. [Rev. version.] New York: Harper & Row, 1981. Includes "Preface" (pp. ix–xii) and "Acknowledgements" (pp. xiii–xiv), in which the author discusses the textual changes made between the London and the New York productions as well as some details of both.

Shaw, [George] Bernard. *Saint Joan*. Ed, Stanley Weintraub. Indianapolis: Bobbs-Merrill, 1971.

Simmel, George. *The Conflict in Modern Culture and Other Essays*. Trans. K. Peter Etzkorn. New York: Teachers College Press, 1968. Includes the 1911 essay "On the Concept and the Tragedy of Culture," pp. 27–46.

———. *Fragmente und Aufsätze aus dem Nachlass und Veröffentlichungen der letzten Jahre*. Munich: Drei Masken Verlag, 1923. Includes "Zur Philosophie des Schauspielers" (pp. 231–65).

Solomon, Robert C. *The Passions*. Garden City, N.Y.: Anchor/Doubleday, 1976.

Staiger, Emil. *Grundbegriffe der Poetik* [1946]. 6th ed. Zürich: Atlantis, 1963.

Stanzel, Franz K. *A Theory of Narrative*. Trans. Charlotte Goedsche. Cambridge: Cambridge University Press, 1984.

States, Bert O. "The Actor's Presence: Three Phenomenal Modes." *Theatre Journal*, 35 (1983), 359–75. Most of this article has been republished as part of Chapter 5 in States's latest book, *Great Reckonings in Little Rooms: On the Phenomenology of Theater*, pp. 157–97. Berkeley: University of California Press, 1985.

Strauss, Walter A. "Albert Camus' *Caligula*: Ancient Sources and Modern Parallels." *Comparative Literature*, 3 (1951), 160–73.

Suetonius, Gaius Tranquillus. *The Twelve Caesars.* Trans. Robert Graves. Harmondsworth: Penguin, 1957. Includes "Gaius Caligula" (pp. 149–79).

Szondi, Peter. *Theorie des modernen Dramas.* Frankfurt: Suhrkamp, 1956.

———. *Versuch über das Tragische.* Frankfurt: Insel, 1961.

Thucydides. *History of the Peloponnesian War.* Trans. Charles Forster Smith. London: Heinemann; New York: Putnam, 1919. Reprinted and revised for the Loeb Classical Library (1928).

Veltruský, Jiří. "Dramatic Text as Component of Theatre." In *Semiotics of Art: Prague School Contributions,* ed. Ladislav Matejka and Irwin R. Titunik, pp. 94–117. Cambridge: MIT Press, 1976.

———. "The Prague School Theory of Theater." *Poetics Today,* 2 (1981), 225–35.

Walpole, Horace. *Correspondence with the Countess of Upper Ossory.* 3 vols. Ed. W. S. Lewis et al. New Haven: Yale University Press, 1965. [Vols. 32–34 of Yale University Press ed. of Horace Walpole's correspondence.]

Watts, Harold H. "Myth and Drama." *Cross Currents,* 5 (1955), 154–70.

Weiss, Peter. *The Persecution and Assassination of Jean-Paul Marat as Performed by the Inmates of the Asylum of Charenton under the Direction of the Marquis de Sade.* English version by Geoffrey Skelton. Verse adaptation by Adrian Mitchell. New York: Atheneum, 1965.

———. *Die Verfolgung und Ermordung Jean Paul Marats dargestellt durch die Schauspielertruppe des Hospizes zu Charenton unter Anleitung des Herrn de Sade.* Edition Suhrkamp no. 68 (1964). Frankfurt: Suhrkamp, 1967.

White, Hayden. *Metahistory: The Historical Imagination in Nineteenth-Century Europe.* Baltimore: Johns Hopkins University Press, 1973.

Wilder, Thornton. *Three Plays.* New York: Bantam Books, 1958. Includes *The Skin of Our Teeth* (pp. 65–137).

Wiles, Timothy. *The Theater Event: Modern Theories of Performance.* Chicago: University of Chicago Press, 1980.

Wilshire, Bruce. *Role Playing and Identity: The Limits of Theatre as Metaphor.* Bloomington: Indiana University Press, 1982.

Index

231

Index

Composite (dual) vision, 18–20, 22–23, 25–28, 30, 32, 51, 69, 106, 115, 138–40, 142, 144–47, 185, 215, 219

Coombs, Ilona, 199

Culture (society), 34, 43–45, 51–52, 127–28, 172

Danto, Arthur C.: *Analytical Philosophy of History,* 69

Da Ponte, Lorenzo, 209

David, Jacques Louis, 181

Derision, 46, 51, 64

Derrida, Jacques, 48

Desire, 34, 36, 56, 70–71, 75–76, 83, 136, 182, 200

Detachment (distance, view from outside), 40–41, 43, 51, 136–37, 140–49, 163–65, 184–85, 217, 219

Dickens, Charles: *David Copperfield,* 157

Diction (*lexis*), 102–3, 108–10, 122, 125, 133

Diderot, Denis: *Paradox of Acting,* 136–38, 142–43, 145

Direct quotation, 18, 29–30, 104, 134, 199

Distance. *See* Detachment

Docudrama, 29–31, 72

Dramatic mode. *See* Modes of discourse

Dryden, John: *Essay of Dramatic Poesie,* 50

Dual vision. *See* Composite vision

Dürrenmatt, Friedrich, 10; *Blinde,* 61; *Es steht geschrieben,* 61; *Romulus the Great,* 38, 49, 52–53, 59–64

Eisler, Hanns, 120

Elam, Keir, 162

Eliade, Mircea, 68

Eliot, T. S., 10, 26, 122; *Murder in the Cathedral,* 38, 49, 52–58, 61, 63–64, 71, 98

Empathy (identification, view from within), 40–41, 43, 51, 136–37, 140–46, 148–49, 164–65, 184–85, 217, 219

Entertainment (through thrill or gratification), 45, 71–73, 75, 149, 177

Epic, 11, 34

Esslin, Martin, 146–47; *Theatre of the Absurd,* 49, 188

Falla, Manuel de, 101

Farce, 33, 46, 49, 63–64, 76, 92, 166

Fear, 46, 51

Festivity, 46, 49–50, 58, 76, 103, 132

Freedom: of action, 76, 80–85, 93, 95–96, 98, 180, 189–90; of research, 116, 130–31

Freud, Sigmund, 25, 42, 169, 195; *New Introductory Lectures on Psychoanalysis,* 171, 217–19

Frisch, Max, 10; *Don Juan or the Love of Geometry,* 89; *Great Wall of China,* 65–67, 76, 85–93, 95–97

Frustration, 33–34, 41–43, 47, 51–52, 76, 93, 98, 167, 200

Fry, Christopher, 20–21, 28

Frye, Northrop: *Anatomy of Criticism,* 44–47, 70–71

Fulfillment, 33–34, 41–43, 47, 51–52, 76, 93, 98, 167, 200, 214

Gadamer, Hans-Georg, 215, 219

Generic categories, 38–39, 48–49, 75. *See also entries for individual genres*

Gilbert, Stuart, 187–88, 191

Giraudoux, Jean, 39

Goethe, Johann Wolfgang von, 102; *Faust,* 32, 66–67, 78; *Götz von Berlichingen,* 77–78

Goffman, Erving, 160; *Frame Analysis,* 216

233

Index

235

Index

Library of Congress Cataloging in Publication Data

Hernadi, Paul, 1936–
    Interpreting events.

    Includes index.
    1. Tragicomedy.   2. Drama—20th century—History and criticism.
3. History in literature.   I. Title.
PN1907.H47   1985   809.2′523   85–4166
ISBN 0–8014–1766–X (alk. paper)